THE SECTIONS
AND THE
CIVIL WAR
1826–1877

by
Clarence B. Carson

To Clyde R. Ray

For a union of States –

Clarence B. Carson

**Dedicated
to
the Memory of
ROBERT W. STODDARD
(1906–1984)**

**Other Books
by
Clarence B. Carson**

The Fateful Turn
The American Tradition
The Flight from Reality
The War on the Poor
Throttling the Railroads
The Rebirth of Liberty
The World in the Grip of an Idea
Organized Against Whom? The
    Labor Union in America
The Colonial Experience
The Beginning of the Republic

A Basic History of
the United States—Book III

THE SECTIONS
AND THE
CIVIL WAR
1826–1877

by
Clarence B. Carson

Beth A. Hoffman
Editorial Consultant

American Textbook Committee
P.O. Box 308
Greenville, Alabama 36037

Grateful acknowledgment is hereby made to Dover Publications for permission to use an extensive number of portraits from *Dictionary of American Portraits*, edited by Hayward and Blanche Cirker and published by Dover Publications, Inc.

First Printing September, 1985

Contents

Chapter 1

Introduction

The Civil War and Reconstruction were primal events in the history of the United States and the most dramatic and pronounced ones in the 19th century. They were events of the order, say, of the French Revolution for the history of France, or, more broadly, of western Europe. Historian Charles A. Beard has referred to the Civil War and its aftermath as "The Second American Revolution."[1] But in fact it was not a revolution in the most basic sense, though it contained a rebellion, and to compare it to the American Revolution understates the extent of the disruption involved. In a large and important sense the American revolution did not profoundly disrupt the continuity of American development greatly. On the contrary, it was the continuation of a movement toward more complete self-government in America and toward limited government that had been underway for a long time. True, there was the break from England, the rejection of monarchy, internal divisions between Patriots and Loyalists, and the charting of an independent course in the world by the United States. But the way had been prepared for these developments and they somehow fit into and are readily absorbed into American history.

Not so, however, the Civil War and Reconstruction; they constitute a major break in the continuity of American history. They could hardly be absorbed into the frame of what preceded them nor what came after. They do not fit within the framework of the Constitution of the United States. There was, and is, no provision in the Constitution for taking military action against any state or combination of them. Nor, for that matter, was there any provision for the withdrawal of a state from the union. The union was voluntarily composed of states and peoples who had come in by action of appropriate majorities. A prolonged and violent civil war would have been sufficiently difficult to overcome and absorb, but there was much more than that, too. It was not a war among groups or organizations spread throughout the country. Rather, it was a war of one section or region of the country against other sections or regions. The split was geographical, not by class, order, or grouping of peoples. A remnant of the former union made war against a new and much smaller union. This set the stage for the harshness of the treatment of the South during the Reconstruction.

Even so, it is possible that the war could have somehow been absorbed into the stream of American history, probably as an unfortunate, regrettable, and abominable episode which was an aberration from it. That was made much more difficult itself, however, by the fact that Union armies pursued it

1

more and more as a total war in the last two years of the fighting rather than
the more limited and restrained wars of the past. But the difficulties of
fitting these events into American history were compounded greatly by
Reconstruction. The vengeful behavior of Congress, the disfranchisement of
many Southern whites, the penalties laid upon the wealth and resources of
the South, and the prolonged evasion of constitutional restraints were too
much to take in and absorb.

Undoubtedly, the impact of these events was felt much more directly and
with greater force in the South than elsewhere. And the memory and
resentment lingered on there long after the desire for revenge or retribution,
or the memory of the animosities had died out or at least were in a state of
remission—elsewhere. Eighty years after the onset of the Civil War, a
Southernor would write:

> The Civil War and Reconstruction represent in their primary aspect
> an attempt on the part of the Yankee to achieve by force what he had
> failed to achieve by political means: first, a free hand in the nation for
> the thievish aims of the tariff gang, and secondly, and far more
> fundamentally, the satisfaction of the instinctive urge of men in the
> mass to put down whatever differs from themselves—the will to make
> over the South in the prevailing American image and to sweep it into
> the main current of the nation.
>
> To that end, he set himself to destroy the Southern world. . . . And
> the land was stripped and bled white—made, indeed, a frontier once
> more. . . .[2]

The South did not absorb the Civil War and Reconstruction into its history,
not, at least, in the version the reconstructionists would impose, not for the
better part of a hundred years anyway. That, however, belongs to a later part
of American history.

There is, however, an aspect of the Civil War and Reconstruction that
needs to be noted here for later reference. There is a sense in which the Civil
War and Reconstruction were a foretaste of what has been writ large in the
20th century, not especially in the United States but for the whole world.
Total war is one aspect of it, but totalitarianism is its more comprehensive
term, and it is animated by what may be described in a paraphrase of Cash as
the urge of men to put down whatever differs from themselves and to make
them over according to some pattern. These patterns are best known as
ideologies in the 20th century.

The Civil War and Reconstruction, then, loom large in the history of the
19th century. Moreover, they are primal events toward which much that
happened in the preceding decades points, leads, and in some measure
conditions. None of this is to be ignored or downplayed. Neither, however,
should these events, however momentous their character, be permitted to

overshadow others which bear no particular relation to them. It is possible, for example, that two books published in 1859—*Critique of Political Economy* by Karl Marx and *Origin of the Species* by Charles Darwin—were of much greater long-range importance to Western Civilization than what followed the attack by the Confederacy on Fort Sumter in 1861. Or, to take a different tack, the invention of the sewing machine, or for that matter, the typewriter, surely were of great importance for the future of America. Andrew Jackson's campaign for the presidency between 1825–1828 was a major shift in American politics. In short, it would be to misconstrue history to focus on any particular development to the exclusion of others.

Actually, the period of the 1820s through the 1860s is an especially rich period in the social, economic, intellectual, and cultural life of the American people. Americans had extricated themselves from the political connections with Europe and they were in the process of becoming self-consciously American, however much they might still retain dependence upon Europe. In architecture, it was the era both of the log cabin and of a Greek revival in public buildings and mansions. (Houses that are often described as colonial in origin are more apt to be Greek revival of the first half of the 19th century than remains of the 18th.) Andrew Jackson was born in a log cabin but built a fine example of the Greek revival mansion, ''The Hermitage,'' outside Nashville. American writers began to develop an American literature, with peculiarly American themes, and began, too, the development of local and regional themes. It was an age of oratory, Greek perhaps in inspiration but very American in its articulation. Great religious revivals swept over America, and religion freed from state control was attuned to the American scene in a proliferation of denominations and sects.

It was above all an era of romanticism, born in Europe it may be, but flowering in America in accord with its own clime. The belief in the supremacy of reason of the preceding age yielded ground to a new emphasis upon feeling, emotion, insight, intuition, and the wonders of the peculiar, the unique, and the individual. Poetry, which had become almost like prose, was freed from much of its bondage and emerged as a specialized art form for the romantics. But romanticism had a hundred facets, and it would be an error to place undue emphasis upon its literary and artistic side. It did include not only New England Transcendentalism and the Medieval revival in the South with the emphasis upon courtly graces and a class structure but also the placing of women upon a pedestal, so to speak, romantic love, the stark contrast between good and evil, the veneration of heroes such as Andrew Jackson, David Crockett, and Sam Houston (and ultimately Robert E. Lee), the love for the tall tale, oratorical flights in speeches, and dramatic religious conversions. Romantics exalted the imagination, and men conceived all sorts of reforms and had visions of utopias.

Nor is it less important to be aware that the mastery of government over the lives of the people had been very nearly broken in America, and after the break from England the bent of the people was to make it a servant. But whether they could achieve the latter, or whether or not it might not hold perils unguessed, for a time government had been restrained and a goodly portion of the population was free. What did Americans make of this large measure of freedom to pursue their own ends? The answer to this question entails the opening up of the West, the clearing of forests, the development of inventions, and the hundreds of ways a growing population made its living and produced wealth. The great story of this period is that of the family farm, of self-employment, of the devices men hit upon to cooperate with one another to achieve their ends, and how people pursued and attained a measure of economic independence. It is true there was chattel slavery over much of the South, and the factory was making its appearance in the North, but the main current of this age was of men managing their own affairs on farms and with small businesses.

In short, there are a goodly number of themes worthy of attention and study during this period of American history. They are themes rich in meaning without reference to the Civil War and Reconstruction. That is not to say that most of them do not have some bearing in one way or another, for they do. For example, it would be difficult to account for the coming of the Civil War without the abolition movement, which was spawned out of the reform ferment which was romantic in its animus. Nor would the excesses of Reconstruction have been likely to occur to the extent that they did without the reformist zeal to make over the South. Rather, it is to say that the people who lived then and the themes by which their lives may be partially comprehended had existence and meaning both within and outside the framework of Civil War and Reconstruction.

Chapter 2
The Rise of Sectionalism

. . . The tendency of universal suffrage is to jeopardize the rights of property and the principles of liberty. There is a constant tendency . . . in the poor to covet a share in the plunder of the rich . . . ; in the indolent and profligate to cast the whole burthens of society upon the industrious and virtuous; and there is a tendency in ambitious and wicked men to inflame these combustible materials.

—Chancellor James Kent, 1821

. . . The great object of . . . government is the improvement of the condition of those who are parties to the social compact. . . . For the fulfillment of those duties governments are invested with power, and to the attainment of the end—the progressive improvement of the condition of the governed—the exercise of delegated powers is a . . . sacred and indispensable [duty]. . . .

—John Quincy Adams, 1825

The Senate and House of Representatives of South Carolina . . . do . . . solemnly PROTEST against the system of protecting duties, lately adopted by the federal government . . . , because South Carolina . . . is, and must ever continue to be, wholly dependent upon agriculture and commerce, not only for her prosperity, but for her very existence as a state. . . .

—Protest against the Tariff, 1828

Chronology

1803—Admission of Ohio to Union.

1812—Admission of Louisiana to Union.

1816—Admission of Indiana to Union.

1817—Admission of Mississippi to Union.

1818—Admission of Illinois to Union.

1819—Admission of Alabama to Union.

1820—Admission of Maine to Union.

1821—Admission of Missouri to Union.

1824—Presidential election.

1825—Adams elected by the House of Representatives.

1826—Panama Congress for Latin America.

1828—Passage of "Tariff of Abominations."

The main division in English America during the colonial period was into colonies, and during the first several decades of the United States it was the states. These were the primary political units and centers of attachments and loyalties. What regionalism or sectionalism there was before the 19th century was occasional, temporary, and informal. True, historians have often divided the region east of the Appalachians into three areas: New England, the Middle Colonies or States, and the South. This division, however, is more for convenience than anything else, with the possible exception of New England. New England did have a homogenous population during the colonial period and the early years of the Republic. There was a New England Confederation for a brief period; the colonies were Calvinist in religious background; and Britain did make a short-lived effort to unite them administratively.

But the main tendency in America up until 1789 was centrifugal, not centripetal. That is, new colonies (or states) tended to be formed in territory originally claimed by older colonies, to spin off from rather than move toward or join them. That was true from the very beginning, when Virginia's grant, or at least Virginia, virtually encompassed English America. Thereafter, new grants were made and new settlements formed from the territory claimed by England. So, colonies multiplied in America: several spun off Massachusetts, for example. There were what might be called central or dominant colonies: Massachusetts, the Penn colonies, and Virginia, as well as South Carolina, perhaps. But there were maverick colonies, so to speak, which did not clearly fit into any configuration. Rhode Island was in New England geographically, but rarely spiritually or politically. It was not clear just where New York fit, if anywhere, and until after the break from England much the same could be said for Georgia. The main tendency throughout the colonial period, however, was for colonies to spin off on their own and to assume a political independence of the others.

This tendency was brought to a virtual halt in the 1780s. The Constitution required that for a new state to be formed within the bounds of an old one the established state must give its approval. Some states had given up their western claims, or agreed to do so in the future, to secure ratification of the Articles of Confederation, and after the ratification of the Constitution, Southern states allowed such new territories and states to be formed as Tennessee and Alabama. Vermont cut away from New York to become a separate state in 1791, but New York's claim had long been disputed. But after these old claims had been disposed of the tendency to spin off ended, except where states had not yet been formed in western lands.

With the Declaration of Independence, the colonies became states, and assumed most of the powers and attributes of independent countries. However, from the outset there was supposed to be a union, and very shortly a confederation was formed of all the states. Though the Articles of Confederation referred to a "perpetual union," a much more likely outcome was that it was occasioned by the revolt and that once the danger was past the confederation would break up. There were many signs that this was taking place in the 1780s. The states paid little heed to the requests and decisions of Congress, and Congress lacked the independence or power to enforce its will. By 1787, such government of the union as existed was virtually at a standstill, and many observers believed that it must be either replaced or the union was at an end. It was replaced, of course, by a government with enlarged powers, and this made for a much firmer union.

It is doubtful that if the confederation had broken up in the 1780s it would have been replaced by regional or sectional confederacies. The point is that sectionalism had not developed as yet in the country. The most clear-cut division in the Constitutional Convention was not between sections but between the large and small states. There was not even a self-conscious Southern section in 1787. Virginia probably voted much more often with Pennsylvania than with South Carolina, for example. The Maryland delegation had difficulty enough agreeing among themselves, much less with anyone else. As for the Middle and New England states, they hardly comprised a self-conscious North, and jealousies among their inhabitants were much more common than were regional attachments.

The first self-conscious section to develop under the Constitution was New England. The particular occasion for its rise was the dominance of the Jeffersonian Republicans and the Napoleonic wars. New England was the seat of the strength of the Federalist Party, was the most conservative region in its religious affinities, and its inhabitants (or leaders) were most apt to be appalled by the ideas of the French Revolution. It is worth noting, too, that in the early 19th century, New England states were not increasing in population as were many other states. Their minority status in the union was impressed strongly upon them by the decline of the Federalist Party. Sectional feeling reached a peak in New England as the Jeffersonians made efforts to thwart British control over shipping during the Napoleonic wars. It was not so much that New Englanders were pro-British as that they were anti-French. The Federalists resented their own impotence, too, and the dominance of a Virginia dynasty. In any case, this New England sectionalism reached a peak during the War of 1812 and had its swan song at the Hartford Convention in 1814.

As it turned out, political parties were the great instrument for dispersing any sectional fervor, so long as no self-conscious section held a deciding majority of the population. It looked at first as if parties might be the focus and instrument of sectionalism. Certainly, the Federalist Party was central to New England sectionalism. But the more it became a New England party the more it declined in national influence. The way the population was distributed over the country, no sectional party had any chance to elect a national candidate. That is not to say that a section could not dominate a party, but that is another story. At any rate, the Jeffersonian Republicans were a national party from the outset, had a considerable following in New England from the outset, and by 1820 had absorbed most Federalists and some of their programs.

Actually, however, states, not sections, were the main divisions in the union in the early years of the Republic. Neither regions nor sections have any constitutional standing or power in the United States. The Jeffersonians tended eventually to unify the nation by defending the states and their position of a strict construction of the Constitution. A strict construction tends to leave the states to the exercise of the preponderance of the power of government and to reduce any occasion for sectional contests. On the contrary, sectionalism is aided and abetted by the use of the national power extensively either for or against some region. That is, people within a section may attempt to use the national government for their ends, prevent its use for something they oppose, or do both. In that case, sections become both important and potentially divisive.

Sectionalism did begin to become a factor in the 1820s and succeeding years. The main issues were the use of government power. And these issues did arise over differences between the sections.

Regional Differences and Changes

The differences which gave rise to sectionalism were not primarily geographical. They certainly were not topographical. There were not great land or water barriers separating North and South. The Potomac is the boundary between Virginia and Maryland, but not between North and South. Nor is there any other body of water or mountain range that significantly separates North from South. The great topographical divider was the Appalachians, and separates East from West, not North from South.

Actually, there were two different basic divisions in the country in the 1820s. One basis of division was political; the other was geographic or topographical. As noted, the topographical division was between East and West, and the line dividing them was the crest of the Appalachians. Actually, this great mountain chain not only divides regions of the country but also several states. Pennsylvania is divided almost in half by the Alleghenies, a part of the Appalachians. Upstate New York is divided from New York City and environs by the mountains, as is Virginia from West

Virginia (then, simply western Virginia). Only from northern Georgia southward is East no longer divided from West by the mountains.

The West was much more part of a natural geographic unit than was the East. It belongs to a vast area which is often referred to as the Mississippi Basin, the northern portion of which extends from the Appalachians to the Rockies. It comprises that region drained by the Mississippi River into the Gulf of Mexico, extending from western Pennsylvania in the East to Montana in the West in the north and from southwestern Virginia and eastern Tennessee to Colorado in the south. So far as water traffic is concerned, the natural seaport for virtually the whole of this region is New Orleans. Thus, in the 1820s it appeared that a major commercial tie of the region that lies to the north is with the south. By contrast, most of the older states in the East had their own natural outlets to the sea: at Boston, Newport, New York, Philadelphia, Baltimore, Norfolk, Wilmington, Charleston, Savannah, and so on. So it was that while there were no great land barriers separating the North from the South in the East, neither was there any great river flowing through them linking them together. They were, however, linked by ports on the ocean.

The basic divisions between North and South were *political*, i.e., established by political authorities. Looking at it this way, there were four sections in the United States in the 1820s. Except for Missouri and a portion of Louisiana, all the states were at that time east of the Mississippi. The sections, excluding the relatively small settled region beyond the Mississippi, consisted of the Northeast, the Southeast, the Old Northwest, and the Old Southwest. The Northeast was divided from the Southeast by the Mason and Dixon Line. This is a line surveyed in the 1760s by the English astronomers Charles Mason and Jeremiah Dixon and is the boundary between Pennsylvania and Maryland. In the debates which led to the Missouri Compromise in 1820, the Mason and Dixon Line was referred to as the dividing line between slave and free states, and after that it came to be thought of as the division between the Northeast and Southeast (or, more loosely, the North and the South). *Slavery* was the difference focused upon, but whether or not a state abolished slavery had been determined politically by the states after the break from England.

The division between the Old Northwest and Old Southwest had been determined much earlier by the Continental Congress. The Northwest Ordinance had divided the territory west of the Appalachians at the Ohio River and had prohibited slavery north of that line. The Missouri Compromise extended the line west of the Mississippi at about the same latitude at which the Ohio empties into the Mississippi, excepting for Missouri, where slavery was to be permitted. Thus, it should be clear that the basic sectional lines were politically determined.

One of the major changes in the early 19th century was the rapid flow of population westward. It became rapid into some areas in the 1790s, when

Robert Fulton
(1765–1815)

Courtesy Independence National Historical Park

Fulton was an engineer, inventor, and entrepreneur. He is best known for devising a method of propelling a boat by steam—inventing the steamboat. Fulton was born in Pennsylvania, apprenticed a jeweller, but went to England to study painting. While there, he met James Watt, became interested in engineering, and began to tinker with inventions. Among the preliminary devices he exhibited in Paris was a submarine. When he returned to the United States, he built the *Clermont* with the aid of Robert Livingston, and put it into operation on the Hudson river in 1807. Among his other inventions were a steam powered warship and machines for spinning flax, for making ropes, and for sawing and polishing marble. He had a remarkable flair for seeing the possibilities in machines for performing work and other tasks.

Kentucky and Tennessee were admitted as states in the union, followed by Ohio in 1803. But the westward movement became a surge after the War of 1812. Organized Indian resistance to settlers was virtually ended east of the Mississippi during that war. Also, the invention of the cotton gin brought short staple cotton into its own as a fabric. By 1820, the population of Ohio exceeded that of Massachusetts, and by 1830 Tennessee was more populous than the Bay State. Many New Englanders moved westward into upstate New York in the early years of the century, and New York had passed Virginia to become the most populous state in the union by 1820. The population of Alabama increased from about 9,000 in 1810 to 309,000 by 1830. Indiana was more populous than Connecticut by 1830.

Probably, the single most important invention commercially in the early years of the Republic, except possibly for the cotton gin, was that of the steamboat. Robert Fulton made a successful steamboat in 1807 and began regular boat service on the Hudson very shortly thereafter. The steamboat opened up new vistas for river transport, especially for the Midwest and upper South west of the mountains. River transport on the Mississippi and its tributaries had been mostly a one-way affair before the invention of the steamboat. Boats or rafts could be floated down the rivers, but once they had reached New Orleans or some other port, that was the end of the line. There was no way to propel a loaded raft up the river. Steamboats, however, could go both ways; thus, whatever the shortcomings of travel on these rivers, a way had been found to transport heavy goods to a seaport.

It took no great foresight by 1825 to see what probably loomed ahead in the future development of America. Population had already surged westward to claim the fertile farmlands of the Mississippi valley. They would be the center of agricultural production in the future. New Orleans would be the major port of the future and probably the largest city in America, dwarfing New York, Philadelphia, Baltimore, and Boston. Even the goods from western New York and Pennsylvania might well flow to the sea by way of New Orleans. The focal point of the commerce of much of America would be in the South. Nor was it improbable that if the commercial lines ran Midwest to South and back again many other ties would be formed. Agricultural America might well absorb much of the commerce of the Northeast and be remote from the manufactures that were developing there.

It did not happen, of course, not on anything like the scale that might have taken place. A great deal of energy, however, went into preventing it from occurring. Much of the history of the middle of the 19th century can be told in terms of a large and determined effort to shift the lines of commerce from the Mississippi toward the Northeast. It is the story of the building of roads, canals, and railroads to be told later, and of the political activities that underlay much of this. The point here is that sectionalism was shaped in considerable measure from the political effort of the Northeast to survive and maintain its dominant role in the union.

There were other regional differences, of course, some of which fueled sectionalism. There were economic differences, some of them attributable to differences in climate, soil, and other geographical factors. For example, textile manufacturing in a factory setting developed for the first time in New England. This was connected with the facts that machinery was turned with water wheels at the time, and that the hilly country in parts of New England provided the rapid streams for force to turn the wheels. Or again, the making of iron was extensive in Pennsylvania because the various ores and materials were available there.

The South remained the major center of the growing of staple crops for export for much of the 19th century as it had been in the 18th century. Tobacco continued to be a major export crop, though competition from many other places made it no longer so profitable to produce. Most of the tobacco was produced in the upper South, and Tennessee and Kentucky now became major tobacco producers as well as the older states. Rice was a major staple crop in South Carolina, and when Louisiana came into the United States, sugar from sugar cane became an important staple. Indigo lost its significance once the break from England ended the subsidy for growing it.

Cotton, as well as rice and sugar cane, illustrates the importance of geography to the crops grown. Tobacco could be produced throughout much of the United States, and it was widely grown. Connecticut was an important tobacco producing state, for example. (Commercially, however, different climates and soils were better suited to growing tobacco used for some purposes than others.) Rice, on the other hand, could only be grown commercially on the marsh lands near the sea, mainly in South Carolina and Georgia. Sugar cane thrived in the climate of southern Louisiana, but requires much too long a growing season to do well very far north. Short staple cotton, the main variety grown after the invention of the cotton gin, does best in the dryer uplands where there is a long hot summer and a long growing season. It could be grown profitably from eastern Virginia (warmed by the winds from the Gulf stream) southward to middle Georgia and thence westward. Cotton became quickly from 1820 onward the most important export staple of the United States as the British demand for it seemed insatiable. In 1792, approximately 2,000 bales of cotton were produced. With the introduction of the gin, it increased rapidly thereafter: by 1800 156,000 bales were produced; by 1810, 340,000; in 1820, 606,000; in 1830, 976,000 bales. In 1830, 596,000 bales were exported to Great Britain, and nearly 90 per cent of the crop was exported to some foreign country. In 1821, South Carolina ranked first among the states in cotton production, Georgia second, and Alabama third. Virtually all the cotton was grown in the South, and the center of cotton growing moved westward over the years.

Slavery was not equally important in the growing of all these staples. Rice and sugar cane were grown commercially almost exclusively on large plantations. The initial expenses in growing rice were too large for small farmers, and it was widely believed, or claimed, that only the Blacks could endure the toil of working it. The milling of sugar cane involved large capital expenses which gave large planters the advantage in this undertaking. On the other hand, cotton and tobacco could be, and were, grown equally well on plantations and on small farms. Indeed, the small family farm had many advantages in tobacco farming because of the delicacy of the plant and the tobacco leaves and the need for intensive cultivation and care. Cotton, too, required intensive care and work, but except for the small plants, there was little that was delicate about it.

Other sections of the country focused on different crops, products, and commercial activities. The Midwest early became the major grain producing portion of the country. More corn than any other crop was grown there, but the most important commercial crop was wheat. New Englanders turned extensively toward manufacturing in the 1820s and afterward. New York had become the most populous state, and New York City had both the largest population and was the most important shipping center in the 1820s. Both New York and Pennsylvania had diverse economies with extensive farming, shipping, and manufactures. But neither the Midwest nor the Northeast, either separately or together, produced as much for export as did the South. Compilations indicate that cotton exports represented nearly 40 per cent of the value of goods exported between 1816–1820. Wheat and flour (mostly Northeast and Midwest in origin) accounted for about 16 per cent; tobacco 15 per cent; manufactured goods 7 per cent; lumber 5 per cent, and rice 4 per cent.

The diversity of goods produced and the differences from region to region need not have produced conflict. After all, the regions complemented one another by their different products and could contribute to the general prosperity. Northerners could engage in shipping and trade while Southerners concentrated on producing staple crops primarily for export. In his Farewell Address, George Washington had pictured how all this might work for the mutual benefit of all: "The *North,*" he said, "in an unrestrained intercourse with the *South* . . . , finds . . . great additional resources of maritime and commercial enterprise. . . . The *South,* in the same intercourse, benefiting by the same agency of the *North,* sees its agriculture grow and its commerce expand. . . . The *East,* in a like intercourse with the *West,* already finds . . . a valuable vent for the commodities which it brings from abroad or manufactures at home. The *West* derives from the *East* supplies requisite to its growth and comfort, and . . . the secure enjoyment of indispensable *outlets* for its own productions. . . ." In short, trade is a mutually beneficial undertaking.

That can be changed, however, when one region or another attempts to use government for its benefit to the disadvantage of another region. Political jockeying, the enactment of legislation for the supposed benefit of one region at the expense of another, can give rise to sectional jealousies and rivalries. This is what Washington and Madison referred to as factions, and they thought them dangerous to the stability of a republic. They are often referred to nowadays as special interest groups, but that does not so well describe what may be their sectional or regional character. Madison believed that factions are unavoidable, but he hoped the great expanse and diversity of the country might keep them from controlling the government for their own particular ends. That, however, did not always happen, and in the 1820s the contests for political power contributed to the beginning of the rise of sectionalism.

The Election of 1824

The political unity forged by the Jeffersonian Republicans began to break up in the early 1820s. For one thing, the growing western states, particularly Kentucky and Tennessee, wanted to make certain they were not shut off from the highest offices in the land. The practice had developed of nominating presidential candidates by party *caucus* in Congress. With the disappearance of the Federalist Party, this meant the nomination of one candidate by Congress, in effect. If the man nominated were then regularly elected, Congress would have assumed the position of choosing the President. The General Assembly of Tennessee lodged a formal protest against the caucus method of nomination in 1823. It declared "that the practice of congressional nominations is a violation of the spirit of the Constitution of the United States."[3] The Constitution, the protest pointed out, had separated the powers and vested election in an electoral college, none of whose members could be members of Congress at the same time.

For another thing, a movement was well underway in state after state to have the electors of the President and Vice-President popularly elected. This was part of a broader movement toward the expansion of the suffrage and giving voters a more direct role in government. By 1828, only 2 states still chose their electors by state legislatures. Clearly, if there was to be a choice by the voters, there must be other candidates than those nominated by a congressional caucus.

At any rate, the caucus system did not survive the election in 1824. It was already so unpopular that most members of Congress did not attend the caucus that was held. Those who did—the "rump"—nominated William H. Crawford of Georgia as candidate. Crawford was Monroe's Secretary of the Treasury, a vigorous defender of the powers of the states, more of a Jeffersonian than not. Unfortunately, he was struck down by a paralytic stroke and was incapacitated for much of the campaign. In any case, other men with larger following became candidates, nominated either by state legislatures or at mass meetings in various places. John Quincy Adams of Massachusetts became New England's candidate, in effect. Andrew Jackson of Tennessee and Henry Clay were the candidates from the west. John C. Calhoun of South Carolina intended to run for President, but after surveying the situation he decided to run for Vice-President instead.

Jackson was probably the best known and certainly the most popular of these candidates. Although he had been active in politics, was in the Senate at the time, his fame was as an Indian fighter, as the victor at the Battle of New Orleans, and for his exploits in Florida. His political ideas were not generally known at this time, if he had any distinctive ones, and he did not feel called upon to take any strong positions. Adams was next in line for the presidency, or so it might be supposed, since he had served prominently as Secretary of State during the two terms of Monroe. But he did not receive the caucus nomination, and his following was mostly in New England. Only Clay had a recognizable program, one which called for a larger role of the federal government in the development of an American economy. It was called the "American System," and the idea was to promote manufactures and agriculture with a protective tariff and to have the federal government play a much larger role in road and canal building.

No candidate received a majority in the vote in the electoral college.

John Randolph of Roanoke (1773–1833)

Randolph was descended from leading Virginia families—the Randolphs and Blands—and was himself a planter, slaveholder, and owner of a vast estate. In his day, he was one of the most famous orators in the country, at a time when oratorical ability was highly prized. He was educated at Princeton, Columbia, and William and Mary. He served in the House of Representatives for many years and for a short period in the Senate. Randolph might have been a great national leader, and he did serve effectively for a good many years as head of the House Ways and Means Committee. His views were in many ways similar to those of Jefferson and Jackson, though narrower and less flexible. He was a defender of state sovereignty, opposed to extending the power of the federal government, and a defender of slavery (though he freed his own by his will). But he was not a party man, drifted away from Jefferson and openly opposed Jackson in the last year of his life, and followed his own standards rather than those of others. Although he was a man of great learning and strong beliefs, historians are more apt to quote him for his wit than for his wisdom.

Jackson led with 90 votes; Adams got 84, Crawford 41, and Clay 37. The Jackson vote ranged from Pennsylvania to South Carolina and Illinois to Louisiana, was national in character, though concentrated in the South and West. Adams took New England, Clay a part of the West, and Crawford two states in the South. The election had to be decided in the House of Representatives, where the vote was by states. Clay was out of the election, having come in fourth, and Crawford could not be seriously considered because of his physical condition; thus, the choice was between Jackson and Adams. Clay threw his support to Adams, who won in the House vote.

When Adams later appointed Clay as his Secretary of State, Jackson's followers charged that a "corrupt bargain" had been made between the two. John Randolph of Virginia declared that Adams and Clay were "the Puritan and the blackleg." Clay challenged Randolph to a duel for slurring his name, but both survived the fray without injury. The main point, however, is that there was much ill feeling about the outcome of the election. The Tennessee legislature promptly renominated Andrew Jackson for President for the election that was nearly four years away, and the race began anew before the old one was hardly over.

The Adams Administration

John Quincy Adams, as had his father before him, came to the highest office in the midst of a struggle for political leadership. The younger Adams, unlike his father, had the additional handicap of coming in second in the electoral vote. Worse still, perhaps, his support was regional, not nationwide. Adams had a good mind, had long experience in government, and was a master of foreign diplomacy. But he had neither the charm, attractiveness, nor popularity to overcome these difficulties. Beyond that, he had a vision of using the federal government in ways that tended to divide rather than unite the country. It would arouse sectional feelings and contests, and did to some extent. Consequently, his administration made little impact on the country, and his was largely a caretaker government between Monroe and Jackson. He succeeded mainly in dividing the Republican Party further and giving impetus to the development of two distinct parties once again.

Ironically, the House had managed to elect a President whose experience and successes had been in the field of foreign relations at just that juncture when, for the first time since the founding of the Republic, foreign relations were least pressing. No longer were European powers a significant menace on American frontiers. The one major area where there might have been some likelihood of diplomatic successes was with the newly independent Latin American countries. But whatever the possibilities, the Adams administration did not succeed in its main effort in this direction.

Simon Bolivar called a meeting of Latin American countries at a Panama Congress in 1826. He invited Great Britain to send a delegation but not the United States. Mexico and Colombia, however, extended an invitation to the United States, and Adams accepted. Bolivar apparently hoped that the Panama Congress would adopt a plan for united or common action by the newly formed republics. There was strong opposition in the Senate both to Adams' failure to get approval at the outset from that body as well as opposition to sending a delegation. In consequence, the mission was so delayed before the Senate finally approved it that the Panama Congress had adjourned before it arrived in Panama. If the United States had managed to have a delegation there, it might have made no difference. British long term policy had shifted away from colonialism toward free trade; they were mainly interested in opening up and dominating markets in Latin America, thus keeping any other foreign power out. They were much more successful in Latin American diplomacy in the ensuing years than the United States, though their policies were not that distinct from those of the United States. The crucial point here, however, is that Adams came up empty in the Panama maneuver and that he was obstructed in the Senate by opposition.

Adams received a more direct defeat in foreign relations from the British in the West Indies. The British West Indies had been a highly important market for American goods during the colonial period. For many years after the War for Independence this trade had been closed to America. When it was eventually reopened, it was still restricted and limited. Adams insisted that the West Indies be fully opened to Americans, and that it be treated as a "right" and not a "privilege." When the British refused, Adams retaliated by restricting British shipping and trade with America. The British, in their turn, retaliated by excluding American ships from the Indies. The upshot was that the United States had less than it started with.

The domestic proposals of Adams met with no greater success and aroused even more determined opposition. In his Inaugural Address, Adams called for more energetic and far-reaching government action than had thus far been undertaken. He recommended "laws promoting the improvement of agriculture, commerce, and manufactures, the cultivation and encouragement of the mechanic and of the elegant arts, the advancement of literature, and the progress of the sciences, ornamental and profound. . . ."[4] To accomplish these ends, he favored not only federally aided road and canal building and protective tariffs but also such things as a national university at Washington, an astronomical observatory (which he referred to as "lighthouses in the sky"), the fitting out of ships with scientific devices for exploration and observation, and so on.

Although Congress did make additional appropriations for the Cumberland Road project and had passed a higher tariff in 1824, it was hardly in a mood for new programs for exercising Federal power. Thus, it took no action along most of the recommended lines. A part of this opposition could be attributed to the Jacksonians in Congress, who were increased by the elections in 1826. Martin Van Buren of New York was a Jackson leader in Congress. John C. Calhoun, too, had tied his fortunes to those of Jackson during this time. Calhoun, Vice-President and presider over the Senate, occupied a crucial post in close votes in the Senate. A higher tariff passed the House in 1827, but the vote in the Senate was tied, and Calhoun voted against it to break the tie, thus defeating the bill.

By this time, the tariff had become a key issue. New Englanders were especially eager for a high, even prohibitive, tariff to protect the home market in textiles from British competition. Some of the manufacturers in the middle states also wanted a higher tariff. On the other hand, Southern states were becoming more determined in their opposition to a protective tariff. Southerners had long favored free trade, but they had yielded ground some during the Era of Good Feeling. But now economic interests were pressing them back to earlier convictions. The South produced and exported mostly agricultural products. They did not need protection from the home

John C. Calhoun
(1782–1850)

Courtesy Library of Congress

Calhoun was born in South Carolina, educated at Yale, studied law in Connecticut
and South Carolina, and was admitted to
the bar in his native state. Almost immediately, he went into state politics, and
in 1811 he entered the United States
House of Representatives, commencing a
national political career that ended only
with his death nearly forty years later. He
first came to national attention as a
"warhawk" preceding the War of 1812,
after which he served as Secretary of War
under President Monroe. Following that,
he was elected Vice-President in 1824.
During his earlier years, he generally took
a nationalist position and even favored a
protective tariff. But as the South began
to become a self-conscious region, he
emerged as a defender of the states from
the encroachment of Federal power. He
cast his lot with Andrew Jackson in the
late 1820s, and was re-elected Vice-
President in 1828. However, Jackson
broke with him in the early 1830s, and
for most of the rest of his life he served
in the Senate. In that position, he developed and set forth what came to be the
"Southern" position about the nature of
the union as the Civil War approached.

market, but they did need a foreign market which depended upon Americans
buying large amounts of goods in foreign trade. A protective tariff worked
against that.

In 1828, a new tariff was passed that was highly protectionist in
character. It was called the "Tariff of Abominations" by its opponents. The
tariff was in some measure at least the work of Jackson's followers, and
there have been charges ever since that they hoped to see it defeated. It
reduced some of the protective duties on textile goods but raised the rates on
raw materials, iron, hemp, and flax. It was expected to favor the Middle
States and the West, but to be unfavorable to New England. Even so, it got

the support of New England as well and passed with the opposition concentrated in the South. Since the Jacksonians of the Middle States and West had voted for the tariff, it took the issue away from Adams in the campaign of 1828.

It did result, however, in the emergence of strong sectional feeling in the South. The South Carolina legislature sent a strongly worded protest to the United States Senate against "it [the tariff] as unconstitutional, oppressive, and unjust."[5] Within a couple of months, the legislatures of Georgia, Mississippi, and Virginia lodged their protests against it as well. The South was showing signs of readiness to take common action as a section, something it had not done thus far.

The Emergence of Two Parties

Between 1825–1828 two distinct factions had taken shape in the Republican Party. They can be identified as the Adams-Clay faction and the Jackson-Calhoun faction. By 1828 they had taken on much of the character of separate parties. The Adams-Clay grouping preferred the title, the National Republican Party, and the Jacksonians called themselves Democrats, or Democratic-Republicans. After Adams' defeat in 1828, Henry Clay assumed the leadership of the party. In the course of the 1830s, it took the name of Whig, thus casting off its nominal connection with the "Republican" name. The Jacksonians, now claiming to be Democrats, nonetheless continued to trace their antecedents back to Jefferson and Madison. Indeed, there was a strong flavor of Jefferson's philosophy in the Democratic Party, but it was both more partisan and appealed more directly to the voters than did the Jeffersonians. (This last, however, may have been the result of the more widespread suffrage in the time of Jackson than of Jefferson.)

While the Democratic Party was very much actuated by ideas in the 1830s and caught up major currents of ideas, it did not arise as a program for anything. It was much more a personal vehicle for the election of General Jackson initially than anything else. To put it another way, the Democratic Party arose in opposition to the programs, policies, and actions of the Adams administration. In the course of the extended campaign from 1825–1828, the Jacksonians formed political organizations in many states and began to gain control over Congress.

Jackson and Calhoun won handily in the election. Jackson carried all the states west and south of Maryland, plus Pennsylvania and New York, though the latter state was divided. Jackson got 171 electoral votes to 83 for Adams. In terms of the election results, only New England appeared to be a separate section. But New England's days of swinging elections with a solid core of votes, which had always been few, were now over. The Southeast, which appeared to be emerging as a self-conscious section, was firmly joined with the West in its vote. The Democratic Party had emerged as a new national party with its solidest support in the South, and it would remain over the next 30 years as the most effective device for defending the interests of the South and keeping it in the union.

Chapter 3
Jacksonian Democracy

In the full enjoyment of the gifts of Heaven and the fruits of superior industry, economy, and virtue, every man is entitled to protection by law; but when the laws undertake to add to these natural and just advantages artificial distinctions . . . , the humble members of society—the farmers, mechanics, and laborers— who have neither the time nor the means of securing like favors to themselves, have a right to complain of the injustices of their Government.

—Andrew Jackson, 1832

The Union: Next to our liberty, the most dear; may we all remember that it can only be preserved by respecting the rights of the States and distributing equally the benefit and burden of the Union.

—John C. Calhoun, 1830

All communities are apt to look to government for too much. . . . But this ought not to be. The framers of our excellent Constitution . . . acted at the time on a sounder principle. They wisely judged that the less government interferes with private pursuits the better for the general prosperity.

—Martin Van Buren, 1837

Chronology

1828—Jackson elected President.

1830—
January—Webster-Hayne Debate.
May—Jackson's veto of the Maysville Road Bill.

1831—Reopening of British West Indies trade.

1832—
March—*Worcester vs. Georgia.*
July—Jackson vetoes recharter of U. S. Bank.
November—South Carolina adopts Nullification Ordinance.

1833—Congress passes Force Bill.

1834—Formal Organization of Whig Party.

21

1836—
  July—Specie Circular Issued.
  December—Van Buren elected President.
1837—Bank Panic.

Andrew Jackson has ever posed difficulties for those who would describe him briefly or grasp him whole. He fits neither the role of an unalloyed hero or an irredeemable villain. Indeed, he was a man of stark contrasts, of temperamental outbursts, of a stern sense of honor, yet he could be reasonable, moderate, and thoughtful. His first biographer, James Parton, described the contrasts and contradictions in the evidence about him this way: "He was one of the greatest of generals, and wholly ignorant of the art of war. A writer brilliant, elegant, eloquent, without being able to compose a correct sentence, or spell words of four syllables. The first of statesmen, he never devised, he never framed a measure. He was the most candid of men, and was capable of the profoundest dissimulation. A most law-defying, law-obeying citizen. A stickler for discipline, he never hesitated to disobey his superior. A democratic autocrat. An urbane savage. An atrocious saint."[6] Such descriptions depended, of course, on who was commenting on him or which of his actions was under discussion. They are exaggerations, too, in most instances; they arise mostly from attempting to apply standards to him by people of different backgrounds or of a different time. He was undoubtedly a volatile man at times, combative and determined, quick to defend his challenged honor, and slow to forgive a slight. But within the framework of his code, his beliefs, and his way of acting, there were recognizable patterns, not contradictions. In any case, what matters here are the things about him and what he did that had an impact on the development of the United States.

There can be no reasonable doubt that Jackson had a considerable impact on the country. He placed his stamp upon a political party which dominated American government from its inception to the Civil War. Only Jefferson's Republican Party had a more consistent and continuous impact. So far as the presidency was concerned, Jacksonian Democrats occupied the office for 24 of the 32 years from 1829 to 1861. More, John Tyler succeeded to the presidency one month after the inauguration of William Henry Harrison in 1841, and he was more nearly a Democrat than a Whig, under whose banner he had been chosen. If his term be counted, it could be said that Democrats actually occupied the presidency for nearly 28 of the 32 years. But Tyler was more of the Calhoun stripe than that of Jackson, did not fit clearly in either party, and probably should not be counted.

It should be emphasized about the others, however, that they were not simply Democrats but also Jacksonians. Van Buren was the hand-picked candidate of Jackson and had exercised considerable influence over him during his years in the presidency. James K. Polk was a fellow Tennessean of Jackson, an early supporter of his, and remained throughout in basic respects a Jacksonian. Franklin Pierce and James Buchanan had been Jackson men from their early years in politics, and the earmarks of Jackson show in their administrations and in their attitudes toward the Constitution.

But Jacksonian Democracy was not simply a political movement; it was political, but it benefited from and caught up currents in the economic, social, and cultural life in America. Socially and culturally, the era of Jackson was the culmination of the long-term trend away from the European class system and continued the trend toward equality before the law. The last vestiges of monarchy and aristocracy had been shed; family background and position by birth no longer counted for so much. The Jacksonians were Americans through and through; if they were still very much a part of Western civilization, it had been winnowed through an American experience which had left it shorn of its outward forms of inequality. The Jacksonians were of the frontier spiritually, if not actually, a product of the westward movement, even when it was only an inland movement from the port cities. Economically, the Jacksonians favored free enterprise, an open field and no favors from anyone. Jacksonian Democracy was a part of an intellectual current as well, a current sweeping through America. If that current has to be given a name, it might best be called romantic individualism. It contained in it a vision of the possibilities of man in America, not simply for a few chosen people but for the generality of people.

Unlike Thomas Jefferson, Andrew Jackson was not himself a man of ideas. He was much more a man of action. Yet he personified the central ideas of a movement, and he was a symbol for the aspirations that underlay it. He was the first President who had been born in a log cabin, though not the last. He had risen from abject poverty to the highest office in the land. He was, in the American idiom, a self-made man. Although he had little formal education, he studied law, became a judge, was a general in the army, served in the United States House of Representatives and the Senate, and was twice elected President. More, he acquired a landed estate, was a slaveowner and planter, built a Greek Revival Southern mansion, and lived the life of a Southern gentleman, when he was not on some sort of warpath. All this he had done without benefit of family background, inheritance, or even marrying a rich widow. He personified the American dream, and he stood for keeping the way open for others.

Although Jackson was not a man of ideas, he had the ability to dramatize ideas and capture the public imagination by doing so. He was the first President to veto legislation with such telling effect. There was a rough and ready way, redolent of the frontier, which he had of confronting and resolving issues. Jefferson preferred to maneuver; Jackson tackled issues head on. And, he brought ideas to life by acting decisively upon them. For whether right or wrong, for whatever motives, he justified his acts as

President in the well-stated language of ideas. Thus, he brought ideas to life by his acts and the justification of them, often quite vividly.

The People's Choice

Andrew Jackson was the first President popularly elected to the office. That is, he was the first chosen by a majority of the voting public. None of this is meant to suggest that earlier Presidents were unpopular or that they might not have been chosen by the voters if the decisions had been made at the polls. The point is that they were not. In the early years, state legislators had chosen the members of the electoral college. They, in turn, had chosen a President, except in 1800 and 1824, when they failed to give a majority to any candidate, and the election was made in the House of Representatives.

Two major changes had occurred in the elections to produce the result of a popularly elected President. One was the development of political parties. The electoral college was devised in the Constitutional Convention mainly as a means to provide an independent source for the election of the President. The Founders considered, but rejected the idea having him elected by Congress. That would have made him too dependent on that body. Nor could they agree to have him appointed by state legislators. Instead, they provided for a distinct one-purpose body—the electoral college. They supposed that the electors would simply vote for the men of their choice, without instruction or prior commitment. It did not work out that way. Political parties were developed early, and thereafter electors were usually expected to vote for party candidates.

The other change was the shift to electing electors by popular vote. The Constitution does not specify who will elect them, so the decision is left to the states. Initially, the electors had been chosen by state legislatures. But by the early 1820s the shift was on to having the electors chosen by popular vote, and by 1828 only Delaware and South Carolina retained the practice of having legislatures choose them. Actually, the shift had proceeded far enough by 1824 that a President might have been popularly elected, but it did not happen that year. It did not happen because none of the candidates got a majority of either the popular vote or the electoral vote. In the election in the House, the candidate who had come in second in both the popular and electoral vote, John Quincy Adams, was elected. In 1828, however, Andrew Jackson got a majority of the popular (as well as the electoral) vote. Thus, he was the first popularly elected President.

The shift to popular voting for presidential candidates had other consequences than popular election, however. One was that before the 1820s men did not actively campaign for the office. There would have been little purpose in campaigning with the general public. When nominations were made by congressional caucuses, there might be some maneuvering in Congress, and supporters of one candidate or another would exert influence in state legislatures. (The early candidates for the office did not usually make any show of desire for high office; more tastefully, they at least appeared to be reluctant. Thus, the maneuvering, if any, was usually done by their supporters.) But with the general voter publicly participating in the election of Presidents, campaigning began to make its appearance much more generally.

Political gatherings to whip up enthusiasm for candidates became common during Jackson's time, and none were more active in this than the Democrats. Supporters of candidates held parades, rallies, tree plantings, barbecues, and the like. A Frenchman, Michael Chevalier, described one such rally for Jackson in 1832:

> . . . I stopped involuntarily at the sight of the gigantic hickory poles which made their solemn entry on eight wheels for the purpose of being planted by the democracy on the eve of the election. I remember one of these poles, its top still crowned with green foliage, which came on the sound of fife and drum and was preceded by ranks of Democrats, bearing no other badge than a twig of the sacred tree in their hats. It was drawn by eight horses, decorated with ribbons and mottoes. Astride the tree itself were a dozen Jackson men of the first water, waving flags with an air of anticipated triumph and shouting, Hurrah for Jackson![7]

It is not surprising, then, that Jackson's first inauguration on March 4, 1829, was attended by great throngs of people, for he was the people's choice and this was their day. It was not a finely organized and orchestrated event; rather people came however they could, in carriages, coaches, "waggons and carts, filled with women and children, some in finery and some in rags,"[8] as Margaret Bayard Smith wrote at the time. They found places to sit or stand as they could. General Jackson walked up Pennsylvania Avenue to the Capitol, a tall, lean figure, dressed in black, his hawk-like face crowned with a shock of white hair. After giving his address, he pressed his way through the crowd, mounted his horse, and rode to the White House. The throngs, meanwhile, had begun to descend on the White House. Mrs. Smith was not there at the first, but she reports what she saw when she arrived this way:

> . . . But what a scene did we witness. The *Majesty of the People* had disappeared, and a rabble, a mob, of boys, negros, women, children, scrambling, fighting, romping. . . . No arrangements had been made, no police officers placed on duty, and the whole house had been inundated. . . . We came too late. The President, after having been *literally* nearly pressed to death . . . by the people in their eagerness to shake hands with Old Hickory, had retreated through the

back way or south front and had escaped to his lodgings. . . . Cut glass and china to the amount of several thousand dollars had been broken in struggle to get the refreshments. . . . "It would have done Mr. Wilberforce's heart good," wrote an observer, "to have seen a black wench eating in this free country a jelly with a gold spoon at the President's house." Ladies fainted, men were seen with bloody noses and such a scene of confusion took place as is impossible to describe,—those who got in could not get out the door again, but had to scramble out of windows. . . .[9]

Some thought that such scenes were reminiscent of the events at the onset of the French Revolution, and there were dark fears about what this might portend for a coming mob rule. But the fears were groundless. These events were only the result of an overly exuberant crowd and the failure to take the necessary precaution. Jackson's first inauguration was an American event, not a foretaste of European revolt but a too casual celebration of what has sometimes been called the rise of the common man. What European revolutionists had vaguely sought in disorderly revolt Americans had already concretely achieved by constitutional government.

Jackson was no "common" man, of course; he was outstandingly uncommon. But he stood for something that was common to many of the people in his day: the aspiration to rise by their own merits without arbitrary obstacles thrown in their way by government. And they apparently saw this in him, for, as his first biographer said: "Andrew Jackson loved the people, the common people, the sons and daughters of toil, as truly as they loved him, and believed in them as they believed in him. He was in accord with his generation. He had a clear perception that the toiling millions are not a class in the community, but *are* the community."[10]

The Meaning of Jacksonian Democracy

When people referred to "The Democracy" in the middle third of the 19th century, they usually meant the Democratic Party. They did not ordinarily think of the United States as a democracy nor describe it that way. The Founders understood that they had established a republic, and that view of the matter still prevailed. It is true that a young Frenchman, Alexis de Tocqueville, toured the United States in the early 1830s. As a result, he wrote a multivolumed work entitled *Democracy in America,* not primarily about the Democratic Party but about the United States. By so doing, he may have given currency to the notion that the United States was a democracy, but his conclusion was an interpretation, not a fact. In any case, Jacksonian Democracy was an impetus within the framework of republican government, not an assault upon it or an attempt to change its basic character.

William Cullen Bryant
(1794–1878)

Courtesy New York Historical Society

Bryant was a poet, journalist, translator, lawyer and newspaperman. He was born in Massachusetts, attended Williams College briefly, studied law, and was admitted to practice. A book of his poems was published when he was only 14, and in the ensuing years others followed.

Although he began the practice of law as a young man, he did not allow that pursuit for long to stifle his literary bent. At the age of 30, Bryant moved to New York City and became an editor on the *Evening Post*. Before long he gained editorial control over the paper and was the chief owner. Thereafter, he busied himself in writing both poetry and prose, as well as translating works in other languages into English. His best known poem is probably "Thanatopsis," which has been published in many anthologies. In the Jacksonian era, he was an outstanding spokesman for the free market.

Nevertheless, the Jacksonians did have an idea of democracy that went beyond political party and that was held or developed by men who were not politicians as well as many of those that were. There was a considerable intellectual ferment in the 1830s and 1840s, a ferment of thought advanced in newspapers, magazines, books, and speeches, and much of it was more or less Jacksonian. Among the Jacksonian thinkers should be included such journalists as William Leggett, William Cullen Bryant (better known in more recent times for his poetry) and William M. Gouge; George Bancroft, the historian, but also involved in Democratic politics; Francis Wayland, president of Brown University; Walt Whitman, who later achieved fame as a poet. These, and others, presented and honed the Jacksonian ideas for public understanding.

The central idea of Jacksonian democracy was the belief in self-government. But they used government in a much broader sense than the formal government. They were referring mainly to individuals and families governing themselves, that is, managing their own affairs. They did believe in a broad popular participation in government by a virtually universal manhood suffrage, but their main emphasis was upon freeing people from

the control of others, including those in formal governments, to manage
their own affairs.

The roots of Jacksonian democracy can be found in the thinking of
Thomas Jefferson. Jefferson, too, had thought of it as democracy. "We of
the United States, you know," Jefferson wrote, "are constitutionally and
conscientiously democrats." He explained it this way:

> We think experience has proved it safer, for the mass of individuals
> composing the society, to reserve to themselves personally the exercise
> of all rightful powers to which they are competent, and to delegate
> those to which they are not competent to deputies named, and remov-
> able for unfaithful conduct, by themselves immediately.[11]

John Taylor of Caroline, himself a Jeffersonian, was a major background
influence on the Jacksonians. Like Jefferson, he believed that farmers were
generally virtuous and that they could be trusted with managing their own
affairs and participation in government. While the Jacksonians did not so
exclusively subscribe to agriculture as he proposed, they did adopt his idea
of the worthiness of the generality of the people. Moreover, his ideas on the
tariff came to be shared by many of the Jacksonians. The tariff, Taylor said,
is "a tax upon the rich and poor of the whole community, all being
consumers, for the exclusive benefit of the rich of one occupation. This is
aristocracy in its worst character."[12]

The Jacksonians did not believe that the generality of people should
control government in order to use it positively for their particular benefit.
On the contrary, they believed that the people generally should control
government so as to limit and restrain it from acting for the benefit of the
few at their expense. That is, they believed in a strict construction of the
Constitution and limited government. Jackson said, "There is but one safe
rule, and that is to confine the General Government rigidly within the sphere
of its appropriate duties. . . . Let us abide by the Constitution as it is written
or amend it in the constitutional mode if it is found to be defective."[13]

Jacksonian journalists drove the point home in publications during these
years. Their central point was to limit government so that people might be
free to manage their own affairs. The *Democratic Review,* which began
publication in 1837, declared in its opening issue:

> The best government is that which governs least. No human deposi-
> tories [of power] can, with safety, be trusted with the power of
> legislation upon the general interests of society so as to operate directly
> or indirectly upon the industry and property of the community.[14]

Why could government not be trusted with this power? Because, "This is
the fundamental principle of the philosophy of democracy, to furnish a

system of administration of justice, and then leave all the business and interests of themselves, to free competition and association; in a word, to the *voluntary principle*."[15]

William Leggett took a similar position and explained it this way: "The fundamental principle of all governments," he pointed out, "is the protection of person and property from domestic and foreign enemies. . . ."[16] When it has done that, he thought, men may be expected to look after themselves:

> As a general rule, the prosperity of rational men depends upon themselves. Their talents and their virtues shape their fortunes. They are therefore the best judges of their own affairs and should be permitted to seek their own happiness in their own way, untrammeled by the capricious interference of legislative bungling, so long as they do not violate the equal rights of others nor transgress the general laws for the security of person and property.[17]

He described this arrangement as the goal and aim of democracy, maintaining that "if government were restricted to the few and simple objects contemplated in the democratic creed, the mere protection of person, life, and property . . . , we should find reason to congratulate ourselves on the change in the improved tone of public morals as well as in the increased prosperity of trade."[18]

Walt Whitman explained the position forthrightly and without mincing words. "Men must be 'masters unto themselves,' " he said, "and not look to presidents and legislative bodies for aid."[19] The route to that goal was to restrain government:

> One point, however, must not be forgotten—ought to be put before the eyes of the people every day; and that is, although government can do little *positive* good to the people, it may do an *immense deal of harm*. And here is where the beauty of the Democratic principle comes in. Democracy would prevent all this harm. It would have no man's benefit achieved at the expense of his neighbors. . . . While mere politicians, in their narrow minds, are sweating and fuming with their complicated statutes, this one single rule . . . is enough to form the starting point of all that is necessary in government; *to make no more laws than those useful for preventing a man or body of men from infringing on the rights of other men.*[20]

The Jacksonians, then, had a theory of democracy, a theory which included limited government, free trade, a society of equals before the law, and each man pursuing his own interests limited only by the equal rights of others. In this way, the energies of each man would be released to make the most for himself and contribute to the general well-being. The spokesmen for the Democracy had imbibed the teachings of the classical economists, of Adam Smith, J. B. Say, and David Ricardo, and had caught the vision of the possibilities of freedom and were pressing for the freeing of enterprise. Andrew Jackson was their champion, and Martin Van Buren was hardly less convinced of the rightness of this cause. In politics, it turned into a campaign against chartered monopolies or any other government benefits held in perpetuity. Some carried these ideas in particular directions that would have undercut the foundations of such a society, but the main thrust of them is described in the above.

Chattel slavery was surely an anomaly in this "democratic creed," as it was within the framework of the Declaration of Independence. Clearly slaves were not permitted to manage their own affairs, and their status was hereditary. Two principles, however, enabled the Democrats to avoid raising the issue in the 1830s and 1840s. One was that slavery was controlled by the states, and since the Constitution gave no power to Congress to deal with slavery (except to prohibit their importation), they could maintain it was not a national question. The other was that slaves were the property of their owners, and property was protected by the Constitution.

Jackson's Administrations

Jackson was undoubtedly one of the more popular Presidents, but it is also true that his administration was rent by controversies. Some of the controversy can be attributed to Jackson's temperament and military background. He was used to making decisions and following them through, did not go out of his way to avoid confrontations, and liked to win. He could be vindictive, too, though he may not have been so much different from others except for his openness about it. It is true also, however, that the focus had now shifted from foreign to domestic affairs, and these are apt to be more divisive. In addition, the thrust of the Democrats against special privilege and chartered monopolies aroused resentments. But whatever the explanation, there were spirited controversies during much of Jackson's eight years in office.

a. Replacing Government Employees

The Constitution is silent about the terms of appointed government employees or when and under what conditions they may be removed from office. The only reference to removal from office of appointed officials is by impeachment, which would apply only to extraordinary cases. It does grant to the President the power to appoint high government officials by and with the advice and consent of the Senate. More, Congress is empowered to authorize the appointment of "such inferior Officers, as they think proper, in the President alone, in the Courts of Law, or in the Heads of Departments." Nothing is mentioned, except for impeachment, about when or how they may be removed from office.

It was an unfortunate omission, for the question has been a subject of controversy throughout much of American history. The makers of the Constitution may simply not have foreseen the difficulties. Or, they may have assumed that the power of appointment carries with it a power of dismissal by the same authority. The evidence available from records of debates in the Constitutional Convention, however, suggests that they did not much expect this particular problem to arise. Their experience on a national level had been that it was difficult to get and keep government employees. It had been difficult to get people to accept appointments to the Continental Congress or to remain in office, once appointed. Thus, there was considerable concern expressed in the Convention about attracting competent people into government service, little to none about getting rid of those who were not wanted. At any rate, there was no explicit provision for dismissing and replacing appointed officials in the Constitution, and no amendment has ever been added to supply the deficiency.

The way Jackson chose to deal with the matter was one of the first controversies to arise in his administration. He was accused of initiating the "Spoils System," and has been pilloried for doing so ever since. So far as the charge had any factual basis, it lay in the fact that a goodly number of appointees from past administrations were dismissed and replaced by people of his own choosing. The origin of the phrase, "Spoils System," was the aphorism, "To the victor belongs the spoils." In this case, it was the spoils of office, and the charge was that he was rewarding the faithful with the fruits of victory.

These charges obscured the problem and made it appear that Jackson was doing something wrong. The problem can be stated much more fairly and objectively than that. In its broadest dimensions, it can be brought into view with some questions. Are all government appointments to be for life (except for impeachment)? If not, when may they be terminated, and by whom? If they are appointments for life, how would a President execute his policies? Would an incoming President not be stripped of most of his powers of appointment and control over his administration? There might well be advantages to keeping many "inferior Officers," both to give continuity to the government and benefit from their experience. But was the President, or the heads of departments, to have no say as to which were to be replaced and which kept? Or, to take a different angle, did government employees have property in their jobs?

Jackson made his answer to these questions in his First Annual Message to Congress. He argued that no person had a right to public office (i.e., government employment), that "He who is removed has the same means of obtaining a living that are enjoyed by the millions who never held office."

In his view, men were apt to be corrupted by long stints of government employment, that, therefore there ought to be rotation in office. As for the expertise they might have or have gained, "The duties of all public officers are, or at least admit of being made, so plain and simple that men of intelligence may readily qualify themselves for their performance." Jackson made a telling point when he declared that under a system in which people were kept indefinitely in public employment, "Office is considered a species of property, and government rather as a means of promoting individual interests than as an instrument created solely for the service of the people." It becomes an "engine for the support of the few at the expense of the many." Therefore, he favored "a general extension of the law which limits appointments to four years."[21]

Thomas Hart Benton (1782–1858)

Benton was an American statesman and orator, and, though less well known than Webster, Clay, and Calhoun, he should be ranked with them for his role in the Senate. He was born in North Carolina, moved to Tennessee, but most of his political activities were from the home base of Missouri. He tried several pursuits—farming, practicing law, and teaching—, but he found his vocation in politics. His early career and movements paralleled those of Jackson, and indeed Benton became friends with Jackson while living in Tennessee. They fell out, however, and were involved in a gunfight brawl, which made them mortal enemies for several years. However, when Jackson began his run for the presidency, Benton supported him and became a Jacksonian for the rest of his political career. He served in the Senate from 1820–1851, and took the lead in the Senate during Jackson's second term in office. He was a sound money man and led the attack on banks and banking. Benton was a nationalist and a Westerner and worked for many years to make public lands available for private ownership.

Jackson did not completely explore the questions nor answer all the objections of the critics. The patronage question remained as an issue. But it was constitutionally logical to propose that presidential appointments be limited to four years. Presidents are elected to four-year terms, and in the absence of prescription (as in the appointment of Supreme Court justices) it would be an unusual grant of power to allow them to appoint the public servants of their successors. That issue had arisen as early as Jefferson's first term in office. Adams had kept Washington's Cabinet, and it was by no means clear that even heads of departments should retire when a new President came to office. Jefferson settled that question for top officials (by replacing all of them), undercut the positions of some of the judicial appointments of Adams by having the law repealed creating the offices. He also removed some of the "inferior Officers" and replaced them with some of his appointees. But those who had government employment continued to try to cling to their jobs when there was a change of administration.

Actually, Jackson did not make a wholesale removal of government employees and replace them with his appointees. During his first year and a half in office he removed only 919 of the over 10,000 government employees from office. During his 8 years as President, somewhere between one-fifth and one-tenth of the officeholders were replaced. A Senate committee to inquire into executive patronage in 1835 voiced greater concern with the growth in the number of government employees than with the removal of earlier ones by an incoming President. The committee noted that government expenditures increased from over $11 million in 1825 to over $22 million in 1833. Government employment had greatly increased along with expenditures, the committee asserted. Thus, the executive had opportunities to increase the number of the party faithful rewarded. The committee deplored this situation and recommended that the government reduce taxes and expenses, thus reducing the opportunities for patronage.

It should be noted that Jackson's position on government appointments was consistent with the Jacksonian philosophy. It was opposed to special privileges for any group, and permanent government employment looked suspiciously like a privileged position. If rotation in office was good for elected officials, why not for appointive ones?

b. Webster-Hayne Debates

For once, Jackson was not directly involved in a major event which took place during his years in office. The Webster-Hayne debates were a Senate affair and did not have much of an immediate impact beyond that forum. They did, however, explode into a sectional controversy and raised the questions of nullification and disunion. On these latter questions, Jackson would have opportunity later to express himself fully.

The debates grew out of a resolution introduced by Senator Samuel Foot of Connecticut in December, 1829. He proposed the restriction of the sale of public lands to those already surveyed and placed on sale at auction. Senator Thomas Hart Benton of Missouri objected strenuously to any restraint on the sale of public lands. He charged the Easterners with attempting to hold on to their industrial workers by cutting off the supply of land in the West. Benton expressed the view that the East was continuing a long-term policy of attempting to stifle the westward movement in order to maintain its own dominance.

The Webster-Hayne debates took place in January, 1830. Senator Hayne of South Carolina rose to take up the argument where Benton had left off. He came out for cheaper public lands on the grounds that the federal government did not need more money (there was already a surplus in the Treasury), and that to receive it would only increase the power of the general government. Moreover, he charged that there were those in "certain quarters of the Union" eager to regulate the disposal of western lands so "as

Daniel Webster
(1782–1852)

Courtesy New York Historical Society

Webster was a famous lawyer, a spellbinding orator, and a statesman. One of his contemporaries said of a speech by him, "I was never so excited by public speaking before in my life. Three or four times I thought my temples would burst with the gush of blood. . . . I was beside myself, and am so still." Webster was born in New Hampshire, attended Dartmouth College, studied law, and soon distinguished himself in the courtroom. He began his national career by a stint in the House of Representatives, 1813–1817, and it was after that when be began to establish himself as an orator among orators. Beginning in the late 1820s he served for several years in the Senate and, after the Webster-Hayne debates, had aspirations to be President as a Whig. He was always a bridesmaid, never a bride, however, so far as the presidency was concerned. He was more of a mover of men by his oratory than a leader of men, which may explain this failure. In any case, he had an impressive career as Senator and Secretary of State and though an opponent of slavery, did not agitate the issue.

to create and preserve . . . a population suitable for conducting great manufacturing establishments.'' It would be a population ''who, having no other means of subsistence, will work for the lowest wages, and be satisfied with the smallest possible share of human enjoyment.''[22] Hayne, a Southerner, had come to the defense of land policies favored in the West. An attempt was going on here to tie the South and West closer together and to gain support from the West against the protective tariff. It was a countermove to that of Clay's American System, which would join the East and West in support of the tariff and other nationalist policies.

Daniel Webster of Massachusetts now entered the debate, and thereafter it was between Hayne and Webster. Webster was already famed as a master of oratory, and in this debate he also demonstrated his understanding of how important it is to decide the issues. He shifted the debate to the question of preserving the union by charging that the tendency of certain ideas being advanced in the South was to break up the union. Hayne rose to the bait and entered into a lengthy defense of state sovereignty, of the rights of the states, and of the importance of maintaining the constitutional balance. Thus, these debates became a dress rehearsal in 1830 of the issues that would rise again and again over the next 30 years and eventually erupt into civil war.

As the debate moved toward its crescendo, it became a spectator event as well. Not only were the galleries of the Senate chamber packed but also the Senate seats and all the space surrounding them. So many Congressmen came to hear the debates that the House of Representatives lacked a quorum to do business.

Probably, the crucial point made by Hayne was that it was the Northern leaders, not Southern positions that were provoking disunion. When they attempted to use the general government for their own special purposes, such as with the protective tariff, theirs was the provocation of disunion. Hayne put it this way:

> Who then . . . are the true friends of the Union? Those who would confine the federal government strictly within the limits prescribed by the Constitution; who would preserve to the States and the people all powers not expressly delegated, who would make this a federal and not a national Union, and who, administering the government in a spirit of equal justice, would make it a blessing and not a curse. And who are its enemies? Those who are in favor of consolidation; who are constantly stealing power from the States, and adding strength to the federal government; who, assuming an unwarrantable jurisdiction over the States and the people, undertake to regulate the whole industry and capital of the country. . . .[23]

It took Webster two afternoons of speaking to give what is known as his ''Second Reply to Hayne.'' He took on Hayne's position that the states had a right to resist what they interpreted as unconstitutional acts by the federal government. That would amount, Webster said, to the right of the states to dissolve the union. Thus, he returned time after time to the theme of preserving the union, finishing with this stirring peroration:

> I have not allowed myself, sir, to look beyond the Union, to see what might lie hidden in the dark recess behind. . . . When my eyes shall be turned to behold for the last time the sun in heaven, may I not see him shining on the broken and dishonored fragments of a once glorious Union; on States dissevered, discordant, belligerent; on a land rent with civil feuds, or drenched, it may be, in fraternal blood! Let their last feeble and lingering glance rather behold the gorgeous ensign of the republic, now known and honored throughout the earth, still full high advanced, its arms and trophies streaming in their original lustre, not a stripe erased or polluted nor a single star obscured . . . ; but everywhere spread all over in characters of living light, blazing on all its ample folds, as they float over sea and over the land, and in every wind under the whole heavens, that other sentiment, dear to every true American heart,—Liberty and Union, now and forever, one and inseparable.[24]

The debate did not, of course resolve the questions at issue. Debates rarely do. The public lands continued to be disposed of by the government, and the tendency of the Democrats was to move toward "squatter rights," called "preemption" at the time, rather than imposing severe restrictions. As for the sectional and constitutional issues raised, the debate aggravated rather than settling these. Undoubtedly, Webster did clothe the position opposed to nullification or state sovereignty with a patriotic aura which, if accepted, made further discussion superfluous. Twenty different editions of Webster's speech were published within a few months, and it circulated by the thousands over the country. It became the best known speech that had ever been delivered to Congress.

c. The Maysville Road Bill

Congress passed a bill in May, 1830 authorizing the building of a road from Maysville, Kentucky to Lexington. President Jackson promptly vetoed the bill. Advocates of the Maysville Road claimed that it was to be a part of the system of roads known as the Cumberland Road. However, Jackson pointed out that the proposed road would be located entirely within one state and that there was no constitutional authority for building intrastate roads. Indeed, the whole question of federal appropriations for internal improvements was mired in sectional and constitutional controversy. The Jeffersonians had doubted there was any constitutional grounds for the federal government to appropriate money for internal improvements. Both

Madison and Monroe had vetoed appropriations for roads. Nor had the constitutional amendments which might have cleared up the matter been forthcoming. There was far from consensus in the country about the desirability of federal aid to road building because of state and regional rivalries that would be aroused by any given project.

Jackson's veto virtually laid to rest the matter of federal aid for road building for nearly half a century. True, the Cumberland Road was finally extended to Vandalia, Illinois by the 1850s, but the later work on this road was done by the states. Nor was this failure to build roads simply political. Roads were not generally competitive with waterways as yet for transporting freight over any long distance. It was too expensive to haul heavy goods by wagon.

d. The Removal of the Indians

Jefferson believed that a place had been found for the location of the Indians with the purchase of Louisiana. Early explorations of the territory west of the Mississippi resulted in the conclusion that much of it was a desert. Indeed, it was referred to for a good many years as the "Great American Desert." That was not accurate, of course, and though the region posed difficulties for settlers peculiar to it, the plan for removing the Indians to this area did not entail the belief that they were being moved to a desert. The plan in the 1820s and 1830s was to move them west of Arkansas and Missouri.

Why move the Indians at all? Why not allow them to occupy their ancestral lands in peace? Or, better still, why not permit them to integrate with the settlers and become citizens? These questions, and related ones, were raised at the time, and they have come up from time to time since then. Furthermore, charges were levied at the time, particularly from the Northeast (where Indians were not a pressing problem), that grave injustices were involved both in the general treatment of Indians and in the manner of their removal. Indeed, it can be argued with a certain plausibility that this whole continent belonged to the Indians and that the European settlers were interlopers. Certainly, the kings of England acknowledged the justice of such claims from time to time, as did the governments of colonies and of the United States regarding lands on which Indian titles had not been extinguished. But the problem with this position is that once Indians had, by treaty or otherwise, relinquished lands to European settlers, there was no longer any general question but only particular questions about this or that plot of land. That is, the general question became moot once any just acquisition of land had taken place by Europeans.

Particular questions have persisted, in many cases, from the earliest settlement to the present. But a lifetime of study by the wisest of men would probably not suffice for making a generalization as to whether European settlers or the Indians acted more justly. Undoubtedly, there were injustices as between Indians and settlers from Europe and between tribes and general and local governments. There was not, however, any common law or common government to settle disputes or differences between them or mete out justice to them.

That was the crux of the problem, and it helps to explain why removal to the West was favored by many national leaders. The Indians were not citizens of the United States, were not counted in the census for apportioning of representatives, and were not generally citizens of the states wherein they resided. The only recognized peaceful means for dealing with them was by treaties or agreements such as are ordinarily worked out with foreign governments. The resort to force was a resort to war; thus, the difficult issues were settled with musket and tomahawk, as Americans then knew. The Indians had their own tribal governments, such as they were, and did not generally desire to be assimilated by or integrated with general American society.

The difficulties and anomalies of the situation were well illustrated by the contests in Georgia with the Cherokee Indians. There was a large enclave of Cherokees in North Georgia. They had adopted pastoral ways along with much of the civilization of the white man. In the late 1820s, they adopted a written constitution and set up as a separate nation within the territorial bounds of Georgia. Georgia refused to acknowledge their independence and proceeded to assert jurisdiction over them. A case—*Cherokee Nation vs. Georgia*—came before the Supreme Court in 1831. The court held that an Indian tribe was neither a state nor a foreign nation in the sense used in the Constitution and, hence, could not assert its rights in the courts of the United States. However, in *Worcester vs. Georgia* (1832) the Supreme Court held that Georgia had exceeded its authority by going upon Indian land, arresting, and imprisoning a man who was residing there in violation of Georgia law. Georgia had no authority over Cherokee land, Chief Justice Marshall said, speaking for the Court: "The Cherokee Nation, then, is a distinct community, occupying its own territory, with boundaries accurately described, in which the laws of Georgia can have no force. . . ."[25] Georgia ignored the decision, indeed, refused to present its case before the court, and Andrew Jackson took no steps to enforce it. Instead, Jackson is alleged to have said: "John Marshall has made his decision, now let him enforce it."

Rather, Jackson was following a determined policy to remove the Indians west of the Mississippi. Some attempts had been made by earlier administrations to get the Indians to move, but little was accomplished. An Indian Removal Act was passed in 1830. Thereafter, Jackson vigorously pushed for the signing of treaties and getting the moves underway. Most of the Indians were in the Southeast, and most of these were induced to sign agreements to move: the Choctaws in 1830, Creeks in 1832, Chickasaws in 1832, and a portion of the Cherokees in 1835. Some of the Cherokees refused to move to the West, but instead moved into North Carolina. The

Seminoles fought an extended war in Florida before most of them were forcibly moved to the West. Indians in the Midwest were also driven out or induced to leave.

Although there was sometimes harshness and always much sadness and travail in the long move, it is probable that the worst long term impact on the Indians was the paternal attitude of the United States government to them. In 1829, Secretary of War John Eaton wrote that "The President views the Indians as the children of the Government. He sees what is best for them. . . ."[26] Jackson pointed out in a message to Congress in 1835 that "a territory exceeding in extent that relinquished has been granted to each tribe. . . . To these districts the Indians are removed at the expense of the United States, and with certain supplies of clothing, arms, ammunition, and other indispensable articles; they are also furnished . . . with provisions for a year after their arrival at their new homes. . . . Funds have been set aside for the maintenance of the poor. . . . And besides these beneficial arrangements, annuities are in all cases paid. . . ."[27]

Thus began the dependence of many Indians on the United States government, a dependence that continued over many years and which sapped the vitality of a people. Jackson was acting in character when he acted vigorously to remove the Indians. It was hardly in keeping with Jacksonian Democracy, however, to establish a perpetual dependence of the Indians on government aid. Perhaps he did think of them as children, but the extended aid tended to perpetuate the status.

e. The Nullification Controversy

Nullification sentiment had been simmering in South Carolina since the passage of the Tariff of 1828 (the "Tariff of Abominations"). It came to a head with the passage of the Tariff of 1832. Jackson had proposed to Congress that the earlier tariff rates should be reduced, and it would have been in keeping with the general Jacksonian position that the duties on goods be lowered to the point that they would serve only as a tariff for revenue. However, the Tariff of 1832 was still very much a protective tariff. The duties on imports that were reduced were on goods with which Americans were not effectively competing with foreigners. Thus, it appeared that the protective tariff was becoming a fixture.

Opposition to the protective tariff was strongest in the South, while Easterners were most apt to favor it. The South was the major exporting region of the United States, and by the 1830s cotton had become the major export in the country. The great world demand for cotton helped to assure that the South would remain primarily an agricultural region. The tariff did not protect the price of cotton, since it was sold on the world market, but it could raise the prices Southerners paid for manufactured goods. Not only, then, did the South not benefit directly from the tariff but also it was generally harmed by it. This was widely understood and believed in the South.

In South Carolina, some of the leaders had taken two positions by 1832. One, they held that the protective tariff was unconstitutional. This was based on the view that taxes could be levied only to meet the authorized expenses of government. But a protective tariff is not levied to meet expenses but rather to exclude goods from the country or raise their prices. Indeed, a protective tariff might actually reduce revenues by making the goods covered so expensive that they could not compete with American made goods. In that case, a duty would bring in little or no revenue. Where was the constitutional authority for such a tariff? The other position was that a state could *nullify* an act of Congress contrary to the Constitution and *interpose* its power between its citizens and the power of the federal government.

The South Carolina Exposition had set forth the doctrine of nullification in 1828. It had been the work mainly of John C. Calhoun, although he did not openly avow that he was the author. At that time, Calhoun was Vice-President, and was re-elected in that year to serve another term, this time under Jackson. Calhoun had ambitions to succeed Jackson as President and may have wished to avoid too close an identification with a sectional and states' rights position. The situation had changed drastically by 1832. Calhoun may have still had presidential amibitions, but there was no longer any expectation that they would be aided by Jackson. Calhoun and Jackson had broken with one another after 1830, and Van Buren had emerged as the person with greatest influence on Jackson. In 1832, Hayne became governor of South Carolina, and Calhoun resigned the vice presidency to accept a Senate appointment from South Carolina. Thus, he came out openly for the doctrine of nullification and argued the South Carolina position on the Senate floor.

In response to the Tariff of 1832, a special convention in South Carolina adopted an Ordinance of Nullification in November, 1832. It declared the tariff acts of 1828 and 1832 null and void and that they were not to be enforced after February 1, 1833. Since Congress would meet in regular session in December, 1832, the delay in nullification going into effect would allow time for Congress to act on the tariff if it chose to do so. Meanwhile, President Jackson acted decisively. He sent additional troops to forts in Charleston harbor and began to concentrate forces in nearby North Carolina. He issued a proclamation in December which stated his position emphatically: "I consider," he said, "the power to annul a law of the United States, assumed by one State, *incompatible with the existence of the Union, contradicted expressly by the letter of the Constitution, unauthorized by its spirit, inconsistent with every principle on which it was founded, and destructive of the great object for which it was formed.*" Nor did he leave any doubt that if necessary he would use the whole force of the United States government to see that the tariff was enforced. "The laws of the United States must be executed," he declared. "I have no discretionary power on the subject; my duty is emphatically pronounced in the Constitution."[28]

Actually, however, neither side pushed the dispute to armed conflict. No other state came to the aid of South Carolina, though there were rumblings of agreement from Georgia and Virginia. The maneuverings continued. South Carolina objected that the United States had no constitutional authority to use force on a state. Jackson replied with the argument that concerted resistance to the enforcement of the laws would be treason by a faction (which is what he claimed the nullification forces were), and that the government was authorized to punish treason. To make sure, however, Jackson asked Congress for authority to use force. Simultaneously, Congress began work on a compromise tariff. The new tariff proposal was the brainchild of Henry Clay, but in pushing it through Congress he had the vigorous aid of Calhoun.

President Jackson signed both the Force Bill and the compromise Tariff of 1833 at the same time. The tariff act provided for the gradual reduction of the tariff over the next several years until it would reach the point where it would be largely a tariff for revenue. South Carolina accepted the new tariff and revoked the Ordinance of Nullification. On the other hand, the convention declared the Force Act null and void. But since there was no longer any occasion for the exercise of force, the dispute was over, at least for the time being.

f. The Bank Controversy

Even before the contest over the tariff had risen to a peak in nullification actions another issue had come to head. This issue arose over efforts to recharter the Second Bank of the United States in 1832. The Second Bank had been chartered to run for 20 years in 1816. Thus, the question of a new charter for it would not ordinarily have come up until 1836. There is ample evidence that Henry Clay and Daniel Webster—National Republicans on their way to becoming Whigs—persuaded Nicholas Biddle, the president of the bank, to seek a renewal for political reasons of their own. They apparently convinced Biddle that Jackson would not dare veto a new charter in the midst of a presidential campaign. There is also good reason to believe that Clay and Webster believed they would have an excellent issue for the campaign should Jackson veto it, which they certainly expected him to do. In any case, Congress passed a new charter in 1832; Jackson vetoed the bill; and he was elected by a landslide victory over Clay.

Actually, the banking issue was central to Jacksonian Democracy, although not all Jacksonian Democrats appreciated it to the same degree. The Second Bank of the United States was the premier example of a chartered monopoly; it was both a monopoly and a major instance of special incorporation. The bank had a monopoly of the deposits of the United States government revenues: that is, all revenue received but not yet paid out had to be deposited in it by law. The bank was incorporated by the United States, which held a portion of its stock, and it was the only such bank in the United States. It held a dominant and privileged position *vis-à-vis* state chartered banks. There was a movement afoot, which largely achieved its goal during the Jacksonian period, to do away with special acts of incorporation. There was some opposition to the corporation itself, but most opposition was to special acts of incorporation. Jacksonians generally felt that incorporation ought to be made available by general acts of incorporation, and this was accomplished in many states by the 1840s.

Nicholas Biddle
(1786–1844)

Biddle was trained in the law, had literary aspirations, started out in diplomacy, but is known to history as a financier. He was born in Philadelphia, graduated from the University of Pennsylvania (at the age of 13), and did some writing and editorial work. He came to the attention of James Monroe when he served as a secretary in the American embassy in London, and Monroe appointed him a director of the Second United States Bank. He became its president in 1822 and served in that position until the bank lost its standing in 1836. Biddle made the bank into a central bank for the United States with numerous branches around the country and a major factor in the American economy. He aroused the opposition and jealousy of the state banks, however, as well as that of the Jacksonians who believed in "hard money." To compound his difficulties, he used the resources of the bank to gain favor with politicians and sealed the doom of the bank with his aggressive tactics.

There was another objection to banking, however. The business of banks at that time was mainly conducted through the issuing of bank notes (paper money) which usually circulated as currency. These bank notes were promises to pay in specie (gold and silver coin usually). Yet banks, including the Second United States Bank, often kept less specie in reserve than they had bank notes outstanding. If so, they engaged in *fractional reserve* banking. This raised the specter of paper money inflation and bank failures. Although it did not reach a peak during Jackson's time, opposition to banking itself was mounting. Jackson himself was a "hard money" man and was fearful about fractional reserve banking. Actually, the Second Bank under Biddle's control had not only met demands for specie regularly but also pressured state banks toward honesty by collecting their notes and demanding payment in specie. None of this changed the facts, of course, that it had special privileges and a monopoly.

Thus, when the bill to recharter the bank came before Jackson he vetoed it. From the outset, Jackson had expressed the belief that the bank was unconstitutional; thus, he took this as his main grounds for vetoing the bill. He was unmoved by the fact that the Supreme Court had earlier declared a United States bank constitutional. That opinion did not remove from him the necessity of deciding the question for himself, he said. Jackson put it this way: "The authority of the Supreme Court must not, therefore, be permitted to control the Congress or the Executive when acting in their legislative capacities, but to have such influence as the force of their reasoning may deserve."[29] He found the bill before him defective on several grounds. In addition to its unconstitutionality, he questioned its monopolistic character, the enrichment of a few men who were stockholders at the expense of many, and feared the power over the government itself accumulating in the hands of those who controlled the bank. On this last point, there is little doubt that Biddle had by making loans and granting favors gained considerable sway over Congress.

Jackson was now determined to bring to an end the privileged position of the Second Bank, though its charter still had nearly four years to run. His veto of the new charter had not been over-ridden by Congress, and his own re-election gave popular affirmation of his course. He ordered the Secretary of the Treasury to close out the government deposits in the bank. The secretary refused to do it. Jackson dismissed him and appointed another in his place. He also refused, so he was dismissed as well. Jackson then appointed Roger B. Taney Secretary of the Treasury, and he proceeded to finish the government's business with the bank. Taney stopped making deposits with the Second Bank; instead, he deposited government funds in select state banks. (Critics dubbed these favored banks as Jackson's "pets.") Meanwhile, the deposits in the Second Bank were gradually withdrawn as the government paid its bills.

Nicholas Biddle retaliated by precipitating a financial crisis. With the withdrawal of government funds, it was undoubtedly necessary for the bank to call in some of its loans. But he went about calling in loans with unaccustomed zeal, and there was a considerable crunch as debtors sought funds. The evidence indicates that Biddle was deliberately reducing the money supply to create a panic and convince Congress of the necessity of rechartering the bank. He wrote a friend that "if the bank were to suffer itself to be misled into the measure of making money plentiful, it will only give to its enemies the triumph of having robbed it with impunity."[30] He did succeed in causing some financial distress, but political efforts to recharter the bank failed, and Biddle eased up on the money supply.

Actually, the country was being flooded with paper money in the last years of Jackson's second term. Speculation, especially land speculation and building projects, was widespread, and these were being fed by paper money. This story belongs mainly with that of expansionism and is told there, but Jackson struck one more blow for hard money that needs to be mentioned here. He issued a Specie Circular in July, 1836, which required, generally, that payments for land (with some exceptions) should be made in gold and silver. This contributed to a bank panic in 1837, but the remainder of that story belongs elsewhere.

Jackson had made a considerable impact on American political life. He had forged a new political party, the Democratic Party, and infused it with the mission of freeing enterprise by removing government-granted privileges. It was a national party, too, which had a large following in the North and South, East and West. Another major accomplishment during these years was the retirement of the debt around 1835. There was such a surplus in the treasury in the mid-1830s that funds were distributed to the states to reduce it. Although domestic affairs dominated during Jackson's years in the presidency, when the occasion arose the government acted decisively and effectively there as well. The trade with the British West Indies was reopened; trade with Colombia was stabilized; a treaty was worked out with Turkey, and difficulties with the French settled. The Constitution provided for a government in which the branches are in tension with one another, in which there is a tension between state and federal government and between the people and the government. This tension was brought to new heights during Jackson's terms in office, but the main result was the restraining of government, which is how the Constitution was expected to work.

Chapter 4
Americans at Work

Americans of all ages, all conditions, and all dispositions constantly form associations. They have not only commercial and manufacturing companies, in which all take part, but associations of a thousand other kinds—religious, moral, serious, futile, extensive or restrictive, enormous or diminutive. The Americans make associations to give entertainments, to found establishments for education, to build inns, to construct churches, to diffuse books, to send missionaries to the antipodes; and in this manner they found hospitals, prisons, and schools.

—Alexis de Tocqueville, 1840

Now my plan is this: I intend to live in La Platte City. I intend to open up a large farm. I can raise hemp, corn or anything. . . . I intend not only to farm simply but I will open a Commission House. I expect to supply the territory with iron nails, lumber, etc., this will not be profitable in itself but will be the great means of building up the city. . . .

—William Larimer, 1855

As my heart is tender and much distressed on the final disposition of my servants, to mitigate the severity of perpetual slavery, it is my will that they be retained on the farm as usual or, should they become dissipated, lazy, or quarrelsome, or roguish, that they be sold to humane masters at the discretion of the Executors. . . .

—From the will of R. M. Cunningham, 1838

The title of this chapter might have been, "Americans at Work and Play," but that would give a wrong impression. That would not be in accord either with what follows or with the lives of Americans in the first half of the 19th century. More important, perhaps, it would disjoin work and play in ways that were not so common then as now, except among small children.

Work was much more integral to all of life for people then than it is for many today. That is, it did not belong in a separate category, boxed off by distances to be traveled to and fro, and occurring in some remote office, factory, mine, mill, or other location. Work was much more likely to be near at hand, done in the midst of family, and spaced over the day and week rather than concentrated in 8-hour, 5-day weeks. Specialization had not set in strongly yet, so that tasks or activities were not nearly so likely to be classified into work or recreation.

Work and play were not necessarily distinct activities, especially for adults, in those days. Except for slaves and in factories, work was not severely disciplined as it has been for us in more recent times. Most people did not yet live by clocks. Work and rest were ordinarily separated by daylight and darkness; in the absence of dependable bright lights most activities and functions were performed during the day. The rhythms of life were usually geared to day and night, the weather, the seasons of the year, the coming in and going out of tides, rain and drought, cold and hot. There were no professional sports and little professional entertainment. Some things that are thought of as sports today were closely related to getting a living then. Hunting and fishing were means of adding to the meat supply for all but the very wealthy. On the other hand, almost any task, if done alongside others, might be made into a game. Thus, men cutting grain with a scythe might race with one another, as they might do in a hundred other tasks. House raisings, quilting bees, corn huskings, and gatherings of that kind were social events, but they were also pleasant ways to get work done.

None of this is meant to suggest that there were not forms of recreation distinct from work for many people. Prize fighting, while sometimes illegal in cities, did take place; there were boxing and wrestling matches. Plays and musical performances were presented in towns and cities. There was horse racing and fox hunting. Minstrel shows were especially popular in the years before the Civil War. Boys played various games with bats, balls, and bases, and by the 1850s baseball was being played in many places across America. But the common attitude was that such play was for children. An Englishwoman who came to America in the 1860s lamented that the "absence of desire for physical sport seems more or less common throughout America, and is very strange in the eyes of those accustomed to the exhibition of animal spirits in the English youth of both sexes. . . . There seems an absolute deficiency of vitality in Americans in this respect. . . ."[31]

Many Americans did indeed consider play and games frivolous, but it should also be emphasized that Americans were likely to get exercise aplenty in their work. In any case, work is the main subject of this chapter, work by which Americans got their livelihood, work by which they tamed the wilderness, cut down the trees in the forest, tilled the soil, harvested their crops, manufactured their products, built factories and mills, transported and stored their goods, raised their animals, and hunted their meat. Work is, of course, the means by which people provide for their needs and wants. But it was and is much more than that. It is the means by which people fulfill their dreams, so far as they do, develop their skills and abilities, realize themselves, accumulate an estate, provide for families, and accomplish things. What moves them to do so, how they organize to work, and how work gets done, changes from time to time and has its history. At any rate, these things are intertwined with work and form the substance of this chapter.

The Voluntary Way

In most important senses, Americans were individualists in the 19th century. They believed in individual liberty and responsibility and had devised institutions to protect the liberty and enforce the responsibility. John Adams had described the situation this way:

> Each individual of the society has a right to be protected by it in the enjoyment of his life, liberty, and property, according to standing laws. He is obliged, consequently, to contribute his share to the expense of this protection, and to give his personal service, or an equivalent, when necessary.[32]

But the responsibilities go much further than toward the government which protects him in his rights. The individual is responsible for providing for himself and his family, for making his own living, and making such provision as he can against periods when he cannot or does not produce enough for himself and his own. In short, individual responsibility is a corollary of individual rights.

The deepest support for this American belief in the primacy of the individual comes from Christianity. The emphasis of Christianity is focused primarily on the individual. Only the individual survives eternally, according to Christian doctrine, not groups, not organizations, not governments— all of which are temporary and temporal. The individual is responsible for his deeds, both good and bad, and will be held to account for them. Within the Judeo-Christian framework, man is held to be free to choose his course, but he is therefore held responsible for what he does with that freedom.

The counterpart to this emphasis upon the rights, responsibilities, and independence of the individual in America was voluntary association for cooperative undertakings. The thrust of America from the time of the early settlements and coming to a head during the American Revolution had been in the direction of cutting away government control and prescription over the lives of the people. During the early years colonial governments had often been restrictive and prescriptive themselves, but by the 18th century they were moving definitely toward restraining government and freeing the individual. Even the bonds of family were loosened somewhat in the wake of the break from England as primogeniture and entail were abolished. The power of the churches was drastically reduced as church membership became a voluntary matter between individual members and the authorities within the churches. Families had long since lost their authority, or most of it, over marriage arrangements, and churches could now no longer intervene with any governmental support. Thus, individuals above a certain age, especially males, were legally on their own, to prosper or fail as they would, to be as independent as they could, and to look after their own affairs. The result, however, was neither anarchy nor any general loosening of the bonds of society. Indeed, the bonds were knit in voluntary arrangements which had their own special strengths and virtues. People often put a great deal of energy into what they have voluntarily chosen to do.

Foreigners were often greatly impressed and amazed by the number and variety of voluntary undertakings in America. Tocqueville, observing the country in the 1830s, noted that "the political associations which exist in the United States are only a single feature in the midst of the immense assemblage of associations in that country. . . . Wherever, at the head of some new undertaking, you see the Government in France, or a man of rank in England, in the United States you will be sure to find an association." Continuing on the same theme, he said: "I met with several kinds of associations in America, of which I confess I had no previous notion; and I have often admired the extreme skill with which the inhabitants of the United States succeed in proposing a common object to the exertions of a great many men, and in getting them voluntarily to pursue it."[33]

Tocqueville explained the willingness of Americans to participate in joint undertakings and mutual aid this way: "The free institutions which the inhabitants of the United States possess, and the political rights of which they make so much use, remind every citizen, and in a thousand ways, that he lives in society. They every instant impress upon his mind the notion that it is the duty as well as the interest of men to make themselves useful to their fellow-creatures. . . ."[34] To that should be added the fact that if people were to have limited government and personal independence, they must not depend upon government to do a great many things which to do would require joint effort. Particularly, this would be necessary in helping to look after those who might in one way or another be unable to look after themselves. President Franklin Pierce vetoed a bill in 1854 which would have provided Federal aid for the care of the insane. He had this, among other things, to say:

> I readily, and I trust feelingly, acknowledge the duty incumbent on us all, as men and citizens, and as among the highest and holiest of our duties, to provide for those who, in the mysterious order of Providence, are subject to want and to disease of body or mind, but I cannot find any authority in the Constitution for making the Federal Government the great almoner of public charity throughout the United States. . . . It would, in the end, be prejudicial rather than beneficial to the noble offices of charity. . . .[35]

President Pierce believed that it was both good and appropriate that charity should be voluntarily provided. The president of Harvard University developed this thought further some years later in opposing a national university supported by the taxpayers. He said that "our ancestors well understood the principle that to make a people free and self-reliant, it is necessary to let them take care of themselves, even if they do not take quite as good care of themselves as some superior power might."[36]

Frederick Marryat, an Englishman who also visited America in the 1830s and wrote about it, also noted that facility with which Americans formed associations. He declared that "the Americans are society mad." He listed 22 of the most prominent benevolent societies in 1834, e.g., American Education Society, American Bible Society, American Sunday School Union, Prison Discipline Society, American Temperance Society, and so on—, but found it necessary to add that there "are many others. . . ."[37]

Indeed, the variety of activities that were performed at one time or another by voluntary associations of people is truly amazing. Wars were usually fought with voluntary armies. (That any other means should be employed to raise an army left Daniel Webster horror struck, as he indicated in opposing the draft in 1814: "That measures of this nature should be debated at all," Webster said, "in the councils of a free government is cause of dismay. The question is nothing less than whether the most essential rights of personal liberty shall be surrendered and despotism embraced in its worst form."[38]) Volunteers formed fire departments, brought law and order (such as it was) along the frontiers, made up the posses which sheriffs used on occasion, organized churches, built schools, orphanages, libraries, hospitals, and joined political parties to effect their aims. (Political parties were not governmental organizations, though they have taken on some of that character over the years.) Men pooled their resources in partnerships, joint-stock companies, and corporations for undertaking large economic endeavors. But it would be easy to come to the conclusion that associations were more formal or enduring than they often were.

For example, much of the movement into territories west of the Mississippi was not by individuals or families alone but in groups or caravans. These were made up of people who voluntarily organized for purposes of moving into a new territory. Those who were moving would assemble at some point, or there might be several assembly places. When they had gathered, they elected a leader or captain, whose duty it was "to direct the order of travel during the day, and to designate the camping-ground at night. . . ." He was also responsible for organizing the whole expedition, such as in the following account: the men and wagons "are generally apportioned into four 'divisions,' particularly when the company is large. . . . To each of these divisions, a 'lieutenant' was appointed, whose duty it was to inspect every ravine and creek on the route, select the best crossings, and superintend . . . each encampment."[39]

Americans did not necessarily take orders well or obey every command, but they were used to organizing in voluntary groups for both short and long-range undertakings. These might range from building a house for a neighbor to building a church which might endure from generation to generation.

Many things in which government has since taken a leading or dominant role were done mostly, or entirely, voluntarily. Schooling was mostly voluntary in the first half of the 19th century. A few northern states and cities did begin to provide some tax support during these years (public school movement discussed in the following chapter), and Massachusetts passed a compulsory attendance law in 1852. Generally, though, it was accepted that that the education of their children was the right and responsibility of parents. Parents did generally provide much of the training of their children, and they often joined with other interested people to provide formal training in schools. Churches and communities of parents often provided schools.

Two developments which began in England were taken up in the United States. One was the Sunday school in the church, which was introduced as a means of teaching reading and writing. In the United States, though, it was rather quickly changed into a place for religious instruction of the children. The other was the Lancasterian Method, devised by Joseph Lancaster of England, who later came to live in the United States. This was a highly regimented system by which the most apt pupils were used to teach the others. The great advantage to the system was that it was not expensive; one schoolmaster could teach a large roomful of students with the aid of what were called monitors, and, since these were themselves pupils, they were not paid for their services. Undoubtedly, too, these monitors learned their lessons well, for they went over them again and again. Colleges, too, were mostly private in financing, and many of them were local in character. Indeed, so many colleges were conceived and started that Francis Wayland of Brown lamented, in 1850: "We have produced an article for which the demand is diminishing. We sell it at less than cost, and the deficiency is made up by charity. We give it away, and still the demand diminishes."[40] An estimate has it that something on the order of 700 colleges had closed their doors by 1860 in the United States.

Any occasion of widespread suffering was apt to call forth voluntary charitable aid from the United States. Greeks received aid in the 1820s, and many Greek war orphans were brought to this country for adoption. "In the autumn of 1832, when the starving people of Cape Verde Islands rowed to a ship hoping to buy food, they were astonished to learn that the vessel had been sent from the United States for the express purpose of relieving their necessities. Individuals and churches in New England, Philadelphia, and New York had heard of their need and had raised thousands of dollars for their assistance."[41] Nor should it be ignored that Americans customarily aided those in their communities and neighborhoods in times of exceptional need. Orphaned children were most likely to be taken care of by relatives. Neighbors shared their goods with those suffering from some misfortune.

Self-Employment the Rule

It would give the wrong impression to place heavy emphasis upon association and voluntary activities, especially in the ordinary workaday world. Americans were individualists, as already noted. Although voluntary cooperation was highly important, especially as an alternative to the compulsion of government, it was more apt to be occasional than not, and frequently a means of getting something done beyond the powers of an individual. In the main, though, Americans went about their own affairs in their own way. They might join wagon trains to get into some new territory, but once there they were likely to go their own way in selecting their own plots of ground and the tending of them.

Self-employment was the rule among Americans of the first half of the 19th century; independence was the goal. Most likely, Americans of the time would not have described their desired approach to making a living as "self-employment." That is a phrase that has come into widespread use in recent times because of its use by the Internal Revenue Service to describe those who are gainfully employed but not in the employ of someone else. But that is a part of what they had in mind. The most common dream of earlier Americans was to have a place of their own, to be beholden to no man, to manage their own work life, to have a competence, as people did say, and, in a word, to be independent.

For most Americans, that was a station to be achieved by themselves, if at all. Some people arrived at it by inheritance, but most did not. In any case, until they became adults, they were dependent upon someone else and usually worked under the direction and control of their parents or other adults. Most youth had to go through a period of apprenticeship, whether at farming or some trade or profession. Then, they had to acquire the capital or land before they could venture out on their own. Land was the easiest thing to come by in America; capital was harder to obtain. At any rate, it was a realizable dream for many to believe that they could one day be on their own, manage their own affairs, and not have to work under the supervision of any other person.

Indeed, such independence was the rule in America before the Civil War. It was the norm. Working in the employ and under the supervision of others was the exception for grown men. The balance was beginning to shift by the 1850s, but self-employment was still the dominant mode of making a living. There were exceptions, of course, that should be noted. Women did not ordinarily attain the status of independence alone. Rather, they usually shared in it as the helpmate of their husbands and were entitled to a way of life in keeping with his means. Slaves were, of course, usually under the direct supervision of their owners or their agents during the whole course of their work lives. Some people did work for wages, and the number and percentage of these increased over the years. But self-employment was still the rule.

The most obvious example of self-employment was that of farmers. A farmer who owned his own land, or was buying it, who provided his capital (equipment, machinery, beasts of burden and brood stock), and tilled his land was clearly independent and self-employed. Such farmers were the most common entrepreneurs in America at that time. Although they chould manage their own affairs, that is not to say that they could do as they pleased, not if they wanted to have a livelihood, that is. Few people are ever able to do that; all who work for a living live under the necessity of doing those things which will enable them to live. The seasons and the weather made their demands upon them, as they ever have upon farmers. Crops must be planted when the ground gets warm in the spring, when there is moisture in the ground, and the earth must be prepared for the seed. They must be tilled at the appropriate times to protect the seedlings from the weeds, and harvested when the time is right. Farmers live under the discipline of the elements, but farming is nevertheless an independent pursuit.

Although farming was the leading mode of self-employment, there were numerous other ones. Hunters and trappers, who shot or trapped animals, skinned them, dried and cured their furs, and sold them, were usually self-employed. Fishermen who went to sea in their boats and sold their catches were independent entrepreneurs. So, also, were those of a great variety of trades: carpenters, brick-masons, barbers, cordwainers, hatmakers, tailors, ironmongers (perhaps), millers, loggers, and a hundred and one others. In the early 19th century, most goods were made by hand, and those that required any degree of skill were done by tradesmen ordinarily. These usually acquired their skills by working for someone else as apprentices and journeymen, but in the course of time they hoped to and might expect to become independent masters of their trade. Professionals, then even more than now, were usually independent or self-employed. They would include lawyers, physicians, surgeons, and perhaps teachers and clergymen. Peddlers, storekeepers, factors, and people who worked on commission were usually self-employed.

Indeed, it was not common for any employer to have many workers for wages in his employ until the 1830s and after. John Jacob Astor who, when he died in 1846, was probably the wealthiest man in America, "Never. . .had. . .personally organized a large office or labor force," says an economic historian, "and the same was true of his great contemporaries."[42] People in the North who could afford them sometimes employed house servants. Ships were, as they had been, mainly operated with workers for wages. A master tradesman might have a few apprentices or journeymen working for him. And as factories became larger and more numerous they would have more and more wage workers. By and large, though, native American men tended to avoid work in factories. It smacked of servitude to them. For example, in 1816, it is estimated that there were around 100,000 people employed in cotton manufactures. Of this number, 66,000 were women and girls, 24,000 were boys and only 10,000 men. In the ensuing decades, immigrants began to come in, and among these there were often many more men willing to work in factories. It should be said, too, that some men did not manage their own affairs well or for whatever reason did not succeed on their own and were drawn into mines and mills for employment.

But the reigning ideal during this era was for a grown man to manage his own work life, and self-employment was the rule.

The Family Farm

America was primarily a land of farmers, and farming afforded the greatest opportunity for most to manage their affairs. Farm land was plentiful and inexpensive. In 1820, Congress lowered the basic price of public lands to $1.25 per acre and reduced the minimum amount that could be bought to 80 acres. Thereafter, a man could buy the land for a farm for as little as $1.00 per acre. Some settlers, however, did not wait for government surveys and auctions. They simply moved in, selected a place, and acted as if they owned the land. In the 1830s, the government passed a pre-emption law which began to give these "squatters" the opportunity to buy the land at the minimum price before the land was offered at auction. By the time of the Civil War there were 163,110,720 acres of improved land in the United States and its territories, much of which had been improved after 1800. There were even more acres of unimproved land still to be opened up to farming.

The preponderance of farmers is indicated by the statistics for gainful workers in the years up to 1860. In 1830, well over two-thirds of the workers were in agriculture. (These figures do not include slaves, who were predominantly agricultural workers themselves.) Even as late as 1850 there were 4,902,000 farm workers in contrast to 2,795,000 non-farm workers. Moreover, most Americans lived in rural settings, either on farms whose houses were usually separated from one another by some distance or in small towns oriented toward rural pursuits. As late as 1860 only just over 16 per cent of the population of the United States lived in towns or cities with populations over 8,000.

Moreover, most farmers lived on family farms. A family farm is one lived on and run basically by one family. Most of the work is ordinarily done by the members of the family. The major exception to the family farm was the plantation operated by slaves. These were located exclusively in the slave states which were either to the south or east of other states. But there were

John Jacob Astor
(1763–1848)

Astor was reckoned to be the wealthiest man in the United States at his death, leaving behind a fortune somewhere between $20–30 millions. He was born in a village near Heidelberg, Germany, moved to London in 1780, and came to the United States to settle in New York City in 1783. Astor got work in a fur store, where he learned about furs and trading in them. With that background, he went into business on his own and was soon deeply involved in the fur trade with the Indians. At one time or another he had trading posts from the Midwest to the Pacific. He even founded the town of Astoria at the mouth of the Columbia river, but it was subsequently taken by the British. Most of his activities were along the Canadian border. Despite all these trading activities, he maintained his business in New York, where he greatly increased his wealth by purchasing real estate in that city.

many more family farms in the South than plantations. In 1850, there were approximately 1¼ million white families in the slaveholding states, all but a small portion of which lived on farms. Only 347,000 of these families owned slaves, comprising only a little more than a fourth of the families. But well over half of the slaveholding families had fewer than ten slaves each. To have a slave or two did not change a farm from being a family farm any more than having a hired hand or two in season changed it in the North. Indeed, a full-fledged plantation required at least 50 slaves, and there were only some 8,000 families in the South in 1850 who had more than 50 slaves each. In short, and however you calculate, most farms in the South, as elsewhere, were family farms.

Family farms were basically *subsistence* farms. At least, they often started out that way, and many did not progress much beyond that point in the course of the 19th century. Typically, a family farm started this way. A young man, or a couple, acquired some land—40, 80, 120 acres, or whatever—by inheritance, by homesteading, by purchase, or in whatever way he could, even by renting. If there was no house on the land, he would build a lean-to or perhaps a log cabin, with or without the aid of neighbors, and construct barns and cribs as he needed them. He would clear lands of trees, if it was wooded country, and plant some of them. As children came, especially if he was fortunate enough to have sons, the land under cultivation would be extended with the aid of the children.

A subsistence farm was one which produced most of the goods for the family's wants and needs. Thus, the farm might grow corn, wheat, potatoes, vegetables of one sort or another, have fruit and nut trees, and have cattle, hogs, and chickens along with other fowls. These would provide the basic foods, which could be supplemented by game from the woods, fish from nearby streams, and wild berries in season. Clothes could be homespun, from wool or cotton, and from hides tanned on the farm. The heat could be from burning logs and tallow candles would provide such light as a family might have. Water was drawn from a well or carried to the house from a spring or stream. Milk might be had from cows or goats. If the farmer's tastes ran that way, wine could be made by fermenting fruits, supplemented by home brew or liquor from a still.

Absolute self-sufficiency, however, was neither the goal ordinarily nor the case in most instances. Even the poorest of farmers traded in the market to some extent. He did so to obtain salt, spices, sugar, perhaps shoes, flour, or whatever he did not grow, make, or build. Also, every farmer would need some cash, if for no other reason than to pay his local taxes, to purchase some new farm animals, or to provide trinkets for those in his household. In any case, most farmers produced some surpluses for the market when they could, and some produced primarily for the market. In the South, small farmers were most likely to produce cotton or tobacco as their main crop. Both of these could be produced on small farms as well as plantations. In the North, grain was most commonly produced for the market: corn most universally and wheat where it could be profitably grown. As cities grew and markets became accessible, dairy and beef and hog farming became increasingly important. By the 1850s, many small farmers produced primarily for the market and bought many of the goods that they wanted in the market.

New farm machinery did not greatly alter farming in the South before the Civil War. One reason for this was that Southern farmers were more likely to invest any surplus wealth in slaves than machinery. Another was that their cash crops did not lend themselves to the use of machines as yet. Both cotton and tobacco were labor-intensive crops, and no way around this was discovered. By contrast, Northern farmers were greatly aided by new farm machinery. John Deere developed a steel plow which was very effective in plowing the prairie soils of the Midwest. By the 1850s he was manufacturing 13,000 such plows each year. The reaper greatly facilitated the growing of grain, particularly since it needs to be harvested very quickly when it has ripened. Cyrus McCormick was the most successful of the developers of a reaper, and in the 1840s he began manufacturing and selling them in large quantities. The large amounts of land available and the relative shortage of labor made labor-saving devices much in demand in the Midwest.

Before leaving the subject of the family farmer one other aspect of it needs mentioning. Family farmers at their best, and subsistence farmers particularly, performed a great variety of tasks and developed a considerable number of skills in providing for themselves and their families. The farmer often learned to be a woodsman, to cut and split logs, to rive boards, to make baskets, to carpentry, make cabinets, butcher animals, perchance to grind corn or make flour, to hunt and trap animals, to build various structures, to sow, tend, and harvest crops, to maintain machinery, to dig wells, to shear sheep, and to do a thousand and one odd jobs. The division of labor was hardly known to him. His wife, too, had of necessity to be a Jill of many trades, as she must sew, mend, spin, weave, make butter and probably cheese, milk and tend cows, tend a garden, dry foods, serve as nurse for the family in time of illness, and do the numerous household chores. The family farm nurtured much of value in American life.

Cyrus H. McCormick
(1809–1884)

McCormick is best known for the invention and development of a grain harvesting machine, the reaper. He was born in Virginia and followed in the footsteps of his father who had been trying for many years to build a mechanical reaper. At the age of 22, Cyrus succeeded in building a machine that would reap grain. After making a variety of improvements on it, McCormick began to build the machines for sale. In 1847, he set up his own manufacturing plant in Chicago and had developed a nationwide business by 1850. He was not only a mechanic and an inventor but also a pioneer in various business methods. He allowed prospective buyers to try his machines in the field, offered deferred payment plans, offered guarantees on what he sold, and used testimonials from users in his advertising. Also, he pioneered in mass production techniques in making his reapers. His invention made it possible to produce much more grain by the family farmer than had been possible before.

The Factory System

The factory system began to develop and take hold in the United States between 1800–1850. By the 1850s, many goods were being made almost exclusively in factories. This system took shape on any scale first in the making of textiles, particularly of cotton goods. The factory method of organization also began to be extended to such heavy industries as iron manufacturing and the making of products such as arms, stoves, harvesters, and the like. The factory system is a system of organizing production in a central location (a building or buildings), of concentrating capital for a particular undertaking, and organizing workers for the production of a good or goods. Associated with it are: the specialization and division of labor, wage work and, usually, payment for work-time (the time spent at work rather than amount produced), and the integration of production by management.

In important respects, the factory system went against the grain of the trend of the developments in America. The trend in work, as already noted, was toward self-employment and for each adult man to manage and direct his own constructive activities. The long-term trend, too, was the freeing of the individual from various fetters and bonds. Indentured servitude was disappearing from the American scene, and the idea of being a servant at all, however compensated, was distasteful to Americans generally. People continued to do work for others, it is true, as all who offer goods in the market do. But their work was becoming increasingly distinct from servitude, as the focus was on the task they performed or the particular job they worked on.

Even slaves in the rice fields, some of the hardest work performed anywhere, were often assigned plots to tend for the day. When they had finished the work, they were free to amuse themselves at other pursuits. An able worker could finish his assigned task while the sun was still high in the sky in the summer, at least some of the time. Among free workers, the trend was to divide up jobs into tasks that could be performed by individual workers, to parcel it out to them, and to pay by the piece or task. The system under which this was done was often called the "putting out" system. Under this system, an enterpriser or entrepreneur, provided the materials, assigned the tasks, and the work was done in the homes or shops of the workers. Thus, spinning, weaving, the making of clothes, shoes, or what have you, could be done without supervision, with the workman taking responsibility for doing the work, and being paid by the piece for what he accomplished. This organization or work, which took into account specialization and division of labor, survived on some scale into the latter part of the 19th century.

Indeed, the invention and development of the sewing machine in the 1840s and 1850s bid fair to breathe new life into household manufacturing.

Several Europeans had devised machines intended for sewing in the 1830s and 1840s, but it was the American, Elias Howe, who made the crucial inventions for making the sewing machine the effective instrument that it became. Another American, Isaac Singer, was the most effective promoter of the machine. The sewing machine was and is individually operated and was then primarily used for the making of shoes and clothes. The machine was then propelled by hand or foot and neither had nor required any outside source of power. Thus, many women acquired sewing machines, and the ready-made clothing industry was basically a home industry for several decades.

But already the factory system had taken hold, and eventually that aspect of manufacturing also moved into a factory setting. Looked at from our point of view after the fact, it may appear that the factory system was almost a natural development. It was not that at all, of course. Much of textile

Elias Howe
(1819–1867)

Courtesy Metropolitan Museum of Art, Stokes-Hawes Collection

Howe invented the sewing machine. He was born in Massachusetts and became an apprentice in a cotton machinery factory as a youth. In this factory and an instrument shop, he developed the mechanical skills and conceived the idea of the sewing machine. In the winter of 1844–45, he devised an effective machine for which he was issued a patent in 1846. American manufacturers, however, were indifferent toward its possibilities, and he leased the rights to it initially to a London corset maker. The relationship with the London manufacturer did not last long, and he returned to the United States where he found that interest had grown in the machine during his absence. Other makers of machines had entered the field in this country as well. For several years, Howe was embroiled in lawsuits with those he claimed had infringed his patent, and he was so far successful in these suits that after 1854 he drew royalties from most of the makers of sewing machines. Not only did he sometimes draw as much as $4,000 per week in royalties, but he also manufactured the machines himself.

production was moved into factories as a solution to a particular problem. The main problem was the power to turn machines that had been invented and to make the purchase and utilization of the machines profitable. Power, however, was the key. As earlier noted, several important machines were invented for much more rapid spinning and weaving of textiles. They were made by the British. The main source of power at the beginning of the 19th century was falling water. It had long been used for such things as saw mills and grist mills, and could be adapted with belts and pulleys for turning these machines. But two things made the congregation of workers in a central location (a factory) necessary. One was the necessity to locate the operation on some stream that would have sufficient force to turn the water wheel. Frequently, the stream would have to be stopped with a dam, water channeled to the wheel, and, as a rule, the mill would have to be located at some place where the water naturally fell for some distance. The second reason was that the building of such a mill was quite expensive, both for arranging the power and purchasing machines. The workers would have to be brought to the plant to operate it. (The alternative source of power at this time was the steam engine, but steam power was much more expensive than water power, and would have required a centrally located factory as well.) The swift flowing streams of hilly New England were often ideal as power sources, and that is one reason that the textile industry was concentrated in that part of the country in the first half of the 19th century.

There were a host of problems connected with the development of the factory system, problems, in many instances, for which there were no ready-made solutions. The first one, for the textile industry, was getting the machines. British law prohibited the export or taking out of the country any of the basic machines; the British were attempting to establish and maintain a monopoly of textile manufactures. Samuel Slater was the first to deal fairly effectively with this problem. He worked in factories in England and learned how the machines were built and worked. He came to America, constructed machines from memory, and eventually went into manufacturing along with others. Other manufacturers managed to obtain the equipment in one way or another.

Capital was required for building the mills, equipping them, acquiring materials, and paying workers initially. The expense of starting such an operation was generally more than any one person could or would wish to invest. The initial method of handling this was for several men to go together as partners or by some sort of joint stock arrangements. By the 1830s, however, general laws of incorporation made the corporate device available in most states for financing factories. Banks, too, came to play an important role in concentrating wealth for investment.

Getting workers for the factories was a major problem. People were hardly drawn in large numbers to work in factories for wages when there was land available, almost for the asking, with which they might become independent. "Skilled men could be imported from Europe," as one writer says, "and apprentices and journeymen bound to learn a craft, but with the lure of free opportunities in the West it was impossible to keep them long. . . . Labor supply was often an insuperable problem."[43] The early textile industry, however, could use women mostly, and Francis Lowell, an imaginative cotton manufacturer, solved the problem this way. He built boarding houses near his factory in Waltham, Massachusetts, and brought in young girls from the surrounding country to operate the machines. The idea was that these girls would work for two or three years, living and working under supervision, before getting married. This system worked so well that it was adopted in other New England towns. Some estimates have it that the workers in the textile industry were as much as 90 per cent composed of women and children. Textile manufacturing was the first major case of women working for wages outside the home in productive activities.

An English visitor to Lowell, Massachusetts described these working girsl and their lives this way: "All were clean, neat, and fashionably attired. . . . They commonly walked arm in arm [going from the factory to their lodgings] without displaying levity. Their general appearance and deportment was such that few British gentlemen . . . need have been ashamed of leading any one of them to a tea party. Next day, being Sunday, we saw the young females . . . going to church in their best attire, when the favourable impressions of the preceding evening were [reinforced]."[44] The girls may have been happy enough generally, but there were certainly inconveniences. They usually worked sunup to sundown for six days per week, were paid perhaps 60 cents per day, and lived six or eight girls to a room under careful supervision.

The factory and wage system, which was becoming widespread by the 1840s, raised other problems and questions beyond that of getting workers. Defenders of slavery—which was now under attack—in the South charged that factories in the North were bringing wage slavery. Orestes Brownson, writing in 1840, declared that "There must be no class of our fellow men doomed to toil through life as mere workmen at wages. If wages are tolerated it must be, in the case of the individual operative, only under such conditions that by the time he is of a proper age to settle in life, he shall have accumulated enough to be an independent laborer on his own capital,—on his own farm, or in his own shop."[45] What he thought might happen may, perhaps, be seen more clearly from the angle of the manufacturers. The manufacturers not only had to find workers but also workers who would do their bidding sufficiently well for them to make a profit. Obedience undoubtedly came easier for women and children at that time than for men, for they were used to being under the authority and direction of a man, or, at least, an adult. But men, too, must be brought under industrial discipline, as it came to be called, as the factory system took on more and more of the production of goods. Moreover, in many kinds of production, small enterprisers, were in competition with the factories, and they could be expected to give careful attention to their work. The factory system made no great strides in papermaking, for example, until the latter part of the 19th century, because it could be done equally effectively on a small scale. However, where large capital investments, such as in textiles and ironmaking, were necessary to produce goods competitively, the factory system tended to occupy the field. The keys to the success of this system were capital concentration and new technology.

Labor unions were not much of a factor in the United States until the time of the Civil War. Although there was a burst of organizing activity in the 1830s, the membership declined after the Panic of 1837 and the ensuing depression. The only unions that survived for very long before the Civil War were craft unions, such as those of sailmakers, cordwainers, typesetters, and the like. They were organized mainly to attempt to control prices (or wages), and the main device to do so was to keep down the number of workers in the craft by preventing competing workers from entering the trade easily. These unions, some of them, did attempt to prevent the development of the factory system, especially by efforts to stop the use of machines. There were no organized groups directly hurt by the use of machinery in cotton manufacturing, for this work had been done in the home earlier, but in shoemaking, for example, there were labor organizations to oppose the introduction and operation of the machines. Generally speaking, less skilled workers, who would work for less, could be used as machine operators.

However, if the unions used violence or coercion against other workers, their organized activities were usually treated as being illegal. For example, the Philadelphia Cordwainers, a union of shoemakers, were brought to trial in 1806. "The indictment included charges that association members conspired to raise wages, refused to work for an employer who paid less than a fixed rate, and prevented workers who were not members of the association from being hired."[46] The members of the union were found guilty and fined. More pointedly, a New York court in 1835, ruled that it was illegal for a union to combine to exclude nonmembers from employment. The court supported its position with this reasoning:

> . . . The man who owns an article of trade or commerce is not obliged to sell it for any particular price, nor is the mechanic obliged to labor for any particular price. He may say that he will not make coarse boots for less than one dollar per pair, but *he has no right to say that no other mechanic shall make them for less.* The cloth merchant may say that he will not sell his goods for less than so much per yard, but has no right to say that any other merchant shall not sell for less price. If one individual does not possess such a right over the conduct of another, no number of individuals can possess such a right. All combinations

therefore to effect such an object are injurious, not only to the individual particularly oppressed, but to the public at large. . . .[47]

Labor unions require a different atmosphere than that which prevailed in America in the first half of the 19th century to make any headway either in organizing workers or achieving their aims. They need a collectivist atmosphere; whereas, Americans were voluntarists, opposing coercion, and individualists. They need a situation where government will either permit them to use coercion or support them in it. Americans had cast off the remains of medieval corporatism and were not favorably disposed to collective coercion. There needs to be a widespread sense, too, that workers are being mistreated. That was a hard case to make for craftsmen, who were generally the better paid or more prosperous of workers. In consequence, labor unions had little success in preventing people from working for what they would, and they hardly had any impact on the development of the factory system.

Perhaps, the main point about these years, however, is the large development and growth of production in the country. The vast expansion of agriculture had resulted in ever-larger production, not only for home use but also for food and fibers to be sold on the market. Industrial production increased broadly and generally, though most of it was concentrated in the Northeast and Midwest. The value of manufactured production increased from under $200 million in 1810 to over $1 billion in 1850. Iron production increased from 60,000 tons in 1810 to 630,000 tons in 1850. Cotton goods produced increased from 17 million pounds in 1810 to 245 million pounds in 1850. Americans freed from British control and mercantile regulations to pursue their own productive ends did so with ingenuity and enterprise. Not all American inhabitants were free, however, and it is now time to consider that type of production.

The Plantation System

Economically, the plantation was a production unit. If it was a small plantation, it might appear little different from a family farm, except for the few slave cabins located near the home of the owner. Large plantations were likely to be much more grand, of course, with the large family dwelling, perhaps surrounded by Greek ornamented columns (or adorned in that way on the front), with its mills, forges, blacksmith shops, slave cabins lining both sides of a kind of street, stables, separate kitchen from the house, and so on. But large or small, the plantation was a production unit. It was a unit of a large industry, so to speak, the cotton-growing industry, the tobacco-producing industry, the rice or sugar cane industry. The plantation was part of an expansive and expanding industry, again so to speak, which, since the invention of the cotton gin, had been expanding westward, across the Black

Belt of Georgia, Alabama, and Mississippi, into the delta region of Mississippi, Louisiana, and Arkansas, and finally into Texas and Missouri. A plantation was not a factory, of course, nor was it a family farm; it had elements of both of these, but it was more than and different from them.

The most distinctive feature of the plantation was that it depended upon slave labor. In the usual formulation, there are three elements of production: land, labor, and capital. On the plantation, so far as it depended upon slaves to do the work, labor was a major part of the capital. That is, slave labor was capital, not a distinct element such as free labor is. The plantation had other capital, of course; it had shops, mills, plows, hoes, horses, and so on. But the major capital investment of the planter was in slaves. It has been reckoned that the value of the slaves at the time of the Civil War was in the vicinity of $400 million.

Plantations produced staple crops for the market. Planters did not ordinarily try to be self-sufficient; they rarely grew enough food nor produced the clothes for the inhabitants of the plantation. Instead, attention was focused upon growing the crop, or crops, that could be sold in the market. Much of their produce was for export to foreign markets, as it had been from the earliest colonial times. Thus, the business of the plantations was the production of cotton, tobacco, rice, sugar, or some other staple for the market.

The plantation was basically organized for this production. The basic work of production was done by field hands. These, whether men, women or children did field work on a regular basis, in season arising before daybreak and leaving the fields around sundown. The length of the midday break might be varied depending upon the heat. Many plantations had an overseer, whose basic job was to superintend the work. He was usually white, was paid a salary, and had the care and discipline of the slaves in his hands. Usually, too, there were "drivers," almost invariably black themselves, who were, in effect, lieutenants of the overseers, often established the workloads of the slaves, and saw to it that the work got done. There were two different basic organizations of the field hands. One was to assign work by tasks, as, for example, a quarter of an acre of land to be tilled in a day. Drivers would not be necessary in this incentive system, for when the slave had completed his task, he was free from work for the remainder of the day. The other system was that of slave gangs working under a driver. The task system was more widely used in rice, hemp, and long-staple cotton production. The gang system was more common in most cotton production.

But a large plantation was a much more complexly organized system than the above would suggest. The slaves were divided into field hands and house servants, and house servants were reckoned to be the privileged slaves. Much skilled work was needed around the plantations, too, and some slaves bettered their conditions by learning such trades as carpentry, masonry, becoming blacksmiths, and the like. Their owners sometimes hired out such slaves to others when they were not busy on the plantation. In short, there was considerable specialization on the plantation, and there was a hierarchy in the positions which slaves held.

Was the plantation a profitable business? The question was raised at the time and has been much examined by historians since. One reason, perhaps the main one, for asking the question has been to try to decide whether slavery would have disappeared in the course of time without direct government abolition. It should be said, at the outset, that slavery showed no signs of dying out in the 1850s. The price of cotton was generally high during this period, its last decade before disruption by war, and the price of slaves rose to new highs. The plantation system was still expanding on the eve of the Civil War; its demise from natural economic causes was well beyond the horizon, if it portended at all.

Undoubtedly, profits were made from the labor of slaves. Planters profited more or less and from time to time; buyers and sellers of cotton, for example, made profits; suppliers of plantations made profits; textile mills made profits; sellers of cotton goods made profits. It would appear, too, that the plantation might have been the most effective system, or the most successful at any rate, for organizing slavery on scale. But there existed nothing much with which to compare it. On the other hand, it was not very profitable for the slaves. They usually began and ended their lives in slavery and accumulated little or nothing in the course of them. Even planters often did not prosper much.

Although the plantation was undoubtedly an economic enterprise, the question of its profitability may not be as revelant as it has been made to appear. It did not exist simply as an economic enterprise; shares in plantations did not sell on stock exchanges, nor were they corporations. The plantation was the central part of a way of life and a family enterprise. It was a way of life for a Southern gentleman and his family, a way of living with status as a keeper of servants and living without physical labor. It was a mode of life to which millions of Southerners who were not slaveholders aspired. Planters generally hoped to make profits, but they were little inclined to turn their back on the plantation and take up some other occupation when it did not. If need be, they went into debt to buy more land and slaves, lived much of their lives on credit, but come what may clung to their plantations and the style of life involved.

Undoubtedly, well-motivated free men produce much more of goods than do slaves. In that broad sense, slavery is uneconomical. But free men produce primarily for themselves (that, after all, is their main motivation), while slaves are made to produce primarily for their masters. So it is that slavery may be profitable for the masters though looked at in terms of the economy as a whole it is not economical. In any case, slavery was not disappearing for economic reasons in the 1850s.

Slavery was unjust, but not necessarily unprofitable.

Chapter 5
Romanticism and Reform

The poets are thus liberating gods. . . . I think nothing is of any value in books excepting the transcendental and extraordinary. If a man is inflamed and carried away by his thought, to that degree that he forgets the authors and the public and heeds only this one dream which holds him like an insanity, let me read his paper, and you may have all the arguments and histories and criticism.

—Ralph Waldo Emerson

Not only was his robe exceedingly white, but his whole person was glorious beyond description, and his countenance truly like lightning. . . . He called me by name, and said . . . that his name was Moroni; that God had a work for me to do. . . . He said there was a book deposited, written upon gold plates. . . , that the fulness of the everlasting Gospel was contained in it, as delivered by the Savior to the ancient inhabitants.

—Joseph Smith, 1823

I am aware that many object to the severity of my language; but is there not cause for severity? I will be as harsh as truth, and as uncompromising as justice. On this subject [of slavery], I do not wish to think, or speak, or write with moderation. . . . I am in earnest—I will not equivocate—I will not excuse—I will not retreat a single inch . . . AND I WILL BE HEARD.

—William Lloyd Garrison, 1831

Chronology

1781—Immanuel Kant's *Critique of Pure Reason.*

1809—Washington Irving's *History of New York by Diedrich Knickerbocker.*

1819—Founding of Unitarian Church.

1823—James Fenimore Cooper's *The Pioneers.*

1826—Founding of American Temperance Society.

1830—Founding of the Mormon church.

1831—Beginning of Garrison's *Liberator*.

1834—1st volume of Bancroft's *History of the United States*.

1836—Formation of Transcendental Club.

1841—Emerson's *Essays* (1st Series).

1845—Edgar Allan Poe's "The Raven."

1846—Female "Declaration of Independence" at Seneca Falls Convention.

1852—Harriet Beecher Stowe's *Uncle Tom's Cabin*.

1854—Thoreau's *Walden*.

A new outlook swept over the United States in the first half of the 19th century, and it had not run its course until the 1880s, if indeed by then. It is generally known as romanticism, though that is more of a convention than a precise description. In fact, there may be no way to describe romanticism precisely. Romanticism, as a movement, had many faces, was more a mood than a set of ideas, and affected different people in quite different ways. Although it can be examined most closely as a literary and artistic move- ment, it had roots in philosophy, and the romantic mood colored and shaded the way people in all walks of life viewed things. It can be seen in the enthusiasm of religious revivals and camp meetings, in the flights of oratory so much admired in that day, in the emotion packed devotion to country in 19th century nationalism, and in the melodramatic episodes in novels. The romantic mood was a revolt against the excessive claims of reason as well as emphasizing the imagination, feeling, emotion, intuition, inspiration, the inner light within the individual and an outward zeal for reform. While man, so long as he remains man, can never entirely abandon reason, romanticism tended to exalt the heart over the head. In that especially, the romantic outlook differed from the preceding age of reason.

Although romanticism took on an American coloration in America, the roots of this outlook were in European thought in the late 18th century. It is usually traced back at least to Jean Jacques Rousseau, whose main works were published in the 1760s. Rousseau celebrated feeling, sentiment, intuition, and the natural man, though the form of his writing appeared to rely on reason, at least in the *Social Contract*, his best known work. By natural man, he meant man as he might be and could be if he had not been warped and twisted by his institutions. "Civilized man," Rousseau said, "is born, lives and dies in a state of slavery; at his birth, he is sewn up in swaddling clothes, at his death, he is nailed in a coffin; so long as he preserves the human form he is fettered by different institutions."[48] In this emphasis, Rousseau was the godfather of romanticism.

But it was the Germans, not the French, who took the leadership in developing the romantic outlook. French is, above all, the language of reason; the very structure of the language tends to bend the minds of those who use it in that direction. By contrast, German is a much more complex and highly inflected language; those who think with it tend to be more aware of a complex of relationships and dependencies. In any case, it was Germans, such as, Kant, Fichte, Jacobi, Goethe, and Schleirmacher who carried the thrust of romanticism forward. Immanuel Kant, a German philosopher, severely limited the role of reason in his major work, *Critique of Pure Reason,* showed that the senses of themselves bring us only bits and pieces of information, and emphasized the active role of the mind in getting knowledge. Subtly, he shifted the ground of our knowledge from reason and the external world inward to our own conceptions of things. Others in Germany followed his lead gladly and carried his insights further. Johann Wolfgang von Goethe, one of the great and diverse minds of the age, in his novels, his poetry, and drama "gives us what is most fundamental," said the philosopher Santayana, "—the turbid flux of sense, the cry of the heart, the first tentative notions of art and science, which magic or shrewdness might hit upon. . . . In fact, the great merit of the romantic attitude is that it puts us back at the beginning of our experience. It disintegrates convention, which is often cumbrous and confused, and restores us to ourselves, to immediate perception and primordial will."[49]

There are many ways to see the German influence: in the philosophy of Kant and Hegel, in the poetry of Goethe, in the incomparable music of Ludwig van Beethoven, and in the *Sturm und Drang* (Storm and Stress) literary movement. The German influence was strong on such English writers as Samuel Taylor Coleridge, William Wordsworth, and Thomas Carlyle. These, in turn, had much influence upon American literature. Some Americans, such as George Bancroft, studied in German universities and drank deeply at the wells of German philosophy. Others got it second hand through the English or by reading of it.

Not too much should be made of the German origins of romanticism, however. While there is no doubt of the German influence upon some Americans, it is quite possible that these only reinforced ideas, beliefs, and attitudes which were already taking hold in this country. What we do know with reasonable certainty is that the first half of the 19th century was a romantic era in both western Europe and America, and that this outlook had an impact on what men said and did. In America, it had great impact on religion, on social organizations, in the development of individualism, on politics, and in the spawning of reform movements. In a national sense, the first half of the 19th century was the youth of America. Romanticism accorded with that youthful spirit, reinforced the widespread belief that if all things were not possible, much was, succored youthful confidence, and fired the minds of many with the idea of bringing America to its place in the sun.

Developing an American Literature

In a sense, romanticism could be considered as a wave which swept over America from Europe. But in a much more important sense, this outlook served to buttress the American determination to be as intellectually independent of Europe as possible. From the time of the Declaration of Independence onward it became almost an American passion to achieve independence from Europe. With independence, with the establishment of the states, with the foundation of a closer Union under the Constitution, Americans were conscious of their differences from Europe. The American political system was different from that of Europe, a point hammered home in the Monroe Doctrine. In the midst of the Napoleonic wars, it seemed to many leaders that America would have to be more nearly economically independent of Europe, else they would be drawn into European wars. The idea began to take shape, too, that American independence and distinctness should give rise to a literature that expressed American ideals, that was cast in the frame of American independence that bespoke an awareness of that which was being brought forth on this continent. Above all, Americans must become literary equals of Europeans. More than a decade before the declaring of independence, John Trumbull of Yale had written:

> This land her Steele and Addison shall view,
> The former glories equall'd by the new
> Some future Shakespeare charm the rising age.
> And hold in magic charm the listening sage.[50]

Joel Barlow stated the vision more powerfully in *The Columbiad*, a major poem conceived by an American and published in 1808:

> Here social man a second birth shall find,
> And a new range of reason life his mind,
> Feed his strong intellect with purer light,
> A nobler sense of duty and of right,
> The sense of liberty; whose holy fire
> His life shall temper and his laws inspire,
> Purge from all shades the world-embracing scope
> That prompts his genius and expands his scope.[51]

But it was easier to conceive of a noble, expansive, and distinctive American literature than to bring one into being. True, Americans had demonstrated both originality and felicity of expression in setting forth their political beliefs during the revolutionary era. If there was to be an American literature, however, they must go beyond the political; indeed, to the extent they achieved their goal of limiting government to that same extent political thought and writing must become secondary in their lives. Moreover, Americans were accustomed to depend upon Europe, especially England, for the bulk of their literature. "Good poems and novels, like good woolens," the historian Nelson M. Blake has said, "were assumed to be products of English origin; homespuns in literature were regarded with suspicion."[52] Printers in America were not eager to risk publishing books by Americans. In the state of the copyright laws it was much easier to pirate an edition by some English author with greatest assurance of financial success.

Yet an American literature did begin to emerge. Romanticism, as it took hold, gave men confidence in their ability to take up American themes. Individuals, such as Noah Webster, gave a spur and encouragement to the undertaking.Webster devoted much activity from the earliest years of the republic to the promotion of a distinctly American language. It would be English in its roots, of that he had no doubt, but it would take on an American vitality and American flavor. To the end that it should, he promoted uniform spelling and grammar by publishing *A Grammatical Institute of the English Language*. His speller became a best seller; in the years before the Civil War, it sometimes sold as many as a million copies a year. Webster thought that language was the key to future greatness for America. "A *national language*," he wrote, "is a bond of national union. Every engine should be employed to render the people of this country *national*, to call their attachments home to their own country, and to inspire them with the pride of national character."[53] He worked during much of his life to build and solidify the language and make it accessible in all of its richness to his countrymen. His crowning achievement was his dictionary. After many years in the preparation of it, he published *The American Dictionary* in two volumes in 1828. It was so thorough that it became the standard for dictionaries in this country.

If there were not printing houses willing to publish American books with any frequency until the 1820s, there were newspapers and magazines aplenty in which shorter pieces could appear. Thus, Americans at first were more likely to write essays, sketches, short stories, and lyric poetry. Nevertheless, there were some novels published before the turn of the century. Susannah Rowson's *Charlotte Temple* was a great success after its publication in America in 1794. So also was Mrs. Hannah Foster's *The Coquette; or The History of Eliza Wharton,* published in 1797. These were sentimental novels, in a sense, dealing with fallen women, who were punished for their sins. Hugh Henry Brackenridge's *Modern Chivalry* was somewhat higher level as literature, since it was a satire on Americans, particularly frontiersmen of the day.

But the first American writer to make an enduring international reputation in fiction was Washington Irving. His first work to make any large impact was his playful history of New York by the imaginary Diedrich Knicker-

James Fenimore Cooper
(1789–1851)

Cooper was born in New Jersey, but his family moved shortly to the lake region of New York state. He attended Yale, but was expelled for insubordination, and never earned his degree. He went to sea for the next several years, first on merchant ships and later in the United States Navy. Most of his life, however, he spent on the beautiful family estate at Cooperstown. Cooper was the first American writer to earn an international reputation for his fiction. He wrote more than 30 novels, several books of travel, and a large assortment of arguments in controversies. His most successful works were on the sea and the American frontier, and these sold in great quantities, both in English-speaking countries and in translation around the world.

bocker. His aim was to call forth the ghosts, so to speak, of his native state, or as he put it, "to embody the traditions of the city in an amusing form . . . to clothe home scenes and places and familiar names with those imaginative and whimsical associations so seldom met with in our new country. . . ."[54] Irving is best known for such short stories as "Rip Van Winkle" and "The Legend of Sleepy Hollow," but he also wrote books on the West, such as *Tour on the Prairie* and *Astoria*.

James Fenimore Cooper achieved even greater success in the development of an American literature. His romantic tales were most often about the sea and the frontier. By so doing, he dealt with two of the most important locales for American history to that point. It is easy for us to forget that America was a seafaring country mainly in the 17th and 18th centuries. Most Americans lived within a few miles of the ocean or near some navigable river not much above tidewater, if any. Their trade and travel were mostly carried on by sea. Moreover, the frontier until well into the 19th century was not far from the sea itself. Thus, it was appropriate for anyone who would make vivid in fiction the American past to write on these themes. The most beloved stories of Cooper were those about frontiersmen and Indians, comprising the Leatherstocking tales. Among these frontier stories were: *The Pioneers* (1823), *The Last of the Mohicans* (1826), *The*

Prairie (1827), *The Pathfinder* (1840), and *The Deerslayer* (1841). Cooper excelled in writing exciting narratives, and his works were replete with brave frontiersmen, bold Indians, daring rescues, confrontations, and narrow escapes, as befitted romantic novels.

Although Cooper was much in vogue in his lifetime and earned an international reputation, the two romantic novelists who have most intrigued, fascinated and baffled critics ever since were Nathaniel Hawthorne and Herman Melville. Hawthorne was a man as much caught up in the Puritan and New England past as was William Faulkner with his Southern past in the 20th century. Above all, he was concerned with the impact of sin on people's lives and how people are caught within the webs of their own making. Hawthorne's most impressive works appeared in the 1850s: *The Scarlet Letter, The House of Seven Gables,* and *The Blithedale Romance.* Although Hawthorne was associated with the Transcendentalists, even lived for a time at Brook Farm, his romanticism was of a different sort from theirs. The project of transcending society, or even our own pasts as individuals, must have struck him as futile. Rather, he was greatly impressed with the idea that the evil which men do lives after them and how people are often overwhelmed by their persistent past. Although he wrote mostly of his own New England, he wrote of great themes which affect all people.

American writers of the 19th century, the most deeply conscious and

Nathaniel Hawthorne
(1804–1864)

Hawthorne was born in Salem, Massachusetts, a seaport that was long past its prime, to a family whose fortunes had been declining for several generations. He graduated from Bowdoin College in Maine and spent several years mastering the art of writing by writing short stories.

Finally, with the publication of *The Scarlet Letter* in 1850, he had a popular success, and he followed this with several other novels which established his literary reputation. Although Hawthorne married a Transcendentalist and reformer, Elizabeth Peabody, he was not for long captivated by either of these interests. Instead, he wrote somber novels mainly that were taken up with the impact of the past upon the present in people's lives.

Courtesy National Archives, Brady Collection

thoughtful of them anyway, still lived under the shadow of Shakespeare, Milton, the King James Version of the Bible, and, quite often, their Puritan backgrounds. That may not be the best way to put it. They were still enlivened and caught up in the great themes of English and Christian literature. Transcendentalists might "transcend" this framework, or think they could. Others, however, notably Hawthorne, Herman Melville, and, perhaps, Edgar Allan Poe, neither thought they had nor thought the transcendence would be so easy, if it could be accomplished. The sense of the past was strong, even pervasive, in Hawthorne's work. Melville wrestled in a broader and deeper way with the presence of evil in the world. The ancient Greeks had come to terms with evil in the tragedy and in quite another way in the comedy. Life is tragic, so many of the Greek dramatists seemed to conclude. Not so, the central teachings of Christianity hold; good ultimately triumphs over evil and justice prevails, if not in this world in the here and now then in the world to come. Melville was caught between these views.

Herman Melville obtained his apprenticeship to life as a sailor. It was not suprising, then, most of his stories and novels were about ships, sailing, and the sea. His early novels of the sea, *Typee* (1846), *Omoo* (1847), *Redburn* (1849), and *White Jacket* (1850), were popular and sold well. Very soon, however, he turned to deeper themes in *Mardi* (1849), *Moby Dick* (1851), and *Pierre* (1852). The themes were either too difficult or his execution inadequate, except, perhaps, in *Moby Dick*. In any case, these works did not sell well nor were they generally critically acclaimed during his lifetime. Although he lived for forty years after the publication of *Moby Dick*, he published very little more. In the 20th century, Melville's work has been revived, and he is now considered to be a major novelist. Undoubtedly, the presence of overwhelming and engulfing evil has much more the feel of truth about it now than in the more optimistic 19th century. A short novel of his, *Billy Budd*, was not published until 1924, long after his death. The story was set on a British warship and concerned a sunny natured young man, impressed by the British, accused by a villainous mate of treason. In his anger, the young man, Billy Budd, struck the mate and accidentally killed him. Although clearly innocent of any intent to murder, Budd was tried, sentenced to death, and executed. The parallel is with the execution of Jesus, and it is an exploration of evil and injustice, and what happens to innocence in their grasp. Melville came to grips with how this world appears bent on soiling and mutilating innocence and appeared to see the necessity for a justice that was ultimately unjust, but it is not clear that he accepted it all as a part of the Divine plan of redemption. The problem with which Melville wrestled can hardly be solved in human terms; it is a Mystery.

Poetry, which had been eclipsed by prose since the late 17th century, had a considerable revival under the impetus of romanticism. The emphasis upon feeling, emotion, intuition and imagination gave rise to much lyrical poetry. Essayists and novelists often broke out in verse in the midst of their prose. Most writers tried their hands at poetry: Cooper, Melville, Emerson (rather more successfully), and there were some excellent poets, among them William Cullen Bryant, Henry Wadsworth Longfellow, James Russell Lowell, and John Greenleaf Whittier. Two poets have stood the test of time, however, better than the others: Edgar Allan Poe and Walt Whitman. But the discussion of Whitman belongs more properly to Transcendentalism.

It has never been quite clear where the discussion of Poe belongs. He was born in Boston but grew up and was educated in Virginia. Even so, he was hardly more of a Southerner than a New Englander, whatever his pretensions. He wrote short stories and poetry, but these were usually quite strange, to say the least. Both are almost beyond time and place, though his stories are often filled with precise detail. It is almost as if he was not of this world; indeed, much of his work appears to lie on the outer edge of sanity. Romantic it was, but it was a romance of mystery, terror, yearning, and suffocation. He liked to unravel mysteries, but he was equally good at conceiving some terrifying experience. Among his better known short stories are: "Cask of Amontillado," "House of Usher," "Red Death," and "Pit and the Pendulum." Well known poems include "The Raven," "Annabel Lee," and "Lenore." Much of his poetry was haunting and disconsolate, as in this last verse from "Annabel Lee":

> For the moon never beams without bringing me dreams
>   Of the beautiful Annabel Lee;
> And the stars never rise but I see the bright eyes
>   Of the beautiful Annabel Lee;
> And so, all the night-tide, I lie down by the side
> Of my darling, my darling, my life and my bride,
>   In the sepulchre there by the sea—
>   In her tomb by the side of the sea.

Much of this literature was as much or more the emergence of American writers on the stage of Western literature as it was the development of a literature about America. This was true also of the historical writing of the period. The writing of history was still very much a literary undertaking, though not primarily imaginative literature. It contributed much, too, to American self-consciousness of nationhood. Peter Force, a printer, collected and published a mountain of documents pertaining to the American past. Biography was a favorite form of American history, and numerous biographies were published. Jared Sparks was the most industrious of the biographers, for he produced more than 70 volumes of one sort or another. George Washington was a favorite subject: Washington Irving produced a five-volume biography and John Marshall did likewise.

The most ambitious of the undertakings on American history was George

Bancroft's multi-volumned *History of the United States*. He conceived American history as the culmination of a long-term movement toward democracy. Although his work was much admired at the time, it was quite often more romantic than realistic. He could write, for example, concerning the American revolt against British action that "With one impulse the colonies sprang to arms. With one spirit they pledged themselves to be ready for the extreme event. With one heart the continent cried, Liberty or Death."[55]

Other historians ranged more widely and wrote more enduring work. William H. Prescott wrote powerfully of the Spanish conquests in the New World. John L. Motley told the story of the emergence of the Dutch during the colonial period. Francis Parkman wrote memorably of the French in the New World and their contest for dominance with the British. Parkman's writings were made much more vivid by his determination to visit the scenes of that about which he wrote. He also wrote about the trek to Oregon and the far West. These historians placed American history within its framework of the European contest for dominance of the New World.

The Transcendentalists

"Whoso would be a man," Ralph Waldo Emerson wrote, "must be a nonconformist." Again, "Trust thyself: every heart vibrates to that iron string." Or, "I shun father and mother and wife and brother when my genius calls me." And, "What I must do is all that concerns, not what the people think."[56]

Emerson was a Transcendentalist. Transcendentalists were New Englanders mostly, as was Emerson; among the better known of them were: Henry David Thoreau, Bronson Alcott, George Ripley, Theodore Parker, and Margaret Fuller. Transcendentalists were romantics, literary people mostly, who contributed to the development of a national literature. But they were sufficiently distinct from the other writers to be considered as a separate category. They were distinguished by their desire to transcend, to rise above, not to conform to the society, the conventions, the culture, and the mores of their communities, state, and country. Even foolish consistency must be ignored, Emerson said, for it is "the hobgoblin of little minds." The aim which guided them, or so they said, was to be themselves, to speak their own thoughts, to consult their inward beings for the truth, and to speak it directly and bluntly as it came to them. They wanted to be and "do their own thing," as a less literate generation would summarize the view more than a century later.

Transcendentalists were a new breed of men on the American continent, the first of their kind, though hardly the last. They might better be called *intellectuals,* if the term can be sufficiently specialized to deal mainly with its most prominent examples. An intellectual, if you will, is one who dwells in the realm of ideas, who makes a profession, so far as he can, of thinking, who rises above the wisdom of the past, the prejudices of his countrymen, and the society within which he resides. He scales the heights of Mount Olympus, as it were, and surveys with an eye toward judging them all other men and social arrangements. (He is apt to be especially critical of his neighbors and his own country.) The distinctive feature of these intellectuals (Transcendentalists in New England), was not the degree of their learning; they might have much or little of that, and presumption often served well enough in its stead. Their distinctive feature was their spiritual distance from society, their cut-offness from it, lack of identification with it, and often so little involvement in its affairs that they did not fall under its discipline.

Such intellectuals began to crop up in Europe by the 18th century. They probably always exist in embryo, but before that time they were usually clergymen and held in check by the discipline of their churches. As the power of the churches declined, they became more numerous. The French *philosophes* were mostly intellectuals of this variety, and were plentiful in the years before the French Revolution. Rousseau was the prototype of such intellectuals. A later philosopher described well some crucial aspects of this intellectual: "Rousseau tried in vain to subject his life to any rule or to organize it in accordance with any plan. He moved constantly from one extreme to the other. . . . Rousseau never felt completely at home in any profession, in any science or doctrine, in any religion. He practiced in succession the callings of engraver, domestic servant, tax collector and official, tutor, music copyist, diplomatic secretary, musical performer and composer, before he found his true vocation as thinker and writer. Brought up in the strict principles of Calvinism, at the first opportunity he renounced Calvinism for Catholic doctrine; but he abandoned this in turn. . . . His life was filled with unsettled wandering. . . ."[57]

"Never completely at home" may well capture the essential feature of those intellectuals of whom the Transcendentalists were the first notable ones in America. None of this is meant to suggest that the Americans were not in many ways admirable men and women, that they were not talented, nor that they were quite so displaced as Rousseau. The Transcendentalists were mostly born in New England and lived most of their lives near where they were born. Thoreau, for example, was born in Concord, Massachusetts and, except for a brief trip to Canada and to the West, spent all his life in the vicinity of where he was born, and is buried in a cemetery in Concord. Emerson, to take another example, was born in Boston but settled in Concord, not far away, as a young man and made his home there for the rest of his life, though he traveled more than Thoreau.

In certain senses, too, the Transcendentalists were more American than other Americans. They were individualists to the hilt. Their commitment to freedom was almost unlimited. Thoreau held that no government that countenanced and protected slavery could be his government. They were, in

Ralph Waldo Emerson (1803–1882)

Emerson was born in Boston, graduated from Harvard (both college and seminary), taught in a school for several years before preparing for and entering the ministry as a Unitarian. He did not last long in that vocation, however, for he soon had doctrinal difficulties over even liberal Unitarian ritual, and he gave up pastoring churches. He became the intellectual leader of the Transcendentalists and spent the rest of his active life lecturing and writing. Emerson was greatly influenced by the English writers Coleridge, Wordsworth, and Carlyle, and twice made lengthy visits in Britain. The mood of his thought was philosophical, but he wrote in epigrams which are often impressive as statements, but do not comprise unfolding paragraphs very well. Although he often spoke favorably of reform as an idea, Emerson rarely approved particular reform efforts. Emerson was much more interested in awakening the genius in people than reforming institutions.

their eyes at least, believers in democracy. But the America they loved was not by any means the America in which they lived; it was an ideal America, an America purified of all its dross and perfected. "No truer American existed than Thoreau," Emerson said at his funeral. "But idealist as he was, standing for abolition of slavery, abolition of tariffs, almost for abolition of government it is needless to say he found himself not only unrepresented in actual politics, but almost equally opposed to every class of reformers."[58] That comes close to capturing the contradictions in the Transcendentalists.

There is no good reason to doubt, either, that the Transcendentalists considerably enriched American literature with their essays, poetry, and occasionally longer works. There is an enduring youthfulness in much of their work, an immediacy in their contact with the object that is not filtered through some conventional view, an inspiration in their call to others to scale the heights and plumb the depths with them. Emerson gained his fame as a lecturer, and many of his lectures were later published as essays. The titles of many of these essays attest their inspirational character: "Self-Reliance," "Spiritual Laws," "Friendship," "The Over-Soul," "Character," "Experience," and "Fate." He also left a memorable analysis of England, from his travels in that country, in *English Traits*. This little book bespoke an awareness that America had assumed its own character distinct from that of the mother country. Thoreau's best-known work, aside from the essay, "On the Duty of Civil Disobedience," was *Walden*. This account of the more than two years he lived alone near Walden Pond in a house of his own building, trying to discover how little of a man's time it took to provide himself with the necessaries of life, was not popular in his lifetime, but it has since become a classic. Margaret Fuller proved not only that women could write other things than romances, but also make a career, of sorts, of journalism. Walt Whitman, in *Leaves of Grass,* did for Transcendentalism what no New Englander could do: cast their exuberant vision into a highly individualist mold of poetry.

But the emergence of a class of intellectuals, so to speak, had a significance that goes beyond their literary accomplishments. American Transcendentalists might not so clearly be aliens in their native lands as was Rousseau, but they were in spirit akin to him in their separation from the ways of their countrymen and in their tendency to view them from an Olympian distance. Transcendentalists tended to see the world in purple colored half-truths. They saw very clearly how tradition, convention, and the work routine of life could subdue and stifle the life of the imagination. On the other hand, they tended to be blind to how we are sustained by tradition, drawn into liberating regularity by convention, and are fulfilled within the framework of the skills of production. That might have been of little account—for Transcendentalists were relatively few in number and of

Margaret Fuller
(1810–1850)

Fuller was born in Massachusetts, vigorously trained by her father to be a prodigy of learning, became a Transcendentalist, and was surely the most brilliant woman of her generation. She taught for a time after her father died, but was soon drawn into the literary circle of the New England Transcendentalists. She started a literary magazine, *The Dial*, wrote essays and poetry, and became a critic for Horace Greeley's newspaper, the New York *Tribune*. Miss Fuller went to Europe in 1846, lived in Italy for several years, and married an Italian marquis. She died in a shipwreck on return voyage to the United States. Her achievements were an inspiration to the movement for equality for women.

limited influence—, but they had a vision of drawing all men up to their heights and of reforming society to accord with their view. "What is man born for," asked Emerson, "but to be a reformer?" We must see to it, he pointed out, that the world not only fitted men in former ages but those of the present time as well.

Indeed, a great reforming zeal swept through much of America during this period, and a goodly number of Americans were caught up in it, as we shall see. Some of the Transcendentalists might stand outside and above much of the reforming effort, viewing it askance, as Emerson tended to do, but *Ideas Have Consequences*, as Richard Weaver pointed out in a book by that name. And Transcendentalists had, if not promoted particular reforms, buttressed the effort to make the world over by their scathing critique of things as they were.

So long as reforms are voluntary, of course, they may have salutary effects, and they are most unlikely to cause any disruptive convulsions in society. When government uses force to make over a society, however, it is quite otherwise. It should be said that Transcendentalists were not generally favorable to any such government effort. Emerson said that "the less government we have the better—the fewer laws, and the less confided power."[59] As for Thoreau, "I heartily accept the motto,—'That government is best which governs least;' and I should like to see it acted up to more rapidly and systematically."[60] A time was not long distant, however, when there would be people who were fired with a reforming zeal who would not scruple to use the power of government. The Reconstruction of the South was in considerable measure the result of such a zeal, and this was but a foretaste of what has been done in many lands in the 20th century. The impetus to this, or at least much of it, can be ascribed to intellectuals, cut loose from their moorings in the societies in which they live.

Southern Literature

Romanticism in the South was quite different from that in the North, especially New England. Transcendentalism made no impact on Southern thinkers and writers. The Southern outlook was rooted in the past, not oriented toward some future transcendence. Man fulfilled himself, Southerners inclined to believe, in the bosom of family, in integral relations with community, in accord with the rhythms of the seasons, and attuned to the enduring patterns of his culture and civilization. Southerners tended to be at home in their world in a way that Yankees often were not, though that world included slavery, planters with huge estates, great diversity in material well-being, and a greater abundance of perspiration than comfort. They were not, for the most part, seafarers, merchant adventurers, or given to manufacturing ventures. Traders they might be, but farmers they usually had been and would be again when they had accumulated the means by

William Gilmore Simms (1806–1870)

Simms was born in Charleston, South Carolina, received little formal education, but was for many years the leading literary figure in the South. He apprenticed himself to a druggist at first, went on to become a lawyer, dabbled in politics occasionally, and eventually became a planter on an estate inherited by his wife. But his main achievements were literary, as an editor and a writer. He wrote poetry, novels, short stories, biographies and history. Simms was best known, however, for his novels of the frontier and the period of the American Revolution. Although he was never greatly appreciated for his literary ability in the South, Simms was a loyal Southerner and devoted to the traditions of the South.

trade. Southerners might appear to be as restless as any other Americans as they forged westward across the more Southerly region, but it was largely a movement to expand Southern ways, or, perhaps more accurately, a way to acquire new lands by individuals and families which they would adapt to Southern habits.

That is not to suggest that the South was entirely different or separate from the rest of the country. On the contrary, Southerners were enmeshed in national politics, tended to be especially devoted to the Constitution, and the Southern economy was a part of the American economy. But in the decades before the Civil War the South was becoming more distinct as a section, Southern consciousness was increasing, and offshoots of the American plant were being nurtured for Southern nationhood. The South as a separate region, to the extent that it existed, was born in defense, in defense of the institution of slavery mainly, but of the laws, customs, and outlook that supported it as well. As abolitionist attacks on slavery mounted, and as the determination to limit and contain slavery was given more strident voice, the South became more and more defensive. Jeffersonian liberalism, so far as it had prevailed, tended to yield ground to conservatism. The political and legal equality of white men was accepted in the South as elsewhere, but Southerners emphasized status more than equality.

Southern literature tended to reflect these Southern attitudes. When it was not defensive of the South, in defending slavery, it sometimes took the offensive against the North, in attacking "wage slavery" in the factory system. There was a considerable pro-slavery literature, though it has long since become of interest mainly to scholars. Indeed, William J. Grayson published a full-length 1600 line poem on the subject in 1856, entitled *The Hireling and the Slave*. In it, he contrasted the condition of the slave in the South with the wage worker in the North, to the advantage of the former. Writing ironically, he declared that the Northerner, with "philanthropic eye"

> Sees the worn child compelled in mines to slave
> Through the narrow seams of coal, a living grave,
> Driven from the breezy hill, the sunny glade,
> By ruthless hearts, the drudge of labor made,
> Unknown the boyish sport, the hours of play,
> Stripped of the common boon, the light of day,
> Harnessed like brutes, like brutes to tug and strain. . . .[61]

By contrast, the life of the slave appears idyllic in Grayson's poetic view:

> And yet the life, so unassailed by care,
> So blessed with moderate work, with ample care,
> With all the good the starving pauper needs,
> The happier slave on each plantation leads;
> Safe from harassing doubts and annual fears,
> He dreads no famine in unfruitful years;
> If harvest fail from inauspicious skies,
> The master's providence his food supplies. . . .[62]

However, Southern literature ranged much beyond the defense of slavery. John Pendleton Kennedy wrote mainly romances of the South. Kennedy was born and educated in Maryland, but his mother was a Virginian. His novel *Swallow Barn* painted a somewhat idealistic view of the Southern plantation, particularly of the planter and his family. The slaves were kept mostly in the background, but when the institution itself did come up for discussion, the idea was advanced that it was a Southern problem, so far as it was a problem, and its solution should be left to the South. *Rob of the Bowl* is a novel set in the early days of Maryland, and is a kind of reminiscence of the religious conflicts in England out of which Maryland was born. Among his other works was a satire on Jacksonian democracy, *Quodlibet*, written in 1840. So far as Southern writers defended the Southern social system, and that was the tendency of Kennedy's work, they opposed equality and wrote sympathetically about the planters.

The most prolific and best-known of the writers in the South before the Civil War was William Gilmore Simms. He was born in Charleston and lived most of his life in South Carolina. In some respects, Simms was the James Fenimore Cooper of the South, writing romances about the colonial period, and about the earlier days of American history. His novels, however, were richer in detail but not nearly so well organized. He lived in the North for several years, where he first gained attention for his work, with such novels as *Guy Rivers* and *The Yemassee*. Simms then returned to South Carolina, married the daughter of a planter, established himself on a plantation, and wrote widely on history, biography, subjects that could be treated in essays, and edited magazines. In the 1850s, he wrote novels once again, among them: *Katherine Walton, The Sword and the Distaff*, and *Eutaw*.

New Churches and Religious Enthusiasm

The general tendency of the romantic outlook was to foster religion of the heart. Although there were still churches that insisted on a rigorous adherence to strictly defined doctrines, there was a decided movement away from emphasis upon doctrine toward concern with an inward experience of salvation. In any case, with the disestablishment of churches it was much more difficult for a denomination to enforce doctrinal purity. Moreover, those churches which were the most evangelical minded and were less concerned with elaborate doctrines grew most rapidly in the 19th century, particularly the Methodists and Baptists. Those churches which were controlled by local congregations prospered also, although the Methodists did retain an episcopal (bishop-controlled) system. Above all, though, it was the emotional appeal which tended to gain converts and build churches, particularly in the more frontier regions.

New denominations appeared in considerable variety from the late 18th century onward. Frequently, they were offshoots of older denominations. The Unitarian church broke away from the Congregational church in New England, a break occasioned because of doctrine rather than any religious enthusiasm or emotionalism. William Ellery Channing led in the founding of the Unitarians who no longer accepted such Christian beliefs as the belief in miracles. This was an extreme move away from religious doctrine toward no specific doctrine at all. Other new denominations formed in this period were the Disciples of Christ, the Church of Christ, the Christian (O'Kellyite) church, Cumberland Presbyterians, and African Methodist Episcopal church. (A Negro Baptist church had been formed before the American Revolution.) Some of the new denominations kept the common name of the older churches from which they split, but modified it new ways: for example, Primitive Baptists, Free-Will Baptists, Republican Methodists, Free Methodists, and so on.

There were religious movements, too, which cut across the bounds of denominations, though they sometimes led to divisions within particular denominations. The most dramatic of these movements was revivalism. The revival movement actually began with the Great Awakening in the 1740s and 1750s, nor did it end then, for revivals continued to occur for the remainder of the 18th century. New outcroppings of revivals in the 19th century gave rise to two new institutions in some Protestant denominations: the camp meeting and the "protracted meeting," the latter becoming eventually regular annual revivals, particularly in rural churches. Revival movements were most likely to sweep across some area along the frontier in the early 19th century. There was good reason for their occurring in frontier regions. Not only were frontiersmen often a rough lot, but also churches and ministers were scarce. When preachers came, and these people got religion, they often did so dramatically.

One of the most famous of the revivals occurred at Cane Ridge, Kentucky. A union meeting of Presbyterians and Methodists was held which lasted from Friday to Wednesday, almost continuously. More than 20,000 people attended the meeting. One of those there described the proceedings this way:

> The noise was like the roar of Niagara. The vast sea of human beings seemed to be agitated as if by a storm. I counted seven ministers all preaching at once, some on stumps, others in wagons, and one . . . was standing on a tree trunk which had, in falling, lodged against another. Some of the people were singing, others praying, some crying for mercy in the most piteous accents, while others were shouting most vociferously. . . . At one time I saw at least five hundred swept down in a moment, as if a battery of a thousand guns had been opened upon them, and then immediately followed shrieks and shouts that rent the very heavens.[63]

People under conviction often manifested various physical signs, such as falling, getting the "jerks," as they were called, going on their knees and barking like dogs, running, rolling, and laughing. The large gatherings from two or more churches became regularized as camp meetings. Revivals in a particular church became regularized as protracted meetings. As the frontier receded, hysteria-filled conversions became much less common.

Religious fervor, aided and abetted by a loosened romantic imagination and heightened by the belief in unbounded possibilities, set the stage for other sorts of developments as well. Religious cults arose, emphasizing the separation of believers from others in distinct communities. Religious leaders found fertile ground in some areas for stirring up excitement and gaining followers. Kentucky appears to have been the most fertile ground for religious revivals that swept all the countryside into their excitement. An area from Vermont stretching across western New York was most prolific of prophets, seers, and others with new revelations. "This was the area," says an historian of these movements, "that was sometimes called the 'burnt' district because it had been swept by so many fires of religious excitement. Anything new in the way of religious belief seemed attractive to the jaded appetites of its inhabitants, and no new sect lacked some following."[64]

William Miller became a prophet of the imminent Second Coming of Christ. He was born in Massachusetts, but his family moved to Vermont when he was a child. Neither as a child nor as a young man did Miller show any indication that he had any particular interest in religion, much less a religious vocation. But as he approached his middling years he was converted, joined a Baptist church, and began to study the Bible earnestly. He became convinced that prophecies in the Bible were all being fulfilled and that the end of time was near. For several years he did nothing about this, but in 1828, he says that he felt a call to spread the word of his discoveries. "I tried to excuse myself," he said, "for not going out and proclaiming it to the world. I told the Lord that I was not used to speaking; that I had not the necessary qualifications for gaining the attention of an audience; that I was very diffident, and feard to go before the world; that I was slow of speech and of a slow tongue. But I could get no relief."[65] Even so, Miller began to lecture, became a preacher, and began to attract converts.

In 1840, during a series of lectures in Massachusetts, Miller met the Reverend Joshua Himes, who took over the publicity direction of what became the Millerite movement. While Miller resisted giving a precise date for the Second Coming, he became more and more convinced that the end of time would come either in 1843 or 1844. Pressed toward a firm date, he let the coming of spring in 1844 be set as a probable date. Well before this the movement had gained a large following in New York, Vermont, Massachusetts, Pennsylvania, and even into the Midwest. Miller and his disciples painted vivid word pictures of the coming fateful day:

> I am satisfied that the end of the world is at hand. . . . Behold, the heavens grow black with clouds; the sun has veiled himself; the moon, pale and forsaken, hangs in middle air; the hail descends. . . ; the lightnings send their vivid gleams. . . ; and the great city of the nations falls to rise no more forever and forever! At this dread moment, look! The Clouds have burst asunder . . . —He comes!— Behold the Savior comes![66]

As the time approached, the Millerites were claiming as many as a million followers. Be that as it may, they were numerous; and many waited in fear and anticipation, some selling their goods, buying white robes, and going upon mountain tops expecting to be gathered in. The world did not end, of course, and Miller reset the date for October 22, 1844. This date produced no more striking results, and the Millerite movement broke up. So ended one of the most dramatic of the religious eruptions of this period.

The development of the Mormon—Church of Jesus Christ of the Latter Day Saints—faith was both less dramatic and had a more lasting impact. Joseph Smith (junior) was the founder and early leader of the Mormon church. Smith was born in Vermont, but the family moved to Palmyra, New York when he was a boy. His father was unsuccessful in his various ventures and moved around frequently. Joseph was known as a shiftless boy as he grew to be a young man.

The distinctive feature of the Mormon faith is that it has a book of scriptures—*The Book of the Mormon*—in addition to the Bible. *The Book of the Mormon* was made available by Joseph Smith and was first published in 1830 through his efforts and those of friends. According to Smith, he was visited by a ''heavenly visitor'' in 1823, that the visitor's name was Moroni, that he was told that God had a work for him to do, and that there were plates of a book deposited nearby. However, Smith was cautioned that the time was not yet right for him to see the plates. Finally, in 1827 he was led to the place where the plates were buried and saw them. At first three witnesses, and later eight witnesses, signed affidavits that they had seen the plates. The plates were said to be inscribed in an ancient language, a language used by lost tribes of Israel, and through devices made available to him Smith was enabled to translate the works into English. Afterwards, the plates were returned to the visiting Angel.

The miraculous elements in Smith's account are not subject to ordinary proof or disproof, of course; they must be accepted on authority or faith, or

Courtesy Church of Jesus Christ of Latter-Day Saints

Joseph Smith
(1805–1844)·

Smith was the founder of the Mormon religion and its leader during the early years. He was born in Vermont, but grew up in New York state. Smith showed few signs as he grew up and got married of having either leadership ability or any great capacity for extended constructive work. Often, he busied himself with such things as looking for gold with a divining rod, with no notable successes. All that changed after he came into possession of *The Book of the Mormon*. After that, he focused his energies and became an leader and organizer of communities.

not at all. This much is clear, however, and is not questioned. Joseph Smith had in his possession in the late 1820s a lengthy manuscript which was the basis of *The Book of the Mormon*. In a recent printing, it runs to over 500 double-columned pages. Even if it were gibberish, which it is not, it would have taken months to compose, or string the words together and transcribe them. An organized work of that length ordinarily requires much longer to do, even for a professional writer, which Smith certainly was not. Smith might have conceived such an imposture, of course, but for a youth in his early twenties, known to be shiftless, with no known extensive accomplishments, to have mustered the tenacity to carry it through to completion almost surpasses belief. On top of that, he was barely literate.

Be all that as it may, the book went to press in 1830. The first efforts at selling copies met with indifferent success, even when the price was reduced to 25 cents per copy. Nor did Smith do any better in his first attempts to organize a church among neighbors in New York. His teachings did attract followers, however, when he moved to Kurtland in Ohio. His greatest achievement, however, was in founding the vigorous settlement at Nauvoo in Illinois. All his undertakings of communities based on the Mormon faith were shortlived, however. There were several reasons for this. In the communities founded by Smith, especially Nauvoo, the Mormon church not only controlled the religious life of the community, but also the political, economic, and social life. When Smith, along with some of the other leaders, began the practice of polygamy, there was dissension among the Mormons. Some of the political and economic activities also provoked resistance. What brought all this to a head, however, was the animosity of non-Mormons in Illinois. A mob-like assemblage of the militia descended on Nauvoo, took Smith into custody, and murdered him. The rest of the community was ordered out of the state then, though they were given time to plan their move.

Brigham Young led the largest group of the remaining Mormons on a long trek westward to the Great Salt Lake. There, in a territory they called Deseret—which later became Utah—they settled, prospered and grew in number. The remoteness of the location, too, gave the Mormons time to develop ways in accord with their own beliefs but which, in the course of time, they could sufficiently modify as to enable them to live peacefully and fruitfully with those whom they call Gentiles. From their center in Utah, they have sent forth missionaries over the whole United States and much of the rest of the world, won many converts, and become an important church in this country.

The Reformation of Society

There was a considerable ferment of reform in the United States in the decades before the Civil War. Much of it was conceived in New England, but some of it spread over the rest of the country in one way or another and sooner or later. Emerson, an apostle of reform as a general proposition, was somewhat astounded at the variety of things somebody or other thought needed reform. ''What a fertility of projects for the salvation of the world!'' he exclaimed:

> One apostle thought all men should go to farming, another that no man should buy or sell, that the use of money was the cardinal evil; another that the mischief was in our diet, that we eat and drink damnation. . . . Others attacked the system of agriculture, the use of animal manures in farming, and the tyranny of man over brute nature; these abuses polluted his food. The ox must be taken from the plough and the horse from the cart, the hundred acres of the farm must be spaded. . . . Even the insect world was to be defended. . . . Others attacked the institution of marriage as the fountain of social evils.[67]

Emerson may have had tongue in cheek regarding some of the reforms, though there is little enough exaggeration in his list. In truth, reforms of all sorts were being advanced; some were of little consequence then or now, while others were big with portent for the future. The reforms that ultimately had impact were those aimed at the reformation of society, and those that were most important, then or later, were the ones that got the force of government behind them.

The romantic outlook itself had no particular posture toward reform. A romantic might be conservative, radical, revolutionary, or be quite uninterested in social institutions. But some of the currents within romanticism fostered the zeal for reform. Transcendentalism, as noted earlier, with its conception of the individual transcending society, and rising above its confines, gave rise to the notion of changing society to make all this possible. Perhaps the most significant idea to gain ground was that of human perfectibility, that man can be perfected by perfecting society. Rousseau had taught that man is good by nature but that he is corrupted by social institutions. That being the case, the solution was to reform society. This idea gained ground from many directions in the 19th century. Unitarians, who cut loose from strict Christian doctrines, were often open to this view. On the other hand, some Christians who continued to hold to the belief in the natural depravity of man claimed that when he was saved—''born again,'' regenerated—he was perfected. Charles Grandison Finney, a prominent revivalist of the mid-nineteenth century, taught this. He said that regeneration

> implies an entire present change of moral character, that is, a change from entire sinfulness to entire holiness. . . . Regeneration then surely implies an entire change of moral character.

Again: The Bible represents regeneration as a dying to sin and becoming alive to God. Death in sin is total depravity. This is generally admitted. Death to sin and becoming alive to God, must imply entire present holiness.[68]

Such a perfected man, Finney declared, "is a reformer from principle. . . ."[69] Finney had in mind general reforms within society, but some of the religious groups of the time, especially those with very distinctive beliefs, sought to separate saints from sinners by living in separate communities.

Several of the reform movements of the time deserve mention, though they cannot be discussed in detail here. Among these are: prison reform, improved treatment of the insane, the temperance movement, peace movement, and women's rights. The movement for prison reform was tied in with the much more extensive use of imprisonment as punishment for crime and the general abandonment of bodily punishment, except in the case of executions. Jails had earlier been used mainly for temporary incarceration, but as imprisonment as punishment became common, there was a move to build special structures for that purpose. Dorothea Dix spearheaded an effort for better treatment of the insane in asylums. The temperance movement was underway in good earnest in the 1830s and 1840s. It had several facets. Some who sought and preached temperance wanted just that—moderation in the use of alcoholic beverages. Others, however, wanted total abstinence, and some churches established the expectation that their members would totally abstain, and even that it was a requirement for Christians. By the 1840s, a move was underway to have state governments prohibit the sale of alcoholic beverages. This prohibitionist movement met with some success in getting laws passed, but there was much evasion, and by the time of the Civil War the effort had been generally abandoned.

Quakers had been pacifists from the outset, but there were efforts in the 19th century to get a widespread movement afoot to get people committed to peace as a goal. An American Peace Society was formed in 1828 under the leadership of William Ladd. This movement never made much headway, however, under whatever name it went. The movement for female equality with men, led by Lucretia Mott, Elizabeth Cady Stanton, and later joined by Susan B. Anthony, got underway in the 1840s. They had greater success in attracting unfavorable attention to themselves than in altering social attitudes, however.

Except for the temperance crusade, most of the above movements had either limited application or limited impact, or both. Three of the movements need more extensive treatment both as examples of the reforming spirit and for their broader significance. They are: the formation of utopian communities, the drive for public education, and the abolitionist movement.

a. Utopian Communities

The utopian communities founded in America in the 18th and 19th centuries came from a variety of impulses. The colony of Georgia, which had utopian aspects, was founded for the humanitarian purpose of providing a new start for imprisoned debtors and the like. Some of them were founded by German religious sects seeking a place to practice their (often peculiar) beliefs. Most of them were more or less religious in origin, but some, such as Brook Farm, were entirely secular in character. Although they differed much from one another, they had some features in common. One was to live separate from the rest of society in their own communities. This was animated, in some measure at least, by perfectionism. They also often shared in common property, placed their property in a community trust, were sometimes incorporated, might live in common barracks, and do tasks in common.

They were usually communistic in tendency, then, and they may even be considered, at least some of them, as forerunners of state socialism. Historian Arthur Bestor aptly characterized the communities as being *communitarian,* to distinguish it clearly from either communism or state socialism. Indeed, they were voluntary in membership; a person could join them if he wished to and they were willing, and leave at will. Some of them, such as Robert Owen's New Harmony settlement in Indiana, were conscious experiments in what came to be called socialism. But most of the communities were relatively short-lived, rarely outlasting their leader, and often dwindling away or breaking up in a few years. In no case did they directly lead to any adoption of socialism or any particular socialist practice. Their influence on socialism was largely negative; socialists disavowed the voluntary community approach in view of the obvious failure of the secular communities.

Still, they are of interest as examples of the perfectionist and utopian ideas which animated them, for these did drive some of the developments in this country. The following were religious communities or settlements: the Shakers led by Mother Ann Lee, the Rappites of Father George Rapp, the Oneida community founded by John Humphrey Noyes, and the Amana Society. The following were the most directly socialist experiments: Robert Owen's New Harmony, Frances Wright's Nashoba, the North American Phalanx inspired by the French socialist Charles Fourier, and Etienne Cabet's Icaria. Brook Farm, famed because of the Transcendentalists who participated, did not fit well in either category.

b. Public School Movement

Utopian communities were by their very nature outside the framework of American society and could have little impact upon it. That they were usually short-lived is a tribute to the freedom, private ownership of property, and opportunities for individuals and families that prevailed generally, and to the drawing power of these compared to the holding power of collectivized communities. By contrast, the public school movement thrust toward the center of American life, affecting Americans generally, and has resulted in a structure which has lasted to the present. It was aimed at the children, impinged upon the family, and entailed the use of government power in ways that endangered, at the least, the life, liberty and property of Americans, or, if not their lives, their liberty and property.

Many, perhaps most, Americans did not favor public schools in the early 19th century. They were little more inclined to governmentally established schools than they were established churches. That is not to say that Americans generally were opposed to learning or even a measure of formal education. They were not. Nor were they generally opposed to schools; there were a good many schools of one sort or another located about over the country. But they were not greatly addicted to schooling, had not yet closely associated schooling with education, and did not suppose that if you wanted to learn something that schools were either the only or best place to do it. If you wanted to learn carpentry, you found a carpenter to teach you; if law, a lawyer; if political theory, a book, or books on the subject. Above all, though, the training and education of their children was primarily the responsibility of parents. Nobody much supposed that it was the duty of the taxpayers to pay for the education of their children, nor the right of the government to impose schools or the taxes to pay for them upon parents or others. Besides which, there were formidable difficulties in many areas, such as differences of belief and religion, which stood in the way of having common schools for all the people.

It was an uphill job, then, for such reformers and enthusiasts for public schooling as there were to make much headway. Indeed, they had only a limited success in doing so before the Civil War. Not surprisingly, the greatest thrust for public schools came in New England and in such Midwestern states as Ohio into which New Englanders had moved. Transcendentalism was almost exclusively a New England phenomenon, and New Englanders showed the greatest enthusiasm for reformist experiments generally. Moreover, Massachusetts had a rather long history of trying in one way or another to impose schools on the towns going back to the early days of the colony. Though the leaders of the public school movement were neither Calvinists nor Congregationalists as a rule, they still had a goodly amount of that busybodiness of some of their Puritan forebears.

At any rate, the leadership in the movement for public schools came mainly from New England. In 1837, the Massachusetts legislature established a state board of education. Horace Mann, one of the foremost advocates of public schools was appointed secretary of the board, and he served in effect as superintendent of education for the state for the next

Horace Mann
(1796–1859)

Mann was born in Massachusetts, graduated from Brown University, studied law,
and practiced it for several years. He became involved in state politics and became
a leader in reform efforts in the Massachusetts legislature. Although he was involved in a variety of reformist activities,
the one that was of the greatest concern to
him was the use of the state government
to promote and centralize direction over
the public schools. (He wanted public
schools to replace private schools.) Mann
took the legislative lead in getting a state
board of education authorized, and became
its first secretary. As secretary, he established a journal to promote public
schools, got teacher's colleges established,
and promoted French and German ideas
on educating children. He also served in
the United States House of Representatives
and as president of Antioch College in
Ohio.

dozen years. During the next dozen years appropriations for the public
schools doubled, the state made large appropriations for school buildings,
teachers' salaries were increased, and three normal schools (teacher's
colleges) were organized by the state. In 1852, Massachusetts passed a
compulsory attendance law. Henry Barnard was given a similar appointment
to that of Mann in Connecticut. Pennsylvania passed a Free School Act in
1834, which divided the state into school districts and enabled the districts
to levy taxes for schools if they chose. Movements in the direction of
establishing some degree of public schools had occurred in most states by
the time of the Civil War.

The public school movement was always more than simply an effort to
have schools provided at taxpayer expense. Nor was it simply an effort to
have an educated electorate as the franchise was extended to more people, as
is sometimes alleged. The most zealous of the reformers were determined to
use the power of the state by way of the schools to break the hold of
religious tradition and the inherited culture and to change society through

the child's training. These American reformers were influenced by European educational reformers such as Rousseau, Pestalozzi, and others who taught that the child was naturally good and needed only an environment within which to unfold. American Transcendentalists usually held similar ideas. They were influenced also by the Prussian schools, where a thoroughgoing system of state-controlled compulsory education was well established. The common school, Horace Mann wrote, "is the greatest discovery ever made by man: we repeat it, *the common school is the greatest discovery* ever made by man. . . . Let the common school be expanded to its capabilities, let it be worked with the efficiency of which it is susceptible, and nine-tenths of the crimes in the penal code would become obsolete; the long catalogue of human ills would be abridged; men would walk more safely by day; every pillow would be more inviolable by night; property, life, and character held by a stronger tenure; all rational hopes respecting the future brightened."[70]

The public school movement is especially significant, because it was the first major effort in the United States which succeeded in linking the power of government to an effort to reform and transform society. It was hardly the last, however. It should be said, too, that local communities continued to control the schools throughout the 19th century, and the schools were generally kept within the framework of local belief and traditions. The early reformers did little more than set the stage for more determined ones later on.

c. The Abolitionists

Abolitionists were those who wished to see slavery abolished, who spoke out against it, were active in getting petitions against it, and often did what they could to undermine it. They were often uncompromising in their positions. Slavery was a sin, an evil unrelieved by any good, and it must go. Charles Grandison Finney, the evangelist, said that slavery "is a great national sin. . . . It is the church that mainly supports this sin. . . . Let Christians of all denominations . . . write on the head and front of this great abomination, SIN! and in three years, a public sentiment would be formed that would carry all before it. . . ."[71] In the heated religious atmosphere of these years, his claim was a momentous one for all who accepted it from Finney or others.

Eventually, the abolitionist crusade became the focus of many of the reformers of this age; abolition became a cause among and above other causes, the most pressing of them all. Reformers in many other causes were usually drawn into the anti-slavery cause and brought much passion to it. William Lloyd Garrison was the bellwether of the cause, holding its standard high after the beginning of the publication of *The Liberator* in 1831. In his very first editorial, he closed with this stirring poem:

Trampling Oppression and his iron rod;
Such is the vow I take—SO HELP ME GOD![72]

The poet, John Greenleaf Whittier, was drawn to the abolitionist cause by
this passionate appeal from Garrison: "The cause is worthy of Gabriel—
Yea, the God of Hosts places himself at its head. Whittier, enlist!—Your
talent, zeal, influences—all are needed."[73] Thus were reform-minded
people drawn into the cause.

Abolitionists were only less popular in the North than the South. They
were generally regarded as troublemakers in the early years, and were likely
to be run out of town in most places in the North for their efforts, if not
worse. Old John Quincy Adams tried time after time in the 1830s and 1840s
to get the petitions of abolitionists made a part of the Congressional record
before he finally succeeded. But by persevering they won more and more to
their cause. By the 1850s, the anti-slavery attitude was even becoming
popular. Harriet Beecher Stowe's *Uncle Tom's Cabin,* published in 1852,
was a best seller as a book, selling 300,000 copies in the first year and over
3 million copies in succeeding years. Not only that, but the story was made
into a play, and Americans saw one production or another in great numbers.

Probably, the abolitionist crusade did not cause the Civil War, but the
zeal of its condemnation surely increased its incivility, and the thoroughness
of Reconstruction was a conflagration spread from fires lighted by
abolitionists.

Chapter 6
Westward Expansion

. . . The nation that possesses Oregon will not only control the navigation of the Pacific, the trade of the Pacific and Sandwich Islands, but the trade of China itself on the Pacific. . . .

—Alexander Duncan, 1843

Seat the United States firmly in Oregon, and the commercial enterprise and wealth of the world will centralize within our limits.

—C. J. Ingersoll, 1844

In the case of California. . . , the advance guard of Anglo-Saxon emigration has begun to pour down upon it, armed with the plough and the rifle, and marking its trails with schools and colleges, courts and representative halls, mills and meeting-houses. A population will soon be in occupation of California over which it will be idle for Mexico to dream of dominion. They will necessarily become independent. . . . Whether they will then attach themselves to our Union or not, is not to be predicted with certainty.

—John L. O'Sullivan, 1845

Chronology

1838—Wilkes Expedition of Pacific Exploration.
July, 1840—Independent Treasury Act.
December, 1840—Harrison elected President.
1841—Tyler succeeds Harrison upon his death.
1842—Webster-Ashburton Treaty.
1844—Polk elected President.
1845—Annexation of Texas.
May, 1846—United States declares war on Mexico.
June, 1846—Oregon Settlement.
1847—Wilmot Proviso adopted.
January, 1848—Discovery of gold in California.
February, 1848—Treaty of Guadalupe Hidalgo.
1849—Department of Interior established.
1850—Clayton-Bulwer Treaty.
1853—Gadsden Purchase.

desire of some to find "elbow room" in which to live in their own ways.
The usual process of settlement went something like this. First came the
explorers, hunters, trappers, and fur traders. From the early days of
colonization to the middle of the 19th century men were drawn westward by
the possibilities of trade with the Indians and of trapping fur-bearing
animals. The second wave of settlers in many areas was that of cattle
growers, those seeking new and unspoiled lands on which to range their
cattle. The third wave was that of row crop farmers, whose uses of the land
often brought them into conflict with the growers of cattle, sheep, and hogs.

The other major theme is not so well known, though it runs as clearly
through the 19th century as the first. In many respects, it is a counter-trend
to that of the westward movement. It is, in its center, the effort within the
older states along the Atlantic seaboard to retain their early dominant
position in the Union. Most of the effort was concentrated, first and last, in
the northeastern states from Maryland northward, and the centers of the
effort were the great seaport cities of Baltimore, Philadelphia, New York,
Boston, and, to a lesser extent, Newport. As early as the Constitutional
Convention in 1787, there were those who feared that the states that might
be formed beyond the mountains would become dominant in the Union.
Some even favored giving them an inferior status when they entered the
Union. Although the location of the capital in the District of Columbia was
not done to establish the dominance of the East—that location was then near
the population center of the country—, it has tended to give an eastward tilt
to American politics. In any case, leaders in northeastern states have labored
quite often to preserve a dominance for that region and its cities over the
United States. The effort has taken many forms: political efforts to restrain
westward expansion, efforts to tie trade routes to eastern port cities, efforts
to develop financial centers, and attempts to control government policy in
ways favorable to eastern dominance. The older states of the southeast never
made such an extensive effort either to restrain the westward movement nor
dominate the West. Southerners generally favored the westward movement,
especially that where slavery might take root, and usually opposed government efforts to tie the west closely to the east.

In any case, the westward expansion was usually entangled in politics, in
foreign affairs, and sectional efforts to use the power of government one
way or another, or to prevent its use by the federal government. Settlers took
the initiative in moving into new areas in the West, but once there they often
raised a clamor to have the federal government to protect them from the
Indians, from foreign powers, or to be incorporated into the United States.

forefront of political concern on more than one occasion, both the
expansion and the political contest over it reached a peak in the 1840s. The
territorial expansion itself was concentrated in the one term of President
James K. Polk, though the impetus to expand had been building several
years before that and continued for several more years. The political
controversies and struggles over expansion reflected sectional interests,
involved relations with foreign countries, and helped to bring the Whigs to
national power for brief periods of time. Above all, though, in the course of
these things the United States acquired territory all the way to the Pacific, a
long western coast line, and vast new lands to be occupied and developed.

Whigs and Democrats

Two vigorous and distinct political parties had emerged by the late 1830s,
the Whigs and the Democrats. Both parties were national parties in the
scope of their following and in the policies they advocated. Although
Andrew Jackson succeeded in building a strong Democratic Party, he had
managed to alienate important elements in the country by such policies as
opposition to a national bank. For various reasons, a goodly number of
Democrats became Whigs. Two other developments of the 1830s helped to
strengthen and increase the role of political parties. One was the adoption of
the national convention as a means of nominating candidates for the highest
offices in the land. This device was first used by a minor party and was
adopted by the Democrats in 1836. The Whigs began the use of the
convention in 1840. The second development was that of national-state-
local party organizations. Some states, notably New York, had strong party
organizations as early as the 1820s or before. The practice became general
in the course of the 1830s, and political parties were both accepted and their
support sought by candidates. They were no longer denounced as factions
but welcomed as a part of the process of popular government. Daniel
Webster admitted, reluctantly it appears, that ''The existence of parties in
popular Governments is not to be avoided, and, if they are formed on
constitutional questions, or in regard to great measures of public policy. . . , it may be admitted that, on the whole, they do no great harm.''[74]
Parties had become the main, if not only, route to political office.

The Whigs, however, never managed to become a continuing force in
American government. The party was organized nationally, had an attractive program, and in Daniel Webster and Henry Clay had two of the most
compelling orators and most famous men in its leadership ranks. Yet the
Whigs never succeeded in enacting most of their program. They could
sometimes undo for a time what had been done, but they could not do. Two

Whigs were elected President: William Henry Harrison and Zachary Taylor. They were both popular generals, better known for their military exploits than political achievements, though Harrison had served in public office. Neither lived long enough in office to finish a term; Harrison died within a month of his inauguration. The Whigs also gained control of one or both branches of Congress for brief spans. All of this was to little avail.

The main reason for the failures of the Whigs was a tendency in the Southern wing of the party. The sectionalism which eventually sundered the Democratic Party prevented the Whigs from gaining effective control of the government from the outset. Southern Whigs were much better anti-Jacksonians than they ever were pro-whig in their impulses. They were suspicious of Jackson's nationalism and turned off by his emphasis upon equality. Though Jackson was himself a slaveholder, the more thoughtful could see that a consistent belief in equality must eventually undercut the foundations of slavery. The Whigs did not stress equality, probably inclined to oppose it, but they were more much more nationalistic, especially in their economic program, than were the Jacksonians. They favored a national bank, protective tariffs, and active program of internal improvements (road and canal building) by the federal government. In addition, the Whigs were lukewarm toward territorial expansion at the crucial time. Southern politicians who pressed for all these things were in considerable danger of losing their constituency. How sectional differences undid the Whigs may be grasped more clearly, however, by examining some of the political events of these years.

The Whigs got their first opportunity to control the government because of the unpopularity of the Van Buren administration. Martin Van Buren's unpopularity can be attributed mostly to the depression which extended through most of his term. Actually what goes by the name of depression is usually the result of a monetary *deflation*. This one certainly was. There had been a large credit expansion (monetary inflation) in the middle of the 1830s, mainly by state banks. The shift of treasury funds from the United States Bank to state banks after 1832 had provided much of the reserves on which credit had been expanded. Jackson did two things which contributed to the deflation. One was to distribute most of the treasury surplus to state governments. This move reduced the reserves of the state banks who held treasury deposits. The other was to issue a Specie Circular in 1836 requiring payments for land to be made in hard money. This move precipitated a bank panic as banks were pressed to find the hard money to redeem their currency. The result was deflation—a reduction of the money supply—and depressed conditions as credit was hard to get and until prices had adjusted downward.

Pressure was put on Van Buren to foster measures to relieve business distress, but he stoutly denied that there was any constitutional authority for such government action, maintaining that in accord with American practice

Courtesy U.S. Deptartment of State

Van Buren was the 8th President of the United States, a leading politician and statesman of the second quarter of the 19th century, and probably more of a Jacksonian than Andrew Jackson. He was born in New York state and retained his residence there for the whole of his life. Although he received little by way of formal education, Van Buren learned the art of political maneuvering in the best school in the country: New York state. During the early years of the Republic, New York was the seedbed both of family-dominated and machine politics; the state was mercurial, too, in its political swinging from one side to the other. At any rate, Van Buren became a force in Democratic politics in his home state, and from that base he moved on to the national scene by coming to the United States Senate in 1821. There, he became a supporter of Jackson, and under Jackson's wing he became successively Secretary of State, Vice-President, and President. Although he was unable to overcome the handicap of an economic depression during his administration, Van Buren played an important part in tying the North to the South in the Democratic Party.

---

people must look after themselves. Nonetheless, many people blamed him and the Democrats generally for the difficulties. Government action had precipitated the bank panic, of that there could be little doubt. Van Buren did not deny this, and he proposed to take action to prevent a recurrence of such a crisis. So far as the federal government was concerned, he thought the root of the trouble lay in the use of treasury funds to expand the credit. To prevent it from happening again, he proposed to take all government funds out of banks and deposit them in an independent treasury. However, it was not until 1840 that an Independent Treasury Act was passed, much too late to have anything but a further deflationary effect on the economy.

Democratic difficulties were Whig opportunities, of course, and in 1840 the Whigs ran and elected Harrison as President and John Tyler as his Vice-President. Henry Clay finally had his opportunity, or so he hoped, to get the main outlines of his American System—protective tariffs, Federal aid for internal improvements, and a national bank—put into operation. It did not work out that way. The Whigs were able to repeal the Independent Treasury Act. Meanwhile, however, Harrison had died, and Tyler succeeded him as President. Tyler was one of the Southerners who had been a Democrat but had become a Whig. The Whigs assumed at first that his conversion had been complete, but it did not work out that way. He vetoed the legislative attempts to establish a national bank, exhibited no enthusiasm for a protective tariff, and opposed any extensive Federal aid for internal improvements. Tyler had continued Harrison's cabinet, but all the mem-

John Tyler
(1790–1862)

Tyler was the 10th President of the United States. He was born in Virginia, educated at William and Mary, and practiced law and politics. He always placed his principles above party loyalty, and quite likely he would have made an outstanding Senator had the 17th Amendment to the Constitution for the direct election of Senators been passed a century earlier. As it was, he was often undone by the pressures to conform to party positions and state legislatures in his times. Tyler was a Jeffersonian Republican when he entered national politics in the House of Representatives. But as the Democrats and Whigs came to dominate he was never able to find a party in which he and his principles could be at home. He could not abide Jackson, though he was a Democrat for a short period. As a Whig, Tyler had more reservations than party commitments. It was as a Whig that he became President on the death of Harrison, but he could not lead the Whigs because he could not subscribe wholeheartedly to their platform. He withdrew from politics after 1845 and did not become active again until Virginia was preparing to secede from the Union.

(1795–1849)

Polk was born in North Carolina and moved with his family to Tennessee as a boy. He graduated from the University of North Carolina and studied and practiced law in Tennessee. His main vocation, however, was politics. He was elected to Congress in 1824 and served without interruption in that body until 1839. Polk was an early supporter of Jackson, and was Speaker of the House of Representatives during the last years of Jackson's and the early years of Van Buren's presidency. He left Congress to become governor of Tennessee, but was not re-elected to that post. Although Polk was not initially considered as a major contender for the Democratic nomination for the presidency in 1844, he was nominated as a "dark horse" and served with distinction in the highest office in the land. Much of his administration was caught up in the Mexican War and territorial expansion, but he also lent his influence to the establishment of an Independent Treasury and the reduction of the tariff.

bers, except Secretary of State, Daniel Webster, resigned because of his bank veto. Thereafter, Tyler inclined more and more toward the Democratic position.

Henry Clay now believed that the time had arrived for him finally to be elected President. He resigned from the Senate in 1842 in order to strengthen the Whig Party and solidify his position as its leader. Van Buren expected to be the Democratic nominee. As the 1844 political season approached, the question of the annexation of Texas was a mounting divisive issue cutting across party lines. Both Clay and Van Buren published letters prior to the nominating conventions questioning the wisdom of annexing Texas in the near future. Andrew Jackson favored annexation, and he let it be known that the Democrats should choose a man in favor of territorial expansion. In any case, Van Buren did not get the nomination because he could not get the two-thirds majority in the convention required for nomination. Instead, the

Democrats nominated a "dark horse," James K. Polk of Tennessee. Polk ran on an expansionist platform and won the election.

All other activities during the Polk Administration were overshadowed by expansionist activities and the Mexican War. An Independent Treasury Act was passed in 1846, and from that time down to the Civil War Federal treasury deposits were kept out of the banking system. Polk had announced at the beginning that he would not seek a second term, and he did not. The Democrats nominated Lewis Cass as their candidate in 1848, and the Whigs nominated General Zachary Taylor, fresh from victorious campaigns in Mexico. Taylor won the election, but the Senate remained under Democratic control, and the Democrats had a plurality of members, but not a majority, in the House. Thus, Taylor lacked a Whig majority in Congress, had he been disposed to push Whig programs. As it was, Congress became much too entangled in the question of the admission of California to the Union to accomplish much else. Taylor died in 1850, and was succeeded by Millard Fillmore. By his support of the Compromise of 1850, Fillmore so

Zachary Taylor
(1784–1850)

Taylor was the 12th President of the United States and a general in the army during the Mexican War. He was born in Virginia, grew up in Kentucky, and later established his residence as a plantation owner in Louisiana. He joined the army in 1806 and, except for a brief period following the War of 1812 and while he was President, served the military for the remainder of his life. His most distinguished service was during the Mexican War, in which he was field commander of American forces for the first year. Taylor became known as "Old Rough and Ready," both for the stern discipline he professed and his willingness to fight. His most remarkable victory was at the Battle of Buena Vista in Mexico, when he confronted an army led by Santa Anna composed of 20,000 men and turned it back with less than 5,000 under his command. His popularity led the Whigs to nominate and elect him President, but he died before finishing the second year of his term.

Whigs. Thereafter, the Whig following dwindled, and the much more vigorous new Republican Party arose in its stead.

Transportation Linking East and West

Commercial transportation was not so much an economic as a geopolitical problem from 1820 down to the Civil War. The international aspects of the problem were largely solved during the War of 1812 and its aftermath, by the Louisiana Purchase, and by the Acquisition of Florida. These activities had brought full control over the river outlets to the Gulf of Mexico and the main seaports for the United States. The development of the steamboat solved the most formidable problem of river transport. The vast region between the Appalachians and the Rockies is drained by a great system of inland rivers which empty into the Mississippi, many of which are navigable all the way to the foothills of the mountains. South of the mountains, in Mississippi, Alabama, and Georgia there are also lengthy navigable rivers which feed into ports on the Gulf, such rivers as the Alabama-Tombigbee and Chattahoochee-Apalachicola.

There was available yet another potential water transport system in the Midwest—the Great Lakes. They are the largest system of inland lakes in the world, and several of them could be, and occasionally have been, traversed by ocean-going vessels. From Lake Superior on the west, the lakes empty into one another southward and then northeastward until they reach the St. Lawrence, which empties into the Atlantic. Actually, however, the Great Lakes were not initially such a boon to water transport for shippers from the United States as might be supposed. There were three major reasons for this. First, there are virtually no navigable streams of any length which empty into the Great Lakes. Therefore, heavy goods could not be brought to them from very far inland to be shipped. Second, there is no natural route by which the ocean can be reached by way of the Great Lakes. The major obstacle is in trying to go from Lake Erie to Lake Ontario. Niagara Falls is an insurmountable obstacle in navigating the river connection. Moreover, the drop from Lake Erie to Lake Ontario is more than 300 feet, in any case, necessitating numerous locks on the canal which was eventually built to bypass the river. Third, there is what may be called the geopolitical obstacle that the outlet to the ocean by way of the St. Lawrence goes through Canadian ports. There is no reason to suppose that this was an international problem, particularly after the War of 1812, since the Canadians would almost certainly have welcomed any transport business thrown their way from the United States. But it would not have solved the geopolitical problem of the Northeast.

The basic geopolitical problem was that the states and cities of the Northeast were in grave danger of losing their commercial pre-eminence in the Union. The situation had sectional implications as well. If the commerce of the Midwest flowed through the channels of the Mississippi and its tributaries, the major economic ties would be between the mid-South and the Midwest. This was no idle pipedream, for the trend was in that direction in the 1820s and 1830s, until it reached its relative peak in the 1840s. This is well illustrated by the growth of St. Louis and New Orleans, the two major ports on the Mississippi. St. Louis is located a few miles south of the confluence of the Missouri and Mississippi rivers, and 200 miles north of the point where the Ohio joins the Mississippi. The growth of St. Louis as a port city coincided with the widespread use of the steamboat after 1817. In 1840, the population was a little over 16,000; by 1850 it was 77,860. In 1854, St. Louis ranked third among cities in the United States in the tonnage passing through it. One historian describes the city this way:

> St. Louis in the forties was a pulsating river metropolis, a mart on the Mississippi second only to New Orleans. Commercial activity along its levee filled travelers with wonder. There in 1847 Philip Hone, the New York merchant, found fifty large steamboats butted against the wharves, taking on and discharging cargo over their bows. As far as the eye could see, he recalled, the docks were piled high with barrels of flour, bags of corn, hogsheads of tobacco, and the products of American industry soon to be lodged in the stores and warehouses of the growing city.[75]

New Orleans was the port of entry to the Gulf of Mexico for virtually the whole of middle America. It grew rapidly after the end of the War of 1812. By 1825, the imports and exports from the city were valued at $17 million; these increased in the next 10 years to $53 million. Between 1830 and 1840 the traffic came close to doubling. By 1847–1848, exports of domestic products exceeded those going through the port at New York City. While New Orleans had not yet become the leading port in all respects in the United States, it seemed destined for that honor.

It is against this background that it is easiest to understand the great effort from the Northeast to form transportation links to the Midwest. Shut off from trade routes for heavy goods by the Appalachians and restricted to a relatively narrow hinterland from which to draw produce, the ports of the Northeast were almost certain to decline if something were not done. The effort was geopolitical in that the problems to be overcome were topographical (also technological) and governments were drawn into the efforts to divert traffic from the southerly route to the Northeast. Historians usually distinguish three eras of these efforts in the years before the Civil War.

Northeast and Midwest was road building. Attempts were made from the early 19th century onward to get Federal support for building highways. Several Presidents, including Jefferson and Madison, recommended action, but doubted that money from revenues generally should be appropriated for the purpose without a constitutional amendment. One route that was used limitedly was to set aside lands that might be sold to provide aid for the building of roads. Other than that method, however, none was ever much accepted by Jeffersonians or Jacksonians. Measures for sustaining road building were vetoed successively by Madison, Monroe, and Jackson. The truth seems to be that there was little support from the South for national road or canal building programs, and as the South began to become a minority region politically Southerners took their stand on the Constitution as their best defense.

In any case, only one east-west improved road was built with any Federal aid. That was the National Pike or Cumberland Road, which extended from Baltimore, begun in 1811, to a terminus in Vandalia, Illinois in the 1850s. Only a part of the road, however, used Federal funds, that portion from Cumberland, Maryland to Springfield, Ohio. Otherwise, such improved roads as were built in the pre-Civil War period were built under state government: some by local communities, some by the state governments, some by private companies as toll roads, financed either by private subscription or by a combination of state aid and private financing. New York had the most extensive road system, with around 4,000 miles of toll roads, and Pennsylvania about 2,400 miles.

It should be noted that most states did not have the same political, geographical, and commercial reasons to build roads, particularly going

THE NATIONAL ROAD

beyond the mountains, that New York and Pennsylvania did. Most of New York lies beyond the mountains, and Pennsylvania is cut in two by the Alleghenies. The western portions of these states are geographically a part of the Midwest rather than the Northeast. Hence, the major road building effort to tie the regions together. Virginia also had considerable territory lying west of chains of mountains, including what is now West Virginia, but excepting for the Shenandoah Valley the region west of mountain chains had few inhabitants. Whatever the reasons, however, Southern states did not exert themselves with extensively improving their roads.

Undoubtedly, improved roads provided a variety of benefits, but however good or long the roads might be they could not much alter the situation for transporting goods, especially heavy ones. Nor could any amount of Federal aid have appreciably changed the situation. The difficulty lay in the much greater expense of land compared to water transportation. The only way to transport heavy goods overland was on wagons pulled by teams of horses, mules, or oxen. The weight that could be transported was limited not only to what the wagon would bear but also by what the animals could pull up the steepest hills. One estimate has it that it was fifteen times more expensive to transport goods by wagon than by boat. To put it another way, it was much less expensive to ship goods from Pittsburgh down the Ohio to the Mississippi, thence to New Orleans, transfer them to ocean going ships, which could travel through the Gulf and up the Atlantic coast to Philadelphia, than to transport them the few hundred miles overland from Pittsburgh to Philadelphia. By the 1830s or before, attention had shifted from road building to other ways to cross the mountains.

2. Era of the Canals

Aside from the failure of improved roads to alter the direction of the flow of transportation, what diverted attention from road building was the success of the Erie Canal. The project was begun in 1818, and was financed by the state of New York. The canal was completed in 1825; it was 363 miles long and extended from Buffalo and Lake Erie to Troy on the Hudson. From its eastern terminus goods could be shipped downstream on the Hudson to Albany and New York City. The Erie Canal was a major breakthrough; for the first time heavy cargoes could be shipped competitively from the Midwest to the Northeast. The average cost of transporting a ton of cargo from Buffalo to Albany was reduced from $90 to $8. More, the Erie Canal tapped the Great Lakes, and could bring cargoes back and forth from western cities such as Chicago and Cleveland. The canal was an instant commercial success.

This success set off a spate of canal building in the United States. In 1816, there was little more than a hundred miles of canals in the country. By 1830, there were more than 1200 miles; by 1840, some 3300 miles; and by

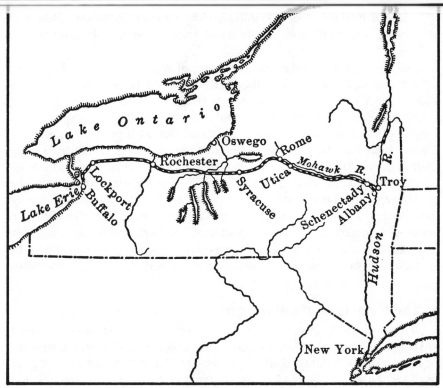

THE ROUTE OF THE ERIE CANAL

1850, some 3700 miles. The great era of canal building, then, was in the 1830s. The most ambitious of the canals was the one known as the Pennsylvania Canal, or the Main Line. It was intended to do for the city and port of Philadelphia what the Erie was doing for New York City. Work was begun on it in 1826, and it was completed in 1834. It was not possible, of course, to build a canal up the eastern slopes of the Alleghenies and down the western slopes. How the Main Line was constructed has been described this way:

> From Philadelphia a railroad traversed the eighty-one miles to Columbia on the Susquehanna. From Columbia a canal ascended the Susquehanna and then traveled westward along the Juniata to Holli-daysburg, where the Allegheny ridge, 2,291 feet high had to be surmounted. The device chosen was the Allegheny Portage Railroad, which mounted each side of the ridge with five inclined planes, interspersed with level stretches. Stationary engines pulled the vehicles

up the inclines; horses pulled them on the level tracks. In this fashion cars or cradles with canal boats were raised from the Juniata and finally let down on the other side into the Conemaugh at Johnstown, whence a canal continued along the route of various rivers to Pittsburgh.[76]

Undoubtedly, this undertaking was quite an engineering feat, but it was largely a failure either in diverting traffic from the Erie or from its normal course down the Ohio and Mississippi rivers.

Otherwise, the most extensive canal building was in Ohio and Indiana in attempts to connect the Ohio and its tributaries with ports on Lake Erie. These canals had the effect both of extending the reach of the Mississippi river system into the eastern Midwest and diverting some river traffic to the Great Lakes and thence to the Erie Canal. Except for Virginia, no extensive canals were dug in the South. The main thrust of this canal building activity, then, was to link the Midwest to the Northeast; major beneficiaries were such cities on the Great Lakes as Chicago, Cleveland, and Buffalo, and New York City in the east. It was also a considerable boon to farming in the northern Midwest. Much of the financing was done by state governments.

c. The Coming of the Railroads

On July 4, 1828, Charles Carroll of Carrollton, the last surviving signer of the Declaration of Independence, lifted a shovel of dirt symbolizing the beginning of construction on the Baltimore and Ohio Railroad. How the cars would be pulled on the tracks had not yet been decided, whether by horses or by a steam engine. Two short railroad lines using steam engines were in operation in England, but it was not yet clear that steam motive power could be adapted to travel by land. But however the cars might eventually be pulled over it, the leaders of Baltimore were bent on building a railroad to the Ohio river in the west. Although Baltimore was the eastern terminus of the Cumberland Road, it was now threatened as a port by canals. The Erie had already made it possible to bring freight from the Midwest to New York City much cheaper than it could be hauled by road, and Pennsylvania had begun the construction of its Main Line. Baltimore would counter with a rail line to Wheeling on the Ohio.

The planners at Baltimore saw possibilities for the railroad, or thought that they did, which few could conceive in the 1820s. Hardly anyone could conceive of any form of transportation replacing water even for inland transportation. After all, water transport had dominated in the carrying of heavy freight since time immemorial. The earliest railroads, even the Baltimore and Ohio, were conceived as supplementing river, lake, canal, and waterway transport by linking them in one way or another to one another or to the ocean. The first successful use of the steam engine to pull a string of cars over a rail line was on the Charleston and Hamburg Railway of

1833, and it was at that time the longest railroad in the world.

It was not many years before the railroad was demonstrating its superiority in many respects to waterways for inland transportation. Trains could run year round, while in the northern portion of the United States frozen streams inhibited travel much of the winter. Travel on the Erie Canal, for example, occurred during a seven-month annual season. Also, low water during summer droughts often occurred on streams, and storms and floods were ever a threat to boats. The major advantage of water travel was that it was less expensive than by trains but much of this was offset except for the heaviest cargoes by regularity, speed, and the fact that rail sidings could bring goods to almost any location. Even so, the early railroads were almost invariably built to and terminated at port cities, either on the rivers, lakes or oceans.

Nor was it many years before rail lines were forging links between the Northeast and Midwest. The first one to do so was the Erie, which was completed in 1851, and extended 483 miles from the Hudson to Lake Erie. Another rail line, pieced together from 10 lines and organized as the New York Central, connected eastern and western New York in the early 1850s. The Baltimore and Ohio was finally completed to the Ohio River in 1852. The Pennsylvania Railroad also completed its main line from Philadelpia to Pittsburgh late in the same year. There were now four main lines which would shortly forge farther westward linking the Northeast with the Midwest.

Indeed, in the decade or so before the Civil War that region of the Midwest between St. Louis, Cincinnati, and Pittsburgh to the South and Minneapolis, Chicago, and Cleveland to the north was honeycombed with railroads. These, in turn, were linked to the trunk lines to the Northeast, in which there were many short lines from Baltimore northward into New Hampshire. Undoubtedly, much of the traffic in freight had been diverted from the Mississippi River and its tributaries to much more direct routes to the Northeast, and the Northeast and Midwest were tied together commercially. It should be emphasized, too, that much of this building of transportation systems was politically supported and some of it politically inspired. State and city governments often sponsored and provided some of the financial support both for canal and railroad building as well as road building. What underlay much of this government involvement was competition among cities—merchants and shippers located in them mainly—for crucial positions on trade routes. This was especially true of Northeastern cities and those located on the Great Lakes.

As already noted, the state of New York built the Erie Canal and operated it. Several Midwestern states sank large amounts of funds into canal building in the 1830s and 1840s. Indeed, some of them extended their credit so far that when the depression came in the late 1830s they failed to make payments or went bankrupt. Despite this unhappy experience, states often played a large role in railroad building. The city of Philadelphia, for example, incurred a debt of $8 million to subsidize railroad building. Although the Baltimore and Ohio railroad was to have been privately financed, both the city of Baltimore and the state of Maryland extended credit for its completion. In the 1830s, the state of Illinois appropriated a total of $19 million in the support of such public improvements as railroads and canals. Ohio passed a law which committed the state to furnish one-third of the capital for any railroad built in that state. Thus, the linking of the Northeast and Midwest was the result of more or less conscious policy of state governments involved.

It should be noted, too, that though canals and railroads often did get built, the government involvement not only spurred hasty and ill-considered building but also placed heavy burdens of taxation on their citizens. One historian has judged about the building to the midpoint of the 19th century: "The experience of building with government-sponsored internal improvements—the Erie being the sole exception—had ended disastrously."[77] Another says that "there was a good deal of fraud and corruption in connection with state aid to railroads, and in later years a number of states repudiated some of their obligations made in connection with railroad construction. Because of the corruption involved and because of the heavy tax burden the people were asked to bear to meet the states' promises, it later became common for state constitutions to prohibit the investment of state money in any private enterprise."[78]

Some clarifying and qualifying remarks may be in order here. First, the building of canals and railroads linking the Northeast with the Midwest did not dry up transportation on the Mississippi by any means. St. Louis continued to be a major port city, and river traffic into New Orleans continued to grow up until the Civil War, though it is reasonable to conclude that it was not nearly so large as it might have been. Second, there was railroad building in the South, though it was hardly on the scale of that in the North. There was one major line connecting Baltimore with Chattanooga, and thence to Memphis and Atlanta. Another rail line was nearly completed linking Chicago with New Orleans when the war began. Otherwise, there were mostly shorter lines leading to ports on the Gulf and Atlantic. Third, once the superiority of rail transportation had been demonstrated undoubtedly many rail lines connecting cities and towns with one another would have been built.

But without the aid of governments, economic, not political considerations, would undoubtedly have been foremost. The Erie Canal might have been built by private enterprise, though it wasn't, but most likely, in view of the lay of the land, attention would have been focused on connecting the Great Lakes with the Mississippi River and in building railroads from

events, but it is reasonable to suppose that some of the states in the South, particularly Tennessee, Mississippi, and Louisiana might have been much more reluctant to secede from the Union had they been more closely tied commercially with the Midwest than they were.

Territorial Expansion

Well before the transportation problems involved in the commercial utilization of much of the land east of the Mississippi had been solved, pressures were mounting for expanding the territory of the United States to the Pacific. Indeed, there was a vast amount of territory west of the continental divide which was but sparsely inhabited. Mexico claimed a huge portion of this territory, in addition to Texas until 1836, but had hardly established an effective rule over it. Americans were not greatly interested in the mountain country, but from the early 1840s onward there was increasing interest in the Oregon country, California, and an already well-developed interest in Texas. As for the mountain country, it formed a necessary connection to the west coast.

a. Texas and Annexation

In 1821, Moses Austin, an American citizen, received permission from the Spanish government to plant a settlement in Texas. He died shortly after receiving the grant, however, and before Stephen F. Austin, his son, could act on it, Mexico achieved its independence from Spain and claimed all Spanish territory from the Southwest to the Pacific. The younger Austin did succeed in persuading the new Mexican government to honor the grant, and even expand it. Thereafter, over the next decade, an increasing number of settlers from the United States poured into Texas. And, though slavery was prohibited by Mexico, a goodly number of slaves were brought in as well. By 1835, there were in the vicinity of 35,000 Anglo-Americans in Texas, while there were very few Mexicans.

Trouble between the Americans and the Mexican government mounted after 1830. In that year, the Mexicans prohibited further American immigration and authorized military occupation of the province. When Santa Anna overthrew the government, the Texans hoped he would be more generous. It did not work out that way, and when Austin was sent to Mexico City to plead their case he was arrested and imprisoned for several months. When Austin returned in 1835, the Texans called a convention, set up a provisional government, and authorized an army. Although the Texans professed loyalty to a constitutional Mexican government, Santa Anna brought a large military force into Texas to subdue the Americans. With four thousand men under his command, Santa Anna laid the fort at the Alamo under siege; the fort was manned by 187 men, including Davy Crockett, and all these were eventually wiped out. In the wake of the siege, Texas declared its independence of Mexico and adopted a constitution of its own. Sam Houston was placed in command of the army, and with a smaller force he defeated and captured Santa Anna at the Battle of San Jacinto. The Mexican army speedily withdrew from Texas and gave no more trouble.

For the next nine years Texas was an independent republic, hence the Lone Star State. Although there was much interest in the United States in acquiring Texas, and many Texans wanted admission to the Union, neither Jackson nor Van Buren took steps to annex the new republic. Sectional differences, particularly abolitionist sentiment which was mounting, made it

Sam Houston
(1793–1863)

Courtesy Gregory's Old Master Gallery

Houston is usually remembered for his leading role in the early years of Texas (the largest city in the state was named for him), but he had been important in Tennessee politics before he ever went to Texas. He was both a Congressman and governor in Tennessee, but he was president of Texas, a United States Senator from that state before he finally became its governor. He was born in Virginia but moved with his family to Tennessee as a boy. At the age of 15, he ran away from home and lived for three years with the Cherokee Indians. Indeed, he left the office of governor of Tennessee to join the Cherokees once again, and he frequently evinced great concern for justice for the Indians. Actually, he had a quite varied life: he fought with Andrew Jackson in the War of 1812 and practiced law for a while. President Jackson sent him to Texas to negotiate with Indian tribes for trade privileges, and while there he became deeply involved in the Texas move for independence. He was appointed commander-in-chief of the Texas army and defeated Santa Anna at the Battle of San Jacinto. This set the stage for his leading role in Texas politics.

would be a slave state, and, if Texas gained all the territory it was claiming,

there might be three or four new slave states. Indeed, the balance of power might shift toward the South. But expansionist sentiment was increasing in the early 1840s. There was renewed interest in Oregon and new interest in California. A trade-off was in the offing for free and slave states. There was a foreign problem as well. Texas had applied for admission to the Union in 1836, and no action had been taken. Thereafter, Texas sought recognition by other nations. Britain and France moved quickly to accord recognition of Texas as an independent country. There was talk in Texas of expanding all the way to California, and in Britain of guaranteeing the boundaries of Texas.

President Tyler presented an annexation treaty to the Senate in early 1844, but it was rejected. The election of 1844, however, changed all that. The Democrats came out for expansion, won majorities in both houses of Congress as well as the presidency. The sense of the election was that the annexation of Texas had wide public support. John Tyler, the outgoing President, recommended to Congress in February, 1845, that Congress pass a joint resolution offering statehood to Texas. The measure passed with majorities in both houses, and Texas accepted the invitation to enter the Union. The United States not only got Texas, however, but also a boundary dispute with Mexico which meant trouble in the future.

b. Acquiring Oregon

President Polk was committed from the outset to acquiring Oregon. In his Inaugural Address on March 4, 1845, he declared that it was his "duty to assert and maintain by all constitutional means the right of the United States to that portion of our territory which lies beyond the Rocky Mountains. Our title to the country of Oregon is 'clear and unquestionable,' and already are our people preparing to perfect that title by occupying it with their wives and children."[79] The only questions remaining were how much of it would be acquired and in what way. "Oregon," at that time, was a vast and indefinite territory, far larger than the present state of Oregon, embracing in the heated American imagination, the area from the 42nd parallel, approximately, to 54 degrees, 40 minutes north latitude, and stretching inland to the continental divide.

Although several countries had at one time laid claim to all or part of this territory, there were only two claimants after the early 1820s: the United States and Great Britain. During that decade, these two countries agreed by treaty to joint authority over and use of the territory. By the early 1840s, Americans had become much more concerned about the possibility of securing private property in the area. There were two major reasons for the change. One had to do with securing seaports along the Pacific coast.

Whaling had become a big enterprise in the northern Pacific by this time, and whalers needed ports from which to operate. Trade with the Orient was an important American activity, and intermediate ports were highly desirable. It should be noted, too, that Americans and the British were major competitors for the Oriental trade. "Commercially," John C. Fremont said in 1844, "the value of the Oregon country must be great, washed as it is by the north Pacific ocean—fronting Asia—producing many of the elements of commerce—mild and healthy in its climate—and becoming, as it naturally will, a thoroughfare for the East India and China trade."[80] Good seaports and sheltered harbors are unusually scarce along the Pacific coast. In contrast to the Atlantic coast, it is not heavily indented, signifying that long rivers emptying into the Pacific are quite unusual. The reason for this is not far to seek; mountain ranges running north and south come very near the ocean in most places, thus diverting any inland rivers. The Columbia river is the major exception to this rule. In any case, the Oregon country contained two major locations for ports: one on the Columbia and the other on Puget Sound.

The other major change was the growth in population of Americans in Oregon in the early 1840s. Earlier, missionaries had gone into this country and brought back accounts of the fertile land and healthy climate, particularly in the Willamette Valley. People began to pour into this area by way of the Oregon Trail in the early 1840s. By 1845, there were approximately 5,000 settlers in the area from the United States. (By contrast, there were only about 700 British, mostly trappers and traders.) These people were not only eager for Oregon to become a part of the United States but also to have a certain claim on their property.

There were other impulses as well behind the move to expand into Oregon. There was what John L. O'Sullivan called Manifest Destiny, the destiny of the United States to spread its institutions across the continent and claim the territory. There was, too, the tacit trade-off between the North and South, by which Texas would be annexed as a potential slave state and Oregon, which no one expected to be a slave region, would be acquired as a counterbalance.

At any rate, President Polk moved quickly to make good on his promises. He approached the British Minister to the United States, Richard Packenham, with the suggestion to divide Oregon at the 49th parallel. When Packenham rejected the proposal without even consulting his government, Polk withdrew the offer. In April, 1846, Congress adopted a joint resolution giving Polk authority to cancel the joint occupation treaty one year after giving notice to that effect. Shortly thereafter, in June, the British Foreign Secretary sent Polk a proposal to divide at the 49th parallel, with the exception of Vancouver Island, and to allow the British free navigation of the Columbia river. The Senate ratified this treaty, and the Oregon question was settled. But the war with Mexico was already underway.

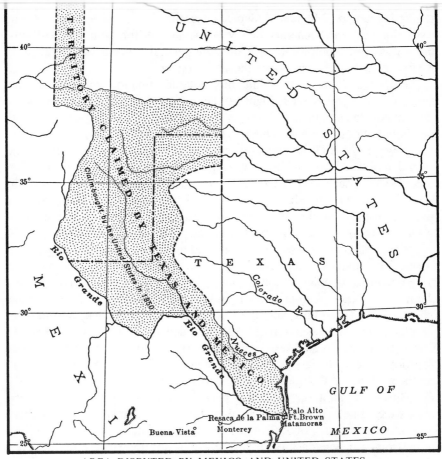

AREA DISPUTED BY MEXICO AND UNITED STATES

c. Mexican War

Mexico's reach considerably exceeded its grasp. Upon effecting its independence from Spain in 1821, Mexico laid claim to an extensive empire in Central and North America. This empire included the present states of Texas, New Mexico, Arizona, Nevada, Utah, California, and portions of Colorado and possibly Oklahoma. The Spaniards, who preceded the Mexicans, did not so much govern as militarily occupy much of this vast territory. More precisely, they set up military posts and the Catholic church sent missions into regions here and there. Nor did they populate much of the area; some colonization, of sorts, took place in California, but elsewhere such Indians as there were, were little disturbed. Mexican independence did not appreciably change the situation, except that the central government now exerting the claims was itself highly unstable. Between 1821 and 1876,

Mexico had two emperors, two regents, several dictators, and enough chief executives to add up to 74 different governments. Indeed, for the first hundred years of Mexican independence there was an average of one revolution per year. Generals vied with one another for the ruling positions, and it was not uncommon for one or more generals to be gathering an army at any given time to take over the government.

The United States moved into this volatile situation when it annexed Texas. Mexico had never recognized the independence of Texas, and when the United States annexed Texas, Mexico broke diplomatic relations with the United States, in effect. This was the usual prelude to war, and there was talk of war in Mexico immediately, and various threats made over the next several months. Polk moved cautiously; he did station an army in Texas under General Zachary Taylor, but he also tried to open negotations with the Mexican government. He sent an emissary to Mexico City to broach the question of negotiations. When the government indicated some willingness to talk, Polk appointed John Slidell as the minister to handle negotiations.

There were two issues already outstanding. One was the boundaries of Texas. The other was claims of the United States against the Mexican government for damages wrought during past revolutionary activity. These claims had already been arbitrated, and the government had made a couple of payments. Then, however, the government had defaulted, and most of the claims had not been satisfied. Polk added to these proposals that the United States buy New Mexico and California. Except as a passageway to California, New Mexico would not have been reckoned to be so important, but the situation in California was precarious. The San Francisco area had a large foreign population, including people from the United States. Rebellions were afoot, and California might fall under British or other foreign control. At any rate, Polk instructed Slidell to negotiate for the Rio Grande as the southern boundary of Texas. For that and the eastern half of New Mexico, the United States would assume the claims of Americans against Mexico. For the western half of New Mexico, Slidell was to offer $5 million, and for California as much as $20 million, or even more.

The Slidell mission was a failure. The Mexican government refused to enter into negotiations with him, despite the fact that Polk had been led to understand that they would. In fact, the government was too weak and insecure to enforce any agreements about concessions it might make, and even to appear willing to do so exposed it to takeover by Mexican generals who were waiting for such an occasion. As soon as Polk got word of Slidell's failure he ordered Taylor's army to the Rio Grande. War appeared to be in the offing, and the move was made to prevent an invasion by the Mexicans.

In early May, 1846, Slidell arrived in Washington, reported to Polk on the Mexican attitudes, and urged war measures. Polk met with his cabinet, and the decision was to ask for a declaration of war. Before Polk could act

Although the Mexican force had been driven back across the river, this warlike action quickened Polk's resolve for war and greatly increased the likelihood that Congress would concur. The President sent the war message to Congress on May 11. After rehearsing the grievances against Mexico and the repeated refusals of the government to make any effort to come to terms, Polk said: "But now, after reiterated menaces, Mexico has passed the boundary of the United States, has invaded our territory and shed American blood upon the American soil. She has proclaimed that hostilities have commenced, and that the two nations are now at war." Therefore, "we are called upon by every consideration of duty and patriotism to vindicate with decision the honor, the rights, and the interests of our country. . . ."[81]

Two days later, May 13, Congress had adopted a declaration of war. There was some opposition to this move, but the war resolution was coupled with a measure providing support for the armed forces. Thus, those who voted against the measure were open to charges of abandoning the armed forces when they were under attack. The war measure passed the House 174-14, and the Senate 40-2.

The Mexicans fought mainly a defensive war. Except for the initial assault across the Rio Grande and a later battle between Taylor's army and Santa Anna's Mexican army at Buena Vista, the Mexicans waited for the Americans to bring the war to them. The result was that it was a war of long marches, extended supply lines, and meeting the enemy on their grounds for the Americans. The grand strategy, as developed by Polk and his advisers, called for a three-pronged assault on Mexican territory in the hope of bringing the government to terms. One prong would be into northern Mexico, another into New Mexico, and a third the taking of California.

Colonel Stephen Kearny was placed in charge of the expedition to take New Mexico. As it turned out, the military side of his undertaking did not amount to much. When he reached the vicinity of Santa Fe with an army of several hundred men, he was supposed to be confronted by a Mexican army of 4,000. As his army approached, however, the Mexicans drifted away, and the one military post in the territory was taken without fighting. The hard part had been the long march overland from Ft. Leavenworth, Kansas to Sante Fe and the exhausting trek through narrow mountain passes. After providing for the governing of the province, Kearny left for California with a part of his small army. Some resistance was encountered during the ensuing winter, but it was put down by the military commander in New Mexico.

The initial taking of California was also accomplished with relative ease. Naval forces were in the vicinity of California ports with orders to take them when war was declared. A military expedition, though small, had also been in California for some while before war came. When it became known that war had been declared, a combined naval and military force under the command of Commodore Robert Stockton took the major coastal cities and declared that California was under American control. This had all been done by August 17, 1846. In September, however, a Mexican revolt broke out, and American forces were mostly driven out of Southern California. Kearny arrived with his small force in California in November. Under Stockton's command, Kearny assembled a sufficient force to defeat the Mexicans, and California was securely under American control by January 10, 1847.

Meanwhile, Taylor's forces operating in northern Mexico had achieved most of their strategic objectives before the end of 1846. Polk's hopes that these peripheral victories would cause the Mexicans to yield were in vain. Central Mexico, which contained much of the Mexican population, was still untouched. Santa Anna, who sought to be the Mexican Napoleon, still had a large army at his disposal as military commander, and he became president of Mexico as well early in 1847. Polk now placed General Winfield Scott in command of an army with the assignment to invade central Mexico and take the capital. A large portion of the army under Taylor was diverted to Scott's

Winfield Scott
(1786–1866)

Scott was a longtime general in the United States army who crowned his military career with his brilliant victories in the Mexican War against Santa Anna. He was born in Virginia, studied law at William and Mary, but was drawn toward the military life from the outset. Scott was commissioned as a captain of artillery in 1808 and remained in the army until 1861. For the last 20 years of his service he was commanding general of the army. He fought in the War of 1812, the Mexican War, and, though a Southerner by birth, commanded the Union army for several months after the Southern states seceded. Between the War of 1812 and the Mexican War he was involved in several Indian wars and with a variety of boundary disputes, as well as supervising the resettlement of the Indians of the Southeast to the Indian Territory. He was the Whig candidate for President in 1852, but the party was badly divided and he lost the election.

It took long marches and several battles in the spring and summer of 1847 until the army stood victorious within the walls of Mexico City on September 14, and a battalion of United States Marines stood guard over the "halls of Montezuma."

Looked at from a later perspective, it would be easy to imagine that the war between the United States and Mexico was a case of a larger power overwhelming a smaller. While it is true that the war making potential of the United States was greater than that of Mexico, in the abstract anyway; the United States produced more goods, had a larger population, and a more effective navy. However, wars are fought in the concrete, not the abstract; they are fought with the men and materials that are available, not with those that might somehow be made available. In these senses, most of the advantages lay with the Mexicans. They had much the larger army at the beginning of the war, and they outnumbered the Americans in virtually every major battle. Moreover, their supply lines were generally much shorter, and they could usually defend from better positions. Americans won the battles not because of numerical superiority but because they were better commanded, were more tenacious fighters, and were willing to keep fighting. Once the tide of battle turned against them, the Mexicans withdrew. The small number of casualties and the brevity of the battles (rarely lasting a whole day) suggest that the Mexican generals were better at bluster than extended campaigns.

At any rate, Santa Anna had been beaten by the time American forces took Mexico City, and there was no longer a Mexican will to continue military resistance. A new Mexican government was formed, and negotiations were soon underway to settle the outstanding issues. Negotiations were conducted between a Mexican commission and Nicholas Trist. The result was the Treaty of Guadalupe Hidalgo, ratified by the United States Senate in March, 1848. The terms were these: (1) the Rio Grande was acknowledged as the southern boundary of Texas; the United States bought California and New Mexico (which included all or parts of several other states, as described above); and the United States paid $15 million for these latter and assumed American claims against the Mexicans up to $3¼ million.

The treaty settled the major differences between the United States and Mexico, but the territorial acquisitions left some thorny political issues to be decided in the United States. Whether and where slavery would be permitted in the territory ceded by Mexico was a hot issue even before the war was over. David Wilmot twice introduced a bill in the House, known as the Wilmot Proviso, providing that slavery should not be introduced in any territory acquired from Mexico. It passed the House twice, but was defeated both times in the Senate. In the midst of these debates, Calhoun put forth the position with considerable fervor that Congress had no constitutional authority to interfere with slavery. These questions were left hanging, but they were harbingers of things to come.

Two other developments round out the discussion of the westward expansion before the Civil War. One was the discovery of gold in California in 1848. The first word of the discovery was passed by James W. Marshall, a New Jersey mechanic, who was erecting a sawmill near Sutter's Fort. It turned out that gold was widespread in the area, and President Polk made this public knowledge in his message to Congress in December, 1848. Seekers after wealth or fortune poured into California by the thousands, so that by the end of 1849 it is estimated that the population of the state had been increased by 100,000. The other development was the Gadsden Purchase. Surveys of rail routes to California indicated that the best southern route might lie south of territory acquired from Mexico. Hence, James Gadsden negotiated with Mexico to purchase the desired land, which now forms southern portions of the states of Arizona and New Mexico. The final price paid for it was $10 million.

Chapter 7

The Coming of the Civil War

*I wish to speak today, not as a Massachusetts man, not as a
Northern man, but as an American. . . . I speak today for the
preservation of the Union. "Hear me for my cause."*
—Daniel Webster, 1850

*The result . . . is to give the Northern section a predominance
in every department of the Government, and thereby concentrate
in it the two elements which constitute the Federal Government. . . . Whatever section concentrates the two in itself
possesses the control of the entire government.*
—John C. Calhoun, 1850

*The real issue in this controversy . . . is the sentiment on the
part of one class that looks upon the institution of slavery* as a
wrong *and of another class that* does not *look upon it as a wrong.
The sentiment that contemplates the institution of slavery in this
country as a wrong is the sentiment of the Republican party.*
—Abraham Lincoln, 1858

Chronology

1843—Southern Baptist Convention formed.

1844—Southern Methodists separate from Northern.

1849—California applies for admission to the Union.

June, 1850—Nashville Convention.

September, 1850—Passage of Compromise of 1850.

1852—Election of Pierce.

May, 1854—Kansas-Nebraska Act.

July, 1854—Formation of Republican Party.

October, 1854—Ostend Manifesto.

1856—Election of Buchanan.

1857—Dred Scott Decision.

1858—Lincoln-Douglas Debates.

1859—John Brown's Raid on Harper's Ferry.

November, 1860—Election of Lincoln.

December, 1860—South Carolina secedes.

February, 1861—Formation of the Confederacy.

March, 1861—Inauguration of Lincoln.

April, 1861—Confederacy takes Fort Sumter.

It was more than a little ironic that the South should secede from the Union. After all, the Union had been forged more than by any others by Southerners. To say that is not to deny that people from all regions of the country had played important roles in making and adhering to the Union. But there can be no doubt that Southerners had been in crucial leadership positions in every stage from the struggle for independence to the extension of the domain to the Pacific.

George Washington had led the Continental Army to victory in the long drawn-out War for Independence. Southerners, primarily the Virginia delegation, took the lead in devising the Constitution of 1787. Washington took the lead once again in establishing the new government under the Constitution. Jefferson led the party which eventually united the country behind it and extended the domain far beyond the Mississippi with the Louisiana Purchase. It was James Monroe, another Virginian who presided over the acquisition of Florida and the Gulf ports, and who set forth American policy in this hemisphere with the Monroe Doctrine. Andrew Jackson of Tennessee made the Democratic Party the main national party, treading a path Jefferson had trod in his day. James K. Polk of Tennessee took the leading role in extending the United States to the Pacific. Indeed, every President who played a leading role in cementing the Union up to the Civil War was from the South. Nor was it in the presidency alone that Southerners had taken the lead. John Marshall of Virginia was the leading jurist on the Supreme Court in construing the Constitution along the lines that made for a stronger Union.

The Union was in considerable measure the handiwork of Southern leaders. That being the case, it is almost as if the South having forged and cemented the Union, having rounded out the continental possessions, having played a leading role in setting the course of the nation, then abandoned their handiwork to start anew. That overstates the case, however, in several directions. In the first place, it was largely another generation from those who had provided the earlier leadership which seceded. Second, it would be an error to conclude that because a man was from the South that he was consciously following some Southern policy or that he necessarily agreed more with his Southern neighbors generally than with people from other parts of the country. Washington said that he was an American first, and that was more or less true of every Southerner in the presidency from the generation before the Civil War.

The South had become a self-conscious section by 1850. The continuing and mounting attack upon slavery as an institution had contributed much to this change. Southern leaders were becoming increasingly sectional in their following and emphasis, defensive of slavery and the South. The change in Southerners was prefigured by changes made by John C. Calhoun over the years. He had been a nationalist and a ''War Hawk'' when he had first come to Congress just before the War of 1812. By 1830, he had taken an uncompromising states' rights position. Still alive in 1850, he warned that the Union stood on the threshold of dismemberment. But one course could save the Union, he said: ''The North has only to will it to accomplish it—to do justice by conceding to the South an equal right in the acquired territory, and to do her duty by causing the stipulations relative to the fugitive slaves to be faithfully fulfilled—to cease the agitation of the slave question, and to provide for . . . an amendment, which will restore to the South . . . the power she possessed of protecting herself'' formerly.[82]

Calhoun pictured the South in 1850 as about to be overwhelmed by the more populous North, and he was saying that the North must yield by providing for protections to the South from the consequences of its minority status. Otherwise, the Southern states would almost certainly secede from the Union. In the same year, Jefferson Davis, a rising politician from Mississippi, declared: ''I see nothing short of conquest on the one side or submission on the other.''[83]

Things had not reached that pass in 1850, as it turned out, but the lines were hardening. There would yet be extensive efforts to arrive at acceptable compromises. But the North would not always yield, and the South was moving toward its own Southern nationalism.

The Last Major Efforts at Compromise

California's adoption of a constitution in 1849 and President Taylor's recommendation that it be admitted to the Union precipitated a political crisis. It was a crisis which Taylor hoped to avoid by swift action, for he urged that Congress ''should abstain from the introduction of those exciting topics of sectional character which have hitherto produced painful apprehensions in the public mind.''[84] But Taylor's hopes were in vain; not only was he trying to hurry Congress but also events were moving much too swiftly in the Mexican cession territory, particularly California, for a Congress which was not yet prepared to deal with them. The gold rush was on, and tens of thousands of people were surging into California, yet Congress had made no provision, or given its approval to any, for governing the territory. The boundary between New Mexico and Texas had not yet been settled and no provision made for the governing of New Mexico. The signs pointed toward the exclusion of slavery from all the Mexican cession territory except that made to Texas. If Congress was to take a hand at all, many Southerners hoped that the Missouri Compromise line would be extended all the way to the Pacific. Yet events were moving fast toward shutting off such a solution, and the anti-slavery forces were dead set against it. Many in the South were talking secession if slavery were precluded from the Mexican cession.

President Taylor offered no solution that would be generally accepted; he wanted California admitted to the Union immediately and no agitation of the other issues. Yet if California were admitted to the Union as a free state, the long-held balance between slave and free states in the Senate would be lost. The North had a majority of Representatives going back to the early years of the Republic, and that majority was gradually becoming preponderant. In times past, when a free state had applied for admission, a slave state had been available to balance the count. But none were in the offing at the beginning of 1850. Moreover, as some Southern leaders pointed out, Delaware, which was technically a slave state, was shifting toward an anti-slavery position. Even without California in the Union as a free state, the balance might be lost. That South would require some concessions, and President Taylor, though he was from Louisiana, was in no mood to take the lead in granting them.

Nor was there any hope from the House of Representatives for leadership in the impending crisis. Not only was the House gravely overbalanced toward the North in its makeup, but also it represented population, not the states.

a. The Compromise of 1850

The task of finding some workable compromise, then, fell upon the Senate. There, free states and slave states were still balanced, and it was a great deliberative body. Though younger men were now thrusting for leadership, the task of presenting and working out a compromise belonged to the great orators of two generations past: Henry Clay, Daniel Webster, and John C. Calhoun. Actually, Calhoun hardly played a constructive role in making a compromise. Rather, he stated what he would have the Southern position to be, without fear or favor. Calhoun was feeble, too weak even to deliver his speech; a fierce fire still burned in his sunken eyes, but he had to be supported by others to walk, and someone else read his lengthy speech.

Clay worked out the compromise; he was its architect and manager. He had lately returned to the Senate, still had the vigor for the effort, and was well suited to the undertaking. Clay was from Kentucky, a slave state, but one not deeply attached generally to the institution. What Clay sought to do was to offer something to all sections, to achieve the admission of Califor-

what was then called an "Omnibus Bill." He described the task, in a series of dramatic speeches in February, 1850, as nothing less than a determined effort to save the Union. The Union was in grave danger, he declared, and "if I can be the means of averting that danger, my health and my life are of little consequence."[85] He was most persuasive in addressing the South, as perhaps only a Southerner could do, and arguing that disunion would achieve none of the ends sought there.

Calhoun's speech dashed cold water on the very possibility of compromise. The North must cease its attack upon slavery and accord to the South its equal place in the sun, he insisted. Webster, on the other hand, when he finally spoke, drove home the point that it was necessary for all sections to compromise. Webster could no longer speak as easily as he once had; the phrases no longer rolled from his tongue with such ease. But he could still call forth dramatic tension as of old.

Webster's love for the Union was undimmed, but his task now was to smooth, not ruffle feathers, and he gave himself to it with a right good will. Although he was from Massachusetts, the very seat of abolitionism, he admitted freely that the South had just cause for complaint by the tenor of the attacks that had been leveled at the region. It was equally true, however, as Webster pointed out, that the North had just complaints about the Southern effort to extend slavery and about the complaints about the character of industrial labor in the North. The sections should yield on these points and compose their differences. The stakes were great. Above all, though, talk of secession should cease. "Secession! Peaceable secession!" he exclaimed. "Sir, your eyes and mine are never destined to see that miracle. The dismemberment of this vast country without convulsion! The breaking up of the fountains of the great deep without ruffling the surface! Who is so foolish . . . as to expect to see any such thing? Sir, he who sees these States, now revolving in harmony around a common center, and expects to see them quit their places and fly off without compulsion, may look the next moment to see the heavenly bodies rush from their spheres and jostle against each other in the realms of space, without causing the wreck of the universe! There can be no such thing as a peaceable secession."[86] That was Webster's ultimate word, and as he described in detail the way the parts of the country were held together and the difficulties of disentangling the states, he was quite convincing.

There were vigorous opponents of any compromise, however. Senator William Seward of New York, who was, in effect, an abolitionist, held that it was a badly misguided idea to permit any extension of slavery. For those who claimed that the Constitution protected all species of property, including slaves, in a territory, he declared: "But there is a higher law than the Constitution, which regulates our authority over the domain, and devotes it

Stephen A. Douglas
(1813–1861)

Courtesy Library of Congress

Douglas was born in Vermont, went to school in New York, and settled in Illinois, where he became the state's most prominent representative on the national scene until the election of Abraham Lincoln to the presidency. Douglas was elected to the House of Representatives in 1843, and to the Senate in 1846. In both, he served on the committee on territories and was deeply involved in both the movement for westward expansion and the slavery question in the territories. Undoubted, he was much more concerned with the development of the West than with slavery one way or the other. His fondest hope was to settle the question of slavery in the territories by leaving it up to the people living there. However, his ideas on popular sovereignty pleased neither side, and his position on that question may well have cost him the presidency.

to the same noble purposes. The territory is a part . . . of the common heritage of mankind, bestowed upon them by the Creator of the universe. We are his stewards and must so discharge our trust as to secure in the highest attainable degree their happiness." This appeal to a higher law became a very important part of the abolitionist weaponry. Finally though, Seward held that efforts to extend and expand the domain of slavery were doomed to failure. "I feel assured," he said, "that slavery must give way. . . , that emancipation is inevitable, and is near . . . ; that all measures which fortify slavery and secure it tend to . . . violence; all that check its extension and abate its strength tend to its peaceful extirpation."[87] On the other hand, Jefferson Davis proclaimed that the opponents of slavery sought power, mastery over the South. "I see nothing short of conquest on the one side, or submission on the other." And the South would not submit, he said. "We will not permit aggressions. We will defend our rights. . . ."[88]

In any case, Clay's "Omnibus Bill" did not pass in that form. It had become clear by the summer of 1850 that it placed too much of a burden upon the individual measures to take them all together. Clay then withdrew

was a master of compromise and parliamentary maneuver. Besides, Douglas was a Democrat, and it was the Democrats, not Clay's Whigs, who gave the compromises the bulk of their support. Under the prodding by Douglas, the measures were passed one by one in August and September. Together, they are known as the Compromise of 1850.

The following acts were passed: (1) the admission of California to the Union as a free state; (2) Texas was paid $10 million for giving up any claims it might have to territory in New Mexico; (3) New Mexico (including a whole region embracing what became Arizona and Utah) was left open to slavery until such time as any portion of the territory should be "admitted as a State, the said territory . . . shall be received into the Union, with or without slavery, as their constitution may prescribe at the time of their admission"; (4) the Fugitive Slave Act, which gave the federal government both the authority and commissioners to return fugitive slaves to their owners; (5) abolition of the slave trade (but not slavery) in the District of Columbia.

Many believed, perhaps because they hoped or wished to believe, that the issues that had been raised had been resolved, and that the question of slavery in the territories had been settled. In fact, however, except for the admission of California, the abolition of the slave trade in the District, and the boundary of Texas, little had been settled. The Northern victories were secure; the South would still have to contest every step of the way for any gains slavery might make. As for slavery in the territories, it would rise again, and that very shortly, to haunt the national councils.

b. The Kansas-Nebraska Act

It was probably the question of the location of the eastern terminus of the proposed railroad to the Pacific that led to the last great compromise effort before the Civil War. There had been talk of such a railroad even before the Polk Administration. But with the acquisition of Oregon and California the pressure for a transcontinental railroad mounted. There were four cities with relatively large populations especially eager to be the eastern terminus: Chicago, St. Louis, Memphis, and New Orleans. Whether the railroad would come to the North or South was a potential sectional issue. In 1853, Congress authorized surveys to be made of the various routes to determine which of them were the most feasible. The surveys did not settle the question, however, for the reports indicated that feasible routes through the Rockies existed all the way from the far north to the lower south. Indeed, several railroads might be built to the Pacific, as there eventually were. In the 1850s, though, it appeared most likely that only one route might receive government support in the near future.

Probably, the best route in terms of the terrain, and the fewest physical obstacles to overcome, would be a southern route. The way was cleared for such a route by the Gadsden Purchase in 1853. This route had the further advantage that there were settlements all along most of the way, and the territories to be crossed had been politically organized.

In early 1854, Senator Douglas of Illinois proposed a bill which might even out the chances somewhat for a Pacific railroad to the Midwest. His bill was for the organization of the Platte River country, commonly called Nebraska, into a territory. This would provide for the settlement of a region through which a railroad might be built. He explained his reasons this way. It was 1,500 miles between settlements in the Midwest and the Pacific, "filled with hostile savages, and cutting off direct communication. The Indian barrier must be removed. The tide of emigration and civilization must be permitted to roll onward. . . . Continuous lines of settlement are . . . demanded. . . . These are essential, but they are not sufficient. . . . We must therefore have Rail Roads and Telegraphs from the Atlantic to the Pacific, through our own territory."[89]

When this proposal met with some objections from the South, he accepted the plan to divide the region involved into two territories, the southern portion to be called Kansas, and the northern Nebraska. So it was that the act is the Kansas-Nebraska Act. The bill not only provided for organizing these territories but also opening them to slavery. Although the whole region lay north of the Missouri Compromise line, the bill provided that the people could decide whether they would have slaves or not and could be admitted to the Union either slave or free. This was in accord with Douglas's doctrine of "popular sovereignty," to leave the decision about slavery up to the people within the territory. The act also repealed the Missouri Compromise as it applied to these new territories.

The bill passed the Senate easily, but the vote was close in the House. Northern Whigs voted against it overwhelmingly, which virtually ended the Whig Party as a national party. Most Southern Whigs became Democrats. A goodly number of Northern Democrats also voted against the bill, indicating future difficulties for the Democratic Party as well. The compromise inflamed passions in the North rather than cooling them, and thereafter opposition to compromise increased in the North as well as the South. Kansas quickly became a battleground between the pro- and anti-slavery forces.

Frustration at the North

From 1854 onward the country moved toward a political rupture and, as it turned out, Civil War. That is hindsight, of course. There were few enough dramatic events during these years to signal the coming eruption. The Senate did not ring with great debates, such as occurred in the hassle over

and less willingness to come to terms with the increasing differences within the framework of the Constitution. Frustrations mounted in the North, and fear increased in the South. The regions were developing along different lines, and unless both agreed not to use the power of the general government for their particular ends, these differences must result in separation or be submitted to determination by force.

a. Changes at the North

Much has been made thus far of the territorial expansion and its relation to the rise of sectionalism. But there was another kind of growth and expansion in which the North was much more clearly distinguished from the South than by the changes in the number of free and slave states, or even population changes. It was in the growing use of technology or capital. So far as the capital of the South was invested in slave labor, expansion was dramatically curtailed with the prohibition of the slave trade in 1808. Thereafter, the prices of slaves tended to rise, and increases of Southern capital investment in slaves did not necessarily represent any great increase in production. By contrast, Northern capital was going increasingly into machines for the production of goods: into textile factories, steam engines for power, iron mills, reapers, and other improvements in the production and trasportation of goods. Nor was there any fixed upper limit to what could be achieved by investment in this kind of capital.

In the 1850s, the output of manufactures nearly doubled, and almost all of it was in the North. By contrast, the output of Southern staples—cotton, tobacco, sugar, rice, and naval stores—increased by only about 25 per cent. It has been estimated that domestic manufactures in 1859 yielded a return of just under $2 billion, nearly ten times as much as the slightly over $200 million of Southern staples. Indeed, the Beards noted that "When Lincoln was inaugurated, the capital invested in industries, railways, commerce, and city property exceeded in dollars and cents the value of all the farms and plantations between the Atlantic and Pacific. . . . The iron, boots, shoes, and leather goods that poured annually from the northern mills alone surpassed in selling price all the cotton grown in southern fields."[90] In short, an economic change of great moment was taking place in the North by way of capital invested in technology.

The North no longer bore the economic earmarks of the colonial past. Much of the economic dependency upon Britain was gone, along with all the political restraints. So far as Northern world trade was concerned, it was a competitor with Britain, not a dependent. By contrast, the South had undergone no great economic change as a result of the political separation from Britain. It still primarily produced staple commodities primarily for export, especially to or through Britain, and it still depended upon sources outside the South for much of its shipping, its manufactured goods, its credit, and so forth. In most of these things, however, the South was much more dependent upon the North now than England. There may be some elements of exaggeration in the following complaint by a Southerner in 1851, but in its details it is near enough to the mark:

> At present the North fattens and grows rich upon the South. We depend upon it for our entire supplies. We purchase all our luxuries and necessaries from the North. . . . The Northerners abuse and denounce slavery and slaveholders, yet our slaves are clothed with Northern manufactured goods, have Northern hats and shoes, work with Northern hoes, ploughs, and other implements. . . . The slaveholder dresses in Northern goods, rides in a Northern saddle. . . , sports his Northern carriage, patronizes Northern newspapers, drinks Northern liquors, reads Northern books. . . . In Northern vessels his products are carred to market, his cotton is ginned with Northern gins, his sugar is crushed and preserved by Northern machinery; his rivers are navigated by Northern steamboats, his mails are carried in Northern stages, his negroes are fed with Northern bacon, beef, flour, and corn. . . .[91]

From the tenor of the above remarks it might be supposed that these things were a source of Southern rather than Northern frustration. In reality, however, both sides to any trade presumably benefit from the activity. If the South provided a market for Northern goods, it is equally true that the North either was or helped to finance and transport to market Southern goods. If Southerners did not wish to buy goods from the North, they were welcome to produce their own. The abiding sources of frustration lay elsewhere. The economic ascendancy of the North was counterbalanced by the political ascendancy of the South, and sometimes thwarted as well. The Northern vision of the development of the nation was different from that of the South. The North was bending toward industry, while the agricultural South was continually entangling the country in its efforts to expand the slave system, a system which many Northerners viewed as belonging to the past rather than the future.

Another source of change concentrated in the North was immigration. A major tide of immigrants poured into the United States in the 1840s and 1850s. There had been a considerable influx of foreigners, mainly into the North, from 1815 onward, but the pace picked up rapidly in the 1840s. The two main sources of these immigrants were Ireland and the German states. Between 1841–1855, approximately 1,600,000 of the Irish migrated to the United States. They settled mostly along the eastern seaboard, in such cities as New York, Philadelphia, and Boston, and the men provided much of the

before the Civil War. Many of the Irish people depended upon the potato as the staple in their diet, and there were repeated crop failures in the late 1840s due to potato rot. Thus, many of the immigrants who came to America were destitute and came to this country out of desperation. They settled in the cities because they had no means either to travel inland or buy or obtain land.

In the decade of the 1850s, 951,000 Germans came to the United States. Several hundred thousand had come earlier, so that in the 1860 census there were 1,300,000 German-born inhabitants. No single reason impelled them to come in such numbers, but these came mainly from the Rhineland and Bavaria. Many of them also settled in the cities, but even more moved into the Midwest and became farmers. They were especially drawn to Wisconsin, because of the similarity of climate and topography to the land from which they had come. A considerable number of Scandinavians also came into the United States in the 1850s, and more often than not they also became farmers in the Midwest.

Both the Irish and Germans who came during this period were usually Roman Catholic. Since they were different in that respect from most Americans, their coming in such numbers spurred both anti-Catholic and anti-foreign feeling. This resentment got some political expression in the "Know Nothing" movement and the American Party, which contributed to the party fragmentation going on in the 1850s. So far as the deepening rift between the North and South was concerned, immigration was significant in these ways. Immigrants swelled the population of the North, thus increasing its preponderance in the Union. They accentuated differences between North and South, for southern whites were not only mostly native-born Americans but also Protestants, and much earlier arrivals from the British Isles. Nor were these recent immigrants likely to sympathize with the South either on slavery, states' rights, or constitutional grounds. As the newcomers formed patriotic attachments, it was much more likely to be to the United States than to any state. Slavery was alien to Europeans, and their aspirations were certainly in the opposite direction from anything smacking of fixed class or caste.

In any case, anti-slavery sentiment mounted in the years before the war. The great popularity of Harriet Beecher Stowe's *Uncle Tom's Cabin* is an indication of the spread of the sentiment in the 1850s. In the 1850s, too, men began to appear in Congress who were leaning toward the abolition of slavery, men such as Charles Sumner and William H. Seward. But it was opposition to the extension of slavery and the Free Soil movement that was most clearly coming to the fore politically. Thus, every attempt either to extend slavery or to giver greater protection by the federal government of the institution, so far as they had any success, increased frustration at the North.

b. Political Ascendancy of the South

As opposition to Southern policies mounted, the political ascendancy of the South became a source of increasing irritation in the North. Southerners had been at the forefront in the determination of national policy for most of the 19th century up to 1860. The two main instruments for this Southern dominance had been the Jeffersonian Republican Party and the Jacksonian Democratic Party. To say that is not to suggest that the leaders of these parties had been sectionalists or that they were were seeking to or did impose strictly Southern views on the nation. On the contrary, both the early Republican and the Democratic parties were national parties, with a national following and many prominent men from all sections of the country. Moreover, every man elected President from the South was a unionist (when and if the issue arose) and a constitutionalist. But there is no reason to doubt that Southern leaders turned back again and again efforts at extensive Federal outlays for internal improvements, high tariffs, and, to a lesser extent, a national banking system. In doing so, they were usually acting in accord with Southern belief. Even so, they were also acting in keeping with widespread belief throughout the country on matters of free trade, the provisions in the Constitution, and the opposition to a national banking establishment. In short, the beliefs which Southern leaders expressed were also American beliefs.

That began to change as sectionalism increased in importance. Such men as James K. Polk still spoke as Americans as late as the last years of the 1840s, but an undercurrent of change was already taking place when he became President. The change was apparent in John C. Calhoun as early as 1830, and it was becoming widespread by 1850. More and more men from the South were becoming *Southern* politicians, jealously and openly defending and advancing Southern interests. Yet the Southern political ascendancy continued apace. This was so mainly because of the crucial role of the South in the Democratic Party. No man could hope to be elected President by the Democrats without widespread support from the South. Democratic control of Congress, too, was dependent upon a large number of Democrats from the South. Moreover, the Democratic Party was so organized unusually in its national convention that its business could only be done by preponderant majorities. Presidential candidates had to be nominated by at least two-thirds of the delegates. The unit rule for voting by states, when it was invoked, also could add weight on any sectional issue. Above all, the South could and often enough did, exercise a *veto* on national policy within the Democratic Party. And a Democratic veto over the years generally meant an effective veto over national policy.

Although no Southerner was elected President after 1848 (Zachary Taylor, a Whig from Louisiana, was the last), the South's position was generally enhanced rather than being diminished during the prewar years.

1852. His was a "dark horse" nomination because agreement could not be reached on any of the leading contenders. His vice-presidential running mate was William King of Alabama, and four of the eight cabinet members were from the South. Pierce was a handsome and genial man who was better known as a follower than a leader. His principles were Jacksonian, and his polities were, if not pro-Southern, inclined in that direction.

James Buchanan, a Democrat from Pennsylvania, was elected President in 1856. He had built his following by careful attention to what the South would and would not tolerate, and though an undoubted constitutionalist and Union man, he was always more than fair to the South. His Vice-President was John C. Breckinridge of Kentucky, and four of the eight members of his cabinet were from the South. Southerners held the majority in the Supreme Court throughout the 1850s. Roger B. Taney of Maryland, a slave state, was Chief Justice, and four of the others were from the South. None of this is meant to suggest that any of the above people acted simply in terms of sectional interests or prejudices, but the evidence shows that the South maintained a prominent role in the Democratic Party until 1860.

This became increasingly frustrating to many at the North. Even after the slave states had lost their balance in the Senate, long after they had become a minority in the House, and the North was beginning to dwarf them in population and had done so productively, the South continued to play an often decisive part in American politics. Most important, the South was in a position to thwart many programs actively sought by Northern politicians with its effective veto power in the Democratic Party. The frustration became more evident as the movements for Free Soil in the West, a more generous homestead act, a Pacific railroad, a protective tariff, and some sort of national banking system gained momentum. Frustration reached its peak, of course, when the South tried to use its political clout to extend slavery.

c. Frustrating Developments

Three events or developments in the mid-1850s heightened frustration at the North, heightened it because it seemed to indicate that the South could use the federal government for its own ends. The first of these is known as the Ostend Manifesto, a diplomatic document drawn up in 1854 as a result of a meeting in Ostend, Belgium. It dealt with the possibility of the acquisition of Cuba by the United States. Cuba was a Spanish possession, and there was talk, especially among Southerners, of expansion into the Caribbean. An occasion for some sort of action occurred when authorities in Cuba seized an American merchant ship in early 1854 because of an error in its manifest. Pierre Soulé, American minister to Spain made strenuous demands for reparations on the Spanish government. The Spanish eventually made a satisfactory settlement, but before this had been done Soulé was instructed by the Secretary of State, with the President's knowledge, to meet with John Y. Mason, minister to France, and James Buchanan, minister to Britain, to propose a settlement of the Cuban question. The result was the Ostend Manifesto.

The paper set forth the interest of the United States in acquiring Cuba, elaborated on the disadvantages of Spanish possession of the island, and proposed that an offer to purchase Cuba be made to the Spanish parliament. If Spain should refuse, and *if* it be determined that the Spanish possession of Cuba threatens the security of the United States, then, the paper declares, "we shall be justified in wresting it from Spain if we possess the power. . . ."[92] The President and Secretary of State disavowed the document, but when it was made public there was an unfavorable reaction in the North. Those who wished to interpret it that way could see evidence of behind the scenes machinations to expand slavery.

A second development, frustrating especially to the anti-slavery movement, was what happened in Kansas after the passage of the Kansas-Nebraska Act. Pro-slavery elements from Missouri came into Kansas in late 1854 and early 1855 and succeeded in electing a pro-slavery territorial

James Buchanan
(1791–1868)

Buchanan was a lawyer, a diplomat, a legislator, Congressman, cabinet member, and President of the United States. He was born in Pennsylvania, educated at Dickinson College, and trained in the law. He was a Jacksonian Democrat, and served Jackson's successors, Polk as Secretary of State and Pierce as minister to Great Britain. In the controversies of the 1850s, Buchanan generally took a pro-Southern position: signed the Ostend Manifesto, favored the admission of Kansas as a slave state, and opposed the Douglas position within the Democratic Party. It was his misfortune to preside over a badly divided country, one bent toward disunion beyond his powers to restrain. Buchanan was firmly committed to the Union and believed that anti-slavery agitation drove the South to secession.

and established a test oath for officeholders. The first round in Kansas had gone to those favoring slavery. The anti-slavery forces were not long in rallying, but it looked for a while as if slavery were on the march in Kansas.

The third event appeared on its face to be much more ominous for the anti-slavery movement. It was the Supreme Court decision in *Dred Scott vs. Sandford* made in 1857. Dred Scott was a slave in Missouri who sued for his freedom on the grounds that he had been taken by his master and lived for several years in the free state of Illinois and the free territory of Wisconsin. The case aroused so many questions that each of the justices wrote a separate opinion. However seven of the justices, including Chief Justice Taney concurred in the decision that the Supreme Court lacked jurisdiction along with the lower federal courts. Two justices dissented. Chief Justice Taney wrote the opinion in support of the decision which probably came closest to expressing the majority opinion, if there had been one. He held (1) that since Dred Scott was a slave of African descent he was not a United States citizen and could not bring suit in federal court; (2) that Congress had no authority under the Constitution to prohibit slavery in the territories (thus nullifying the Missouri Compromise); and (3) that residence in a free state did not automatically free a slave. On this last point, it appears that the federal government had no power to prohibit slavery anywhere.

The decision gave great comfort to those in the South who had been contending for the main points that Taney made. In brief, no decision for or against slavery could be made until a territory adopted a constitution and became a state. Taney's reasoning was that if Congress had no such power, then neither could a territorial legislature, acting under the authority of the United States have such a power. The anti-slavery cause had, at the least, been dealt a severe blow.

Fears at the South

The North drove the South out of the Union. More precisely, the agitation against slavery as an evil and sinful institution by those who advanced the position in the North drove the South out of the Union. Former President James Buchanan recognized this as he reflected on what had happened during the years when the armed conflict raged. He wrote,

> An entire new generation had now come upon the stage in the South, in the midst of the slavery agitation. . . . [They] had grown up . . . amid assaults upon their rights, and attacks from the North upon the domestic institution inherited from their fathers. Their post-offices had been perverted for the circulation of incendiary pictures and publications intended to excite the slaves to servile insurrection. In the

North, the press, State legislatures, anti-slavery societies, abolition lecturers, and above all the Christian pulpit, had been persistently employed in denouncing slavery as a sin, and rendering slaveholders odious. Numerous abolition petitions had been presented to Congress, from session to session, portraying slavery as a grievous sin against God and man.[93]

The repeated charge that slavery was a sin, and the mounting clamor against it as an evil, strained, stretched, and eventually broke the fraternal ties between North and South. Undoubtedly, many who repeated the charges did not intend that the South would, or that they could, withdraw from the Union. But men who believe in the reality of sin and evil do not readily and forever endure the charge that one of their established institutions is by its very nature evil. It was a divisive charge; it separated Northerners and Southerners, and that on deep and precarious grounds. It is one thing to declare that men are sinners—a position accepted by Christians—, and quite another to declare that men are continually entailed in sin by a legal institution which pervades a society. Such a view puts those who maintain the institution beyond the pale, makes of them enemies ultimately, and comes close, when it does not, to proscribing association with them. Given Southern pride, such charges, when they became widespread enough, could lead only to bloodshed and separation.

Two events may help to illustrate how the imputation of evil led to *ad hominem* (personal) attacks and the severing of the bonds of fraternity. The first was the Sumner-Brooks affair in 1856 in the midst of trouble in Kansas. The events occurred in the Senate of the United States. Senator Charles Sumner of Massachusetts, an ardent anti-slavery man, rose in the Senate to give a speech entitled "Crime Against Kansas." In the course of the speech he attacked both Senator Douglas of Illinois and Senator Andrew P. Butler of South Carolina. Butler was a uniformly courteous and courtly man, never apt to give offense. And, he was absent from the Senate when the speech was given. Yet, Sumner charged that Butler "has chosen a mistress to whom he has made his vows, and who, though ugly to others, is always lovely to him, though polluted in the sight of the world, is chaste in his sight—I mean the harlot, Slavery." As for his state of South Carolina, it suffered from the "Shameful imbecility from Slavery. . . ." Moreover, he said of Butler, "He shows an incapacity of accuracy, whether in stating the Constitution or in stating the law, whether in the details of statistics or the diversions of scholarship. He cannot open his mouth, but out there flies a blunder."[94] Sumner was equally harsh in his denunciation of Douglas, but Douglas was there to and did defend himself ably.

Actually, Sumner might have accomplished little more than to have made himself universally hated by his excesses. Senator Cass of Michigan denounced the speech immediately in no uncertain terms. But Representa-

Charles Sumner
(1811–1874)

First and last, Sumner was an anti-slavery man and, ultimately, an abolitionist. He was embroiled in the contest over the expansion of slavery in the 1850s and a Republican leader in the Senate throughout the 1860s. Sumner was implacable in his determination to defeat and reconstruct the South, as well as to free the slaves. He graduated from Harvard, attended Harvard Law School, and became involved in the New England reform movements almost from the outset. He served in the Senate from 1852 until his death in 1874, though he was absent for three years during which he recovered from the beating by Preston Brooks. During most of the 1860s he served as chairman of the Senate Committee on Foreign Affairs.

tive Preston Brooks of South Carolina, a kinsman of Butler, determined to avenge him. Two days later, he entered the Senate just after it recessed, found Sumner in his seat, and beat him unconscious by repeated blows with a cane. It took Sumner three years to recover, and Massachusetts allowed his seat to remain vacant for the period of his absence as a protest to the beating. On the other hand, Southern newspapers applauded Brooks's actions. The Richmond *Whig* declared that "The only regret we feel is that Mr. Brooks did not employ a horsewhip or cowhide upon his slanderous back instead of a cane." The Petersburg *Intelligencer* did express regret that Brooks "dirtied his cane by laying it athwart the shoulders of the blackguard Sumner."[95] University of Virginia students sent canes to Brooks to signify their support. Obviously, the sense of fraternity and fellow feeling was seriously affecting both North and South.

The second event occurred in April, 1860, when feeling was mounting toward the breaking point. Representative Owen Lovejoy took the floor in the House to denounce slavery. "Slaveholding," he asserted, "is worse than robbing, than piracy, than polygamy. . . . The principle of enslaving human beings because they are inferior . . . is the doctrine of Democrats, and the doctrine of devils as well; and there is no place in the universe outside the five points of hell and the Democratic party where the practice and prevalence of such doctrines would not be a disgrace."[96] So saying, he moved over to the Democratic side of the House, gesturing and shaking his fists at Democrats and slaveholders. Some of the Southern Congressmen objected vociferously to his leaving his seat and coming to their side. An altercation broke out and a crowd assembled on the floor. Though order was restored, one Southerner wrote, "I never said a word to anybody but quietly cocked my Revolver in my pocket and took my position in the midst of the mob, and as coolly as I write it . . .now, I had made up my mind to sell my blood out at the highest possible price."[97]

The south did not secede from the Union simply because opponents in the North labeled slavery a sin, of course. Those Southern states which seceded did so after it became clear that those who were determined to stop the spread of slavery and undermine it had gained power over much of the government. Above all, the states which led in secession did so when all doubt had been removed that they had no hope of using the government effectively for expanding and maintaining slavery. The whole tenor of much that happened from 1855 onward set the stage for secession, and much that happened aroused fears about the future course of events.

Many Southerners pinned their hopes upon Kansas becoming a slave state. Not only had pro-slavery elements from Missouri entered Kansas and formed a government, but hundreds from the lower South also migrated, whether temporarily or permanently, to Kansas. They succeeded, as already noted, in organizing the first territorial government. However, the free state forces also moved to and did succeed in organizing a government of their own. There were then two governments in Kansas in 1856, neither regularly elected, nor able to maintain order. Kansas was divided into armed camps, the one receiving support from the South and the other from the North, mainly from abolitionists. A number of atrocities were committed, but the most infamous was a raid led by John Brown. Brown and his party descended upon the cabins of some pro-slavery families at night and murdered five men.

The anti-slavery forces adopted a constitution and applied for admission to the Union on the basis of it. The application came before Congress in 1856. It passed the House, but was rejected by the Senate. President Pierce sent a governor and troops to restore order in Kansas. They succeeded, but under Buchanan's appointee the pro-slavery forces gained control of a territorial government once again. They adopted a constitution in 1857, the Lecompton Constitution, as it was called, and applied for admission as a slave state. Since most of the free state elements had not taken part in either the convention or the vote on the constitution, it had the opposition of Douglas in the Senate and it was clear it would not pass the House. A compromise was worked out providing for sending the Constitution back for an election in which voters generally would participate. The Lecompton Constitution was defeated by the voters, and Kansas remained a territory. Kansas almost certainly was lost to the slavery cause. Equally important, a major rift in the Democratic Party opened. President Buchanan had favored

it. Not only did Buchanan oppose Douglas, who was the leading candidate among the Democrats for President in 1860, but also many Southerners opposed him.

The deepest fears at the South were of slave rebellion, of slaves turning against their masters and going on a rampage. This had happened in Virginia in 1831 when Nat Turner, a lay preacher who had visions of leading his people out of bondage, went on a rampage. With several confederates, he first murdered his master and his family. Then he gathered more followers, got guns and liquor and went on a killing spree through the countryside. In all, 13 men, 18 women, and 24 children were butchered. Turner was captured, tried, and hanged, along with several of his gang. But the memory of it remained, and agitation against slavery was reckoned to be potentially quite dangerous throughout the South.

Moreover, the Fugitive Slave Act, a major concession to the South in the Compromise of 1850, had not worked well. Major efforts to thwart attempts to capture and return runaway slaves were made in Northern states. Several states passed what were called Personal Liberty laws to thwart the slave catchers. "In general, they provided that certain . . . officers of the State should act as counsel for any one arrested as a fugitive; that negroes who were so claimed should be entitled to the benefits of the writ of habeas corpus and of trial by jury; they prohibited the use of the jails of the State for detaining fugitives. . . ."[98] In addition to taking such measures to evade the enforcement of Federal law, there was a widespread organized effort to help slaves escape to Canada. It was called the Underground Railroad, and it is estimated that over several decades as many as 75,000 slaves were helped to escape from their owners.

But the final blow came as the result of the organization and rapid growth of the new Republican Party, a sectional party of the North, as it turned out. A party was organized in Michigan in 1854 under that name and spread rapidly to other states. The Republican candidate for President in 1856, John C. Fremont, came in second to the winner, Buchanan, getting a total of 114 electoral votes. The party drew its following from Free Soilers, Northern Whigs who abandoned their party in droves after the Kansas-Nebraska Act, dissident Democrats, anti-slavery people generally, and minority parties. It opposed the repeal of the Missouri Compromise, favored the admission of Kansas as a free state, was against the extension of slavery, favored government aid for a Pacific railroad, and a federal program to support internal improvements.

While no political party which hoped to elect candidates could please the abolitionists, it was bent from the beginning toward the containment of slavery. Indeed, by 1858, the party was pushing the slavery issue aggressively. In that year, William H. Seward, a leading candidate for the Republican presidential nomination two years later, declared that the contest between slavery and freedom was an irrepressible conflict. "It is an irrepressible conflict," he said, "between opposing and enduring forces, and it means that the United States must and will, sooner or later, become either entirely a slaveholding nation, or entirely a free-labor nation. . . . It is the failure to apprehend this great truth that induces so many unsuccessful attempts at final compromise between the slave and free states, and it is the existence of this great fact that renders all such . . . compromises, when made, vain and ephemeral."[99] In short, to compromise on the slave question was to move the whole country closer to being a slave nation.

An even more virulent anti-slavery position was taken by those in the Republican Party who advanced the views of Hinton Rowan Helper. In 1857, Helper had published a tract under the title *The Impending Crisis*. He proposed to divide the South against itself by organizing the non-slaveholding people of the South against the slaveholders. The result would

---

William H. Seward
(1801–1872)

Courtesy U.S. Department of State

Seward was the foremost national leader in the formation of the Republican Party and served as Secretary of State under Lincoln and Johnson. He was born in New York, graduated from Union College, and was admitted to the practice of law. His career in state and national politics spanned the years from the presidency of John Quincy Adams through those of Andrew Johnson. In succession, he was associated with the National Republican, Anti-Masonic, Whig, and Republican parties. After being elected to the Senate in 1849, Seward immediately distinguished himself as an anti-slavery Whig. He opposed the Compromise of 1850 and the Kansas-Nebraska Bill. Technically, he was not an abolitionist, but he did all in his power to contain and restrain the spread of slavery. He was a leading contender for the Republican nomination to the presidency in both 1856 and 1860, but did not receive it either time, probably because he had been both too outspoken and shifting in his positions on slavery. He was a leader in forming foreign policy in both the Lincoln and Johnson administrations.

the abolition of slavery. In the book, he addressed the slaveholders in this fashion:

> Thus, terror engenderers of the South, have we fully and frankly defined our position; we have no modifications to propose, no compromises to offer, nothing to retract. Frown, sirs, fret, foam, prepare your weapons, strike, shoot, stab, bring on civil war, dissolve the Union, nay, annihilate the solar system if you will—do all this, more, less, better, worse, any thing—do what you will, sires, you can neither foil nor intimidate us; our purpose is as firmly fixed as the eternal pillars of heaven; we have determined to abolish slavery, and so help us God, abolish it we will![100]

The book was not only commended by Senator Seward but also others who had it circulated in large numbers in the campaign in 1860.

Abraham Lincoln emerged in 1858 as a possible Republican candidate for President. He was nominated for Senator by the Republican convention in Illinois to run against the Democrat, Stephen A. Douglas. In the course of the campaign, they engaged in what have gone down in history as the Lincoln-Douglas Debates. Although Lincoln lost the election in the state legislature, he got national publicity for the debates and was widely known in 1860. Lincoln had made his "House Divided" speech during the Republican state convention. He had said, " 'A house divided against itself cannot stand.' I believe this government cannot endure permanently half slave and half free."[101] In that speech and the ensuing debates, he insisted that the only way to perpetuate the Union peacefully was for the nation to follow a course toward the ultimate extinction of slavery. "I have always hated slavery, I think," he said in one of the debates, "as much as any Abolitionist . . . , I have always hated it; but I have always kept quiet about it until this new era of the introduction of the Nebraska bill again."[102] In Lincoln's Cooper Union address in New York in early 1860, he asked what would satisfy the South. "This, and this only," he answered, "cease to call slavery *wrong* and join them in calling it *right*. And this must be done thoroughly—done in *acts* as well as in *words*."[103] While it was never clear beforehand exactly what Lincoln would do about slavery as President, it was abundantly clear that he was opposed to it.

One other event—John Brown's raid on Harper's Ferry arsenal—occurred in 1859 which needs to be reported. The fiery Brown had conceived a plan to foment a slave rebellion in the South. Financed by Northern abolitionists, he assembled a small band of men and seized the Federal arsenal at Harper's Ferry, Virginia. A detachment of Marines under the command of Colonel Robert E. Lee took the arsenal and captured John Brown. He was tried for treason and conspiracy, found guilty, and hanged.

The raid stirred up feeling in the South, where Brown's activities were not only blamed on the abolitionists but also on the Republicans. On the other hand, John Brown was hailed as a martyr by abolitionists and eventually became a symbol of an undying spirit to put down slavery in the North. Feeling was outrunning reason.

The Election of Lincoln and Secession of the South

The election of Lincoln sealed the fate of the Union as far as the states of the lower South were concerned. The Republican Party had taken shape as a sectional party, and the nomination of Lincoln as standard bearer did nothing to change that fact. His election to the presidency, then, signified the rallying of the people of the North to a party opposed to the aims of the South.

A united Democratic Party might conceivably have changed the results in the election of 1860. Certainly, it was the only party with a national following still in the field. Moreover, it was the party through which the South had retained most of its political ascendance over the years. But the Democratic Party came unraveled in 1860. The break between Buchanan and Douglas in 1857 had signaled what was to come. When the Democrats met in convention at Charleston it became clear that Douglas was the choice for presidential nominee of a majority of the delegates. Many of the Southern leaders could not accept that prospect. Douglas's popular sovereignty position and his demonstrated determination to be even handed about slavery in the territories did not set well in the South. Many of their leaders wanted partisans, not judges; they wanted to use the federal government to extend slavery. That they could not have from Douglas or any platform drawn by his followers.

At any rate, a goodly number of Southern delegates withdrew from the Democratic convention when it appeared that Douglas might carry the day. Charleston was not a friendly place for the convention after that, if it had been before, and the Democrats moved to Baltimore to continue their deliberations. There, Douglas was nominated by the regular Democrats. The seceding Southern Democrats then met and nominated John C. Breckinridge of Kentucky on a slavery expansion platform. Another group, mainly remnants of the Whig and American parties, nominated John Bell of Tennessee as their candidate on a Constitutional Union ticket.

In the election, Lincoln got 180 electoral votes, Breckinridge 72, Bell 39, and Douglas 12. Though Lincoln got a minority of the popular votes cast, he had a handy majority of the electoral votes. He carried all the free states, except a portion of New Jersey. But Lincoln did not receive a single vote in 10 of the Southern states. So far as the evidence shows, Lincoln won because of the concentration of the vote, not because of the division of the

had united behind Douglas, he might have won states in the North which left the Democratic fold to vote for Lincoln. The breakup of the party made it certain long before the election that Douglas could not win.

A movement was already afoot before the election among some of the states to secede if Lincoln were elected. Seven states seceded as a direct consequence of the election of Lincoln. South Carolina seceded in December, 1860; Mississippi, Florida, Alabama, Georgia, and Louisiana in January, 1861; and Texas in February. Delegates to a convention of the seceding states met in Montgomery in February, adopted a provisional constitution, and elected a President and Vice-President for the Confederate States of America. All this activity had been carried out in an orderly fashion. The procedure of secession was to have an election for delegates to a state convention, to meet in convention, and to adopt ordinances of secession. This was done in accord with the Southern understanding of what would be in keeping with the United States Constitution. It had, after all, been ratified by states acting through conventions. Could they not "unratify" it—secede from the Union—in the same fashion? Opinions on that question differed greatly, however.

Northern orators, statesmen, and politicians had been maintaining for several decades that the Union was indissoluble, that once a state joined it was a member in perpetuity. It was widely held as an article of faith, particularly in the North. On the other hand, what was to be done about it if a state did secede, or take measures to do so? Could force be used to conquer and hold a state—a political body acting with the consent of its electorate—in the Union? President Buchanan, who remained in office until March 4, 1861, believed firmly that the Union was perpetual. A state could not secede constitutionally, because there was no provision in the Constitution for such an action. On the other hand, neither was there any provision in the Constitution for the federal government to use force on a state. His decision, then, was to collect the revenues and enforce the laws as best he could, but take no further action.

President Buchanan undoubtedly hoped that the seceding states could be drawn back into the Union. Efforts were going on, particularly in the upper South, to arrive at an agreement that would be generally acceptable. None were successful. Lincoln also sought to persuade the seceding states to return to the fold, so to speak. In his Inaugural Address, delivered March 4, 1861, he tried to reassure them on the slavery question, by quoting from what he had said in earlier speeches: "I have no purpose," he had said, "directly or indirectly, to interfere with the institution of slavery in the States where it exists. I believe I have no lawful right to do so, and I have no inclination to do so."[104] He insisted, however, that the Union was perpetual, that no state could leave of its own will, and that if it was a compact among the states it could only be dissolved by all of them, not by any portion of them. He would, therefore, continue to enforce the laws to the best of his ability, but he would force nothing, or so he seemed to say, for he declared, "In your hands, my dissatisfied fellow countrymen, and not in mine, is the momentous issue of civil war. The government will not assail you."[105]

But Lincoln had the means to force the Confederacy to assail the United States, or at least to fish or cut bait. There were still Federal forces at some ports in the Confederacy, most notably at Fort Sumter in Charleston Harbor. Most Federal forces had surrendered to the states in which they were located, but not those at Sumter. But they could not hold out indefinitely, because the fort is on a small island and would have to be provisioned. Buchanan dispatched a ship to reinforce the fort, but it was turned back by fire from the shore batteries. Lincoln delayed a decision as to what to do about Fort Sumter until early April. At that point, he notified South Carolina authorities that a ship was on its way to provision the fort. Clearly, the Confederacy could not continue its course as an independent country with Federal forces occupying a major harbor entrance. Thus, South Carolina requested the commander in the harbor to surrender. When he refused, Confederate forces opened fire, and the fort was surrendered on April 13, 1861. Lincoln declared that an insurrection existed and sent out a call for troops from the states.

Faced with the possibility of fighting for or against the Confederacy, four more slave states seceded: Virginia, North Carolina, Tennessee, and Arkansas. Four slave states did not secede—Maryland, Delaware, Kentucky, and Missouri—though there was much division among them on the question. When Virginia seceded, a large number of counties in western Virginia seceded from Virginia, and were eventually admitted to the Union as West Virginia. Mayor Woods of New York City had proposed that the city should secede from the state and become a free city in January, 1861, but nothing came of it. The secession had now ended; civil war followed.

Chapter 8
The Civil War

If their whole country [the South] must be laid waste, and made a desert, in order to save this Union from destruction, so let it be. I would rather, sir, reduce them to a condition where their whole country is to be repeopled than perpetrate the destruction of this people through our agency.
—Thaddeus Stevens, 1861

My paramount object in this struggle is to save the Union, and is not either to save or destroy slavery. If I could save the Union without freeing any slave, I would do it; and if I could save it by freeing all the slaves, I would do it; and if I could do it by freeing some and leaving others alone, I would also do that.
—Abraham Lincoln, 1862

After four years of arduous service, marked by unsurpassed courage and fortitude, the Army of Northern Virginia has been compelled to yield to overwhelming numbers and resources.
—Robert E. Lee, 1865

Chronology

1861—

April 15—Lincoln declares seceding states in Rebellion.

April 19—Lincoln declares Naval Blockade of South.

July—First Battle of Bull Run.

1862—

January—Battle of *Monitor* and *Merrimac*.

April—Union occupation of New Orleans.

May—Homestead Act.

July—Pacific Railway Act.

August—Second Battle of Bull Run.

September—Battle of Antietam.

1863—

January—Lincoln's Emancipation Proclamation.

1863—

February—National Banking Act.

May—Battle of Chancellorsville.

July 1–3—Battle of Gettysburg.

July 4—Fall of Vicksburg.

September—Union forces occupy Chattanooga.

November—Lincoln's Gettysburg Address.

1864—

May—Battle of the Wilderness.

September—Fall of Atlanta.

November—Lincoln re-elected.

1865—

April 9—Lee surrenders at Appomattox Court House.

April 14—Assassination of Lincoln.

April 18—Johnston surrenders to Sherman.

The Civil War was the most massive and destructive war ever fought in the Western Hemisphere. Indeed, it dwarfs all the other wars in which the United States has fought on this continent. In terms of casualties, more American lives (North and South) were lost in the Civil War than in any other in which we have been engaged. Indeed, the total casualties were greater than for all other of the major conflicts combined. The Union and Confederate dead reached a total of over 600,000; whereas, the total American dead in all other major wars in which the United States has participated through the Korean war amounts to less than a half a million. Of course, the totals for all combatants in both world wars of the 20th century far exceed these, but the figures include only American losses.

There are several reasons for the large number of casualties during the Civil War. One major explanation is that the armies in combat were much larger than they had been in earlier wars. American armies engaged in a battle in the War for Independence rarely numbered more than 5,000 troops. Even as recently as the Mexican War, an army of 15,000 was rare in any given battle. Yet at the Battle of Fredericksburg in December, 1862, General Burnside's Union army had 113,000 men, and Lee had 75,000 at his disposal. Indeed, the Army of the Potomac (Union) often numbered more than 120,000 troops, and the Army of Northern Virginia (Confederate) sometimes rose to around 100,000. But the size of the armies is more of an indication of the scale of the war than an explanation of the large number of casualties. Two other circumstances are important to that.

One was the development of more effective and deadly weaponry. Although breechloading rifles were becoming available, and a forerunner of the machine gun (Gatling gun) was invented during the war, the most common weapon used was the muzzle-loading Springfield rifle. Even so, it could be loaded at the rate of two rounds per minute and was highly accurate. Much more effective artillery was also in use. The other circumstance was that despite the large numbers of men involved and the much more effective weapons, the battle tactics of the past were still in use. Men were still massed at the point of attack, charged into battle in rank upon rank, did so in broad daylight, and were often exposed at close range to the full fury of enemy fire. Warfare was mainly concentrated on destroying an army, causing it to flee, or procuring its surrender. It should be noted, too, that the state of medical practice was such and hygiene so neglected that more than half of those who died succumbed to disease rather than battle wounds.

Major changes in warfare did occur during the war, however. The Civil War was a transitional war. It marked a transit from the more civilized limited war fought by gentlemanly codes, at least in theory, to the kind of unlimited total war that reached its peak, thus far, in World War II. At the outset, both sides conceived of it as a limited conflict, and the leaders proposed to follow high codes of conduct. For example, General McClellan, commander of the main Union army for a considerable portion of 1861–1862, wrote to Lincoln to advise the following policy:

> This rebellion has assumed the character of a war; as such it should be regarded, and it should be conducted upon the highest principles known to Christian civilization. . . .
>
> In prosecuting the war, all private property and unarmed persons should be strictly protected . . . ; all private property taken for military use should be paid or receipted for; pillage and waste should be treated as high crimes; all unnecessary trespass sternly prohibited, and offensive demeanor by the military toward citizens promptly rebuked. . . .[106]

While war necessarily unleashes passions not easily contained, most of the military leaders both North and South undoubtedly intended to fight a limited war. By 1864, however, Union generals had come to the fore who believed it was necessary to destroy the will to make war and the warmaking potential of the South. "War is hell," said General William T. Sherman, and he contributed much to making it so for the South, as his army cut a destructive swath across Georgia in late 1864. This was but the most dramatic of the evidence that a shift toward total war was taking place.

The shift toward total war was in some measure a reflection of changes in war aims in the North. Both sides professed limited aims in the beginning.

The states of the Confederacy sought only recognition of their independence of the United States; in their view, it was a War for Southern Independence. They did not seek to conquer or overwhelm the North, and they retained that limited goal to the end. Both Lincoln and Congress affirmed that theirs were limited goals in the first year of the war. The Crittenden-Johnson Resolution, passed in July, 1861, declared that this war "is not waged upon our part in any spirit of oppression, nor for any purpose of conquest or subjugation, nor purpose of overthrowing or interfering with the rights or established institutions of those States, but to defend and maintain the supremacy of the Constitution and to preserve the Union, with all the dignity, equality, and rights of the several states unimpaired; and that as soon as these objects are accomplished the war ought to cease."[107] These were, on their face, limited goals.

It has generally been accepted that slavery was the issue over which the war was fought. Yet the sense of Congress at the outset was that the matter at hand was constitutional. Alexander H. Stephens, the Vice-President of the Confederacy, believed so tenaciously that the war was fought over differences in interpretation of the Constitution and the nature of the Union that he wrote a two-volume work after the war to prove it. Stephens summed up his position in this way in the "Introduction." "It is a postulate, with many writers of this day," he said, "that the late War was the result of two opposing ideas, or principles, upon the subject of African Slavery." While he agreed that it was the result of two opposing principles, he denied that the differing principles were about slavery. "But the opposing principles which produced these results in physical action were of a very different character from those assumed in the postulate. They lay in the organic Structure of the Government of the States. The conflict in principle arose from different and opposing ideas as to the nature of what is known as the General Government. The contest was between those who held it to be strictly Federal in its character, and those who maintained that it was thoroughly National. It was a strife between the principles of Federation, on the one side, and Centralism, or Consolidation, on the other.

> Slavery, so called, was but the *question* on which these antagonistic principles, which had been in conflict, from the beginning, on . . . *other questions,* were finally brought into actual and active collision with each other on the field of battle.[108]

The position Stephens was maintaining was this. The South held that the Union was a compact of states, that it had been formed by states existing prior to the Union, and that states had come into the Union as the result of people acting within already-formed political bodies. The states retained their independence as political bodies. By contrast, he charged, the North had developed the view that the Union was the result of an act of the people, that it was therefore indissoluble, and that the logical consequence of that belief was to concentrate all power in the central government. The states were the primary and enduring bodies, in his view; the United States became the basic and enduring body in the Northern view. Resistance and secession by the states was a necessary possibility, by the Southern view; it was an impossibility in the Northern view.

While Lincoln would not have agreed with the whole of the position described by Stephens, he did make clear in various ways that the basic issue was constitutional. He held that a state could not secede or otherwise leave the Union, and he declared that states attempting to do so were in rebellion. It was his constitutional duty, he declared, to enforce the laws and put down the rebellion. Given these antagonistic principles, it is reasonably clear that they were the immediate cause of the war. If either side had been prepared to yield, there would have been no war, and it is possible that all the bloodshed and destruction might have been avoided. That is, if the South had conceded that the Union was perpetual and that the majority could ultimately rule within it, there would have been no occasion for secession and war. On the other hand, if the North, or its leaders, had accepted the right of peaceful secession, there might have been no occasion for war. None of that happened, of course, but the conjecture does put into relief the most immediate cause of the war.

In the course of the war, however, the war aims of the North shifted. There were undoubtedly those from the beginning who wanted to use the war for much more than simply preserving the Union. But by 1863 they were becoming sufficiently numerous to effect government policy. They were thrusting to make the war a crusade against slavery and for the transformation of the South. In 1862, Wendell Phillips, a fiery abolitionist, described what he thought ought to be done:

> I hold that the South is to be annihilated. I . . . mean the intellectual, social, aristocratic South—the thing that represented itself by slavery and the bowie-knife, by bullying and lynch law, by ignorance and idleness. . . . I mean a society which holds for its cardinal principle of faith, that one-third of the race is born booted and spurred, and the other two-thirds saddled for the first to ride. . . . That South is to be annihilated.[109]

While this was not yet the language of politicians, there were men in Congress, such as Ben Wade, Charles Sumner, Thaddeus Stevens, William Fessenden, and John Bingham who were pushing the country toward the view that the South must be made over. And it was this urge to reform and transform that thrust the Civil War toward total war and added much to the ferocity of the destruction in the closing two years of the war.

The Sinews of War—North and South

There can be no doubt that the Union had many of the advantages during the war. It had an established government, a system of credit and taxation, and the recognition of foreign powers generally. Twenty-three states remained in the Union with a total population of around 22 million people. The Confederacy, by contrast, consisted of only 11 states with slightly over 9 million. Moreover, of this smaller population, 3,654,000 were Negroes, mostly slaves, and the Confederacy did not use any of these as soldiers. Two-thirds of the farms were in the Union, over four-fifths of the factories, and approximately two-thirds of the railroad mileage. There were nearly thirteen times as many industrial workers in the Union as in the Confederacy. The value of goods manufactured in New York state alone was four times that of the Confederacy. Only 4 per cent of the locomotives and 3 per cent of the firearms in the country were built in the South in 1860.

The Union had a navy at the beginning of the war, though it was small, and no great advantage. The advantage here lay in the potential in the North of building ships and outfitting them. In July, 1861, the Union reported 82 ships in commission. The number grew steadily until there were 671 vessels under commission by December, 1864, and approximately 51,000 sailors. The Confederacy never had any comparable number of ships, and never had more than 4,000 sailors at any one time. Above all, the Confederacy did not have the ship-building potential. The situation of the South has been described this way: It "had neither shipyards (save Norfolk, which was soon lost, and Pensacola, which was inadequate and also, finally lost), nor workshops, steam mills or foundries, except on the most limited scale. . . . There was not, in the whole Confederacy, the means of turning out a complete steam engine of a size suitable for ships. The timber for potential Confederate ships still stood in the forests; the iron required was still in the mines . . . ; the hemp required for ship ropes had actually to be grown. . . ."[110] Hence, many of such ships as the Confederacy had were either captured Union ships or purchased from abroad.

Not all the advantages lay with the North, however. The military leadership of the Confederacy was generally superior to that of the Union, for the first three years at least. Many Confederate officers had attended West Point and fought in the Mexican War. One hundred and eighty-two general officers in the Confederacy had earlier served in the United States Army, 148 of them trained at West Point. Among the storied generals was the one who stood above all the rest, Robert E. Lee. Lee was offered a top command in the Union army, but when his native Virginia seceded, he cast his lot with the South. And there were other military leaders of high repute, such as T. J. (Stonewall) Jackson, Jeb Stuart, Leonidas Polk, Albert S. Johnston, Joseph E. Johnston, Ambrose P. Hill, and Daniel H. Hill. And, though the ordinary soldier of the Confederacy was often ill-clad and poorly equipped, plus being individualistic and resistant to discipline, he was often fierce in battle. There is much evidence through much of the war that man for man the Confederate army was often the superior of the Union army.

At the outset, too, there was much more enthusiasm for their cause and confidence among Southerners. Of their military prowess, Southerners who had anything to say had little doubt; if it came to fighting, they would make quick work of the North. They had a quite different view of their economic strength than historians have since held. They were the great exporting region of the United States. Cotton was king, and as soon as European countries, Britain especially, were denied cotton, they would recognize the Confederacy and come to its aid. They would not permit the shutting off of a major source of agricultural staples. Moreover, the South had long been the seat of free trade sentiment. And that was much more in accord with European thought than the protectionist policies of the Republicans. However, this line of reasoning left out of account some crucial factors. One was vigorous European anti-slavery sentiment, particularly in England. The

Robert E. Lee
(1807–1870)

Lee was born in Virginia, a descendant of a long line of Lees who were prominent in the history of that colony and state, as well as the founding of the United States. He graduated from West Point and entered upon a military career which ended only with the defeat of the Confederacy. Lee fought in the Mexican War with distinction, served as superintendent of West Point and as a colonel of the United States Cavalry. When Virginia seceded and war came, he made the difficult decision to resign his commission and offer his services to the Confederacy, despite the fact that Lincoln offered him field command of the Union army. The first year of the war he acted mainly as adviser to Jefferson Davis. After that, he was field commander of the Army of Northern Virginia and, in the last months of the war, commanding general of Confederate armies. After the war, he was head of Washington (later Washington and Lee) College until his death.

need for cotton abroad was not so great in the early part of the war either. The last two cotton crops had been unusually large, and warehouses in Europe were filled to overflowing. Possibly decisive victories, such as the taking of Washington or the capture of a major Union army, might have turned the tide and brought foreign recognition of the Confederacy, but such victories never occurred.

Although such things are difficult to assess, there were indications that the Confederacy was more unified behind a cause than was the Union. To the extent that this was so, there is a ready explanation for it. The Confederacy was fighting for independence, a noble cause in the American past, and Confederate leaders were not slow to point out such parallels as there might be with the American War for Independence. By contrast, the Union cause was of necessity one of conquest and some degree of subjugation, however much Lincoln and Congress might protest against this interpretation, at least in the beginning.

In any case, it was difficult to unite what remained of the country behind a dubious cause. There was much sympathy for the Confederacy at the beginning, and even more opposition to the idea of conquering the seceding states. Sympathy was no doubt strongest in the slave states that remained in the Union. Large numbers of men from Kentucky and Missouri fought on the Confederate side. The Secretary of State of Maryland said of the seceding states: "Why not let them depart in peace and save the horrors of a Civil War?"[111] When the Maryland legislature assembled after the formation of the Confederacy, it adopted a resolution, saying: "That Maryland implores the President . . . to cease this unholy war, at least until Congress assembles; that Maryland desires and consents to the recognition of the independence of the Confederate States."[112]

Ultimately, Missouri was kept in the Union by the use of military force, and Maryland was intimidated by Federal troops during the ensuing election in that state so as to assure a loyal control of the government. That is not to say that either had the necessary majority for secession, but both had strong Confederate sympathy.

Sympathy for the Confederacy was not so strong elsewhere, but there was much opposition to a policy of conquest. Democrats in the North hardly favored Lincoln's policies and some, known as Copperheads, were castigated as disloyal. New York City, as indicated earlier, was much less than enthusiastic about the war. As far along in the war as March, 1863, the New Jersey legislature declared that "at no time since the commencement of the present war has this State been other than willing to terminate peacefully and honorably to all a war unnecessary in its origin, fraught with horror and suffering in its prosecution, and necessarily dangerous to the liberties of all in its continuance. . . ."[113]

While there were pockets of Unionists in the South during the course of the war, the Confederacy suffered much more from the looseness of the confederation, which was at the heart of the very reason for its existence. By their very acts of secession, the states proclaimed themselves sovereign and independent of any central power. Though the constitution did convey extensive powers upon the Confederacy, similar to those in the United States Constitution, the states did tend to withhold cooperation with the Confederate government in ways that hampered the war effort. As the war wore on, this probably told more against the Confederacy than any similar independence by Northern states did on the Union because it had fewer resources in the first place.

Although it was hardly predictable, it turned out that the Union had much stronger political leadership than did the Confederacy. Both Lincoln and Jefferson Davis took seriously their constitutional roles as commanders-in-chief of their armed forces. Judging by their backgrounds, Davis appeared to be much better suited to leadership than did Lincoln. Both men had been born in Kentucky, but there the resemblance ended. Lincoln had grown up along the frontier in Kentucky and Indiana, finally settling in Illinois. He had little schooling, but he studied law and became a well-known lawyer at Springfield. Before being elected President he did have some political

Abraham Lincoln
(1809–1865)

Lincoln was the 16th President of the United States. He was born in Kentucky, grew up in Indiana, and settled in Illinois. He had little schooling, only enough, most likely, to learn to read, write, and cipher, and he studied enough law on his own to be admitted to the bar. Lincoln became a well-known trial lawyer, even acted for several corporations, served several terms in the Illinois legislature and one term in Congress as a Whig. He became a Republican in 1856 and ran for the Senate against Stephen A. Douglas in 1858, but lost. However, his debates with Douglas brought him to national attention, and he was nominated for and elected President in 1860. In temperament, Lincoln was a romantic nationalist, and as President his consuming passion was to save the Union. He forged a Unionist ticket in 1864, with Andrew Johnson, a Democrat, as his running mate, and won handily.

experience in the state and national legislature but no executive experience. His military experience was too scanty to be worth mentioning. By contrast, Davis was a Mississippi planter, trained at West Point, had both military and executive experience, and had emerged before Lincoln as a national figure. He had served as Secretary of War under President Pierce, and he served in the Senate until his state seceded from the Union.

Lincoln was tall and ungainly, laconic of manner, and a backwoods lawyer in appearance. Beneath the surface, however, there were large reserves of resourcefulness and tenacity. He was determined to win the war from the outset, and despite what some had believed—that they could control him to their own ends—he made it clear from the beginning of his administration that he was his own man. Although he brought little or no military knowledge to his task, he did have a clear grasp of the broad strategy of the war, though he spent much of the war seeking generals who would execute it effectively. Neither the Union nor the Confederacy had what could be called a central military command—a general staff—for much of the war. Lee served as Davis's top military adviser for the first year, and Lincoln had various advisers. General Grant was made com-

Jefferson Davis
(1808–1889)

Courtesy National Archives, Brady Collection

Davis was President of the Confederate States of America and earlier served in the United States Army, House of Representatives, Senate, and as Secretary of War. He was born in Kentucky, but later moved to Louisiana and then Mississippi. He attended Transylvania College in Kentucky and graduated from West Point. After several years in the army, he resigned and lived on and worked his plantation in Mississippi. He fought in the Mexican War, and followed a political career during the interwar years. When the Confederacy was formed, he became its first, and only, president. At the close of the war, he was captured by Union troops and was held in prison for two years under threat of trial for treason. When he was paroled, he went to Canada and Europe before eventually returning to Mississippi. He spent much of his later years writing about the Confederacy.

mander of all Union military forces in 1864, and thereafter the North did have a unified command system. Most historians agree that Jefferson Davis was much less effective as commander-in-chief than Lincoln. He took too much on himself in military matters, and interfered in local command situations. Perhaps his prior military experience gave him too much confidence in what he could do.

The Strategy of the War

At the beginning of the war, neither side believed that it would be a long drawn-out war. Hence, no complex strategy would be required. The Confederates believed that it would only be necessary to show their determination by winning a decisive victory on the field of battle. Then, the Union would accept Southern independence as a fact. On the other hand, Lincoln only sought three-month enlistments at the outset (Congress was not yet in session), and this could be taken as a sign he thought the war might be brief. It began to become clear, however, after the First Battle of Bull Run that it might well be a protracted conflict.

The Union strategy was much the more complex of the two. This was necessarily so, because it was ultimately necessary for the Union to conquer the Confederacy. The broad strategy, as it worked out, was to isolate the Confederacy from the rest of the world, divide the Confederacy by severing the transportation links, and having divided it to conquer it. It should be noted, however, that much of the Union effort during the war was focused on capturing Richmond, the capital of the Confederacy, and that this does not quite belong to the isolate, divide, and conquer strategy. The two capitals—Washington and Richmond—were only about 130 miles apart, and only two rivers—the Potomac and Rappahannock—posed any major obstacle in reaching one from the other. Throughout the war the two major armies—the Union Army of the Potomac and the Confederate Army of Northern Virginia—generally defended the capitals of each from the opposing side, and the Union army made numerous forays in an attempt to take Richmond.

Lincoln declared a blockade of all Southern ports in April, 1861. Considering the size and condition of the Union navy at that time, the blockade could hardly have been effective. But the Confederacy cooperated, for reasons of its own, by declaring an embargo on foreign shipments for the time being. President Davis hoped to make European countries short of cotton and thus move to recognize or otherwise aid the Confederacy. It did not succeed, and by the time the Confederacy removed the embargo the blockade was becoming more effective. The Union pursued with considerable vigor throughout the war the effort to bottle up Southern shipping facilities.

Confederate strategy was mostly defensive, and its task was easier and simpler than that of the Union. The Confederacy had no designs on Union territory, though there were efforts to induce the other slave states to secede. The main efforts were centered on Kentucky, Missouri, and Maryland, and there was fighting in Kentucky and Missouri, as well as one battle fought in Maryland. Otherwise, the main strategy was to defend Confederate territory and defeat such armies as attacked. Indeed, Confederate strategy was defective in that it left so much of the initiative to the Union. The location of the capital at Richmond may well have dictated the concentration of forces in Virginia and have resulted in the loss of territory west of the mountains, which was ultimately decisive in the war. A more centrally located capital, at Chattanooga, say, which was a major railhead, might have resulted in arraying forces in such a way as to hold much of the South.

Early Stages of the War 1861–1863

The Confederacy was well ahead of the Union in assembing a sizeable army. Jefferson Davis had called for a hundred thousand volunteers in March, and Southerners rushed in large numbers to fill the quotas. Since the Union had no large army immediately following the fall of Fort Sumter, it might have been possible for the Confederate army to take Washington. Indeed, the capital was in a highly exposed position, surrounded by a more hostile than not Maryland, and faced across the Potomac by a seceded Virginia. But the Confederacy did not launch an attack, and the Union began to assemble and train an army.

By July, both the Northern press and politicians were pressing for a major attack on the South. So it was that General Irvin McDowell led an army into Virginia on July 21. A goodly number of civilians in Washington thought the battle would be a gala occasion, so they decided to attend. "A throng of newspaper correspondents, sightseers on horse and foot, and congressmen in carriages with ladies and picnic hampers, came out to see the sport."[114] It was hardly that; it was the First Battle of Bull Run. The Union army met a Confederate force under the command of General P.G.T. Beauregard at Manassas or Bull Run, and the first major engagement of the war took place. A smaller Union army had been sent to cut off Confederate General Joseph Johnston's forces from reinforcing Beauregard, but the additional Confederate forces evaded the army and arrived in time at the battle site. At first, the Union army appeared to be winning, but when the Confederate reinforcements arrived, they turned the tide. General T. J. Jackson's troops stood like a "Stonewall," it was said, and thus he acquired the nickname which helped to make him famous. Following Jackson's successful stand, Confederate forces counterattacked; Union troops panicked, and the fighting turned into a rout. Union troops retreated in disorder toward Washington. Confederate forces were both too weary and disorganized to pursue, so that the Union army escaped.

George B. McClellan
(1826–1885)

Courtesy New York Historical Society

McClellan was a professional soldier, born in Philadelphia, and educated at West Point. Immediately upon graduation, he fought in the Mexican War, where he served under General Winfield Scott. McClellan had shown a particular aptitude for engineering, and he was called back to teach it at West Point after the war. In addition to this undertaking, he was assigned to a number of engineering projects during the interwar years and was sent to Europe to study other armies. He left military service in the late 1850s, but returned to take a command at the outbreak of the Civil War. He was soon called to command the Army of the Potomac and was its commanding general in both the Peninsula campaign and at the Battle of Antietam. However, he was a better planner and trainer of soldiers than battlefield commander, and after Antietam he was never offered another command. He was the Democratic nominee for President in 1864, and was elected governor of New Jersey in later years.

It was now clear, to Lincoln at least, that a long, hard war lay ahead. He replaced McDowell with General George B. McClellan, and made him head of the Union armies. McClellan was young, vigorous, thorough, and probably the most beloved by his troops of any Union general. The army was thereafter greatly enlarged with long-term enlistments, and a thorough training program introduced. For all his promise as a commander, McClellan had some glaring weaknesses. He talked a better version of war-making than he fought. He did not respect his commander-in-chief, Lincoln; indeed, he despised and looked down on him. He was a Democrat and suspected of being a Southern sympathizer, though there is no reason to question his loyalty to the Union cause. Above all, though, he was slow to act. During the fall and winter of 1861–1862, he planned and planned and trained and trained, prompting Lincoln to comment: "If General McClellan does not want to use the army I would like to borrow it."[115] For all that, he was almost certainly the most effective military leader on the Virginia front until Ulysses S. Grant took over in 1864.

But while McClellan trained the main army, Union forces were by no means all halted in their tracks. A series of campaigns, most of them involving relatively smaller numbers, often combined naval and army detachments, were going on along the Southeast coast, on the Gulf coast, and on the Mississippi and its tributaries. Most of the naval outlets of the South along the East coast were taken in the summer and fall of 1861. In the following winter and spring Union force was focused on control of the lower Mississippi and its tributaries. It took no great insight to see that the fate of the Confederacy hinged to a great extent on the control of the Mississippi from its mouth northward to its junction with the Ohio at Cairo, Illinois, and probably a portion of the Ohio. Two states in the Confederacy lay west of the Mississippi in their entirety—Arkansas and Texas—, and most of Louisiana as well. If the Union controlled the lower Mississippi these states would be cut off from the Confederacy except by way of the Gulf, and, except for Texas, they would be largely cut off from the Gulf of Mexico.

Thomas J. (Stonewall) Jackson (1824–1863)

Jackson was born in Virginia, worked to support the family of his widowed mother as a youth, but was able to attend and graduate from West Point. He accepted a commission in the army, fought in the Mexican War, and after that served out his enlistment. In 1851, Jackson was appointed professor of artillery and science at Virginia Military Institute. When the Civil War came, he joined the Confederate forces and was given a command. Many of his exploits were as a commander of small, mobile forces in the Shenandoah Valley, but he is most famous as a subordinate to Lee in his victorious battles. Jackson was a master of maneuver and mobility, and the swiftness with which he moved his army enabled him to fight detached engagements as well as join the main army for major battles. He was wounded and died as a result of shots mistakenly fired at him by his own troops following the Battle of Chancellorsville.

Moreover, the main water routes of Tennessee—the Mississippi, the Cumberland, and the Tennessee, the latter two which empty into the Ohio river, could be controlled as well. Missouri would be largely inaccessible to the Confederacy, too. In short, the Confederacy could be sundered by controlling the Mississippi and its tributaries.

This was the prize sought in a multi-pronged military and naval assault by Union forces begun in the early winter of 1862. In January, Union troops under General George Thomas defeated Confederates at the Battle of Mill Springs in Kentucky. In February, General Grant took Fort Henry, the major defensive position on the Tennessee, and Fort Donelson, the defense of Nashville, on the Cumberland river. In early April, Union General John B. Pope broke the northernmost Confederate defensive position on the Mississippi by taking Island number 10 off southern Missouri. On April 6th and 7th occurred the engagement that has gone down in history as the Battle of Shiloh. General Grant marched south with an army of 40,000 to Pittsburg Landing, Tennessee, just north of the state of Mississippi. He was met by 45,000 troops under the command of Confederate General Albert S. Johnston.

On Sunday, April 6, General Johnston's troops launched a surprise attack, and they had the better of the fighting during the remainder of the day. Indeed, a less plucky commander than Grant would have probably beat a hasty retreat, for his troops had their backs to the river and could have been

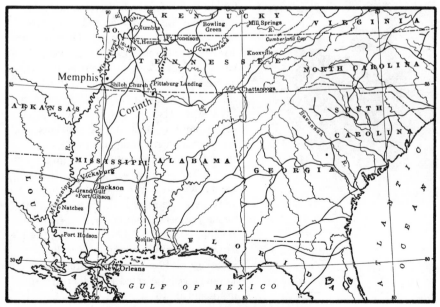

CAMPAIGNS IN THE WEST 1862-1863

surrounded. However, Grant did get reinforcements, and on the next day he counterattacked. General Johnston was killed, and Beauregard, who assumed command, retreated to Corinth, Mississippi after several more hours of desperate fighting. Western Tennessee was now under Union control, but Grant's victory had been bought with a heavy price in loss of troops, and he did not pursue the Confederate army.

In mid-April Commodore David Farragut, with troops aboard his ships, led a fleet up the Mississippi toward New Orleans. The navy destroyed Confederate fortifications on the way and took the city of New Orleans, when the troops met no organized resistance. Thus, the largest city and most important port in the Confederacy fell on April 25, 1862. On June 6, Union gunboats destroyed resistance at Memphis. By the beginning of the summer, then, most of the Mississippi (excepting Vicksburg and a port in Louisiana) was under Union control, along with a considerable portion of the navigable tributaries. The western portion of the Confederacy was deeply infiltrated with Union force, though it was not yet entirely lost.

Ulysses S. Grant
(1822–1885)

Grant was the 18th President of the United States and victorious commanding general of the Union armies in the Civil War. He was born in Ohio, grew up on a farm, and graduated from West Point. He fought under Generals Taylor and Scott during the Mexican War and was several times promoted for bravery. Grant left the army in 1854 and spent several years at a variety of jobs with little distinction. He entered the army immediately after Lincoln sent out a call for volunteers for the Civil War. Through 1863, he was involved entirely in western campaigns, and his reputation rose and fell as he succeeded or failed in battle. Two things became clear eventually: He was a fighter, and he was determined to win. These traits were the ones Lincoln was looking for in a general, and he made Grant commanding general of the armies in 1864. After the war, Grant served briefly as Secretary of War under Johnson, was nominated and elected President in 1868 and again in 1872.

Meanwhile, the war had finally resumed in earnest in the East. Despite the rapidity of telegraphic and rail communication, the Mississippi river was still remote from the seats of power of both the Union and the Confederacy, and the belief still prevailed that the war would be won or lost in Virginia and the surrounding country. (European countries were apt to be even less impressed than Americans with strategic victories or defeats along the Mississippi.) At any rate, as the spring of 1862 approached, Lincoln ordered McClellan to go on the attack. He had a choice to attack directly into Virginia or to make a more roundabout assault by way of the Chesapeake Bay. In either case, Richmond would be the goal. McClellan preferred a combined naval and military assault from the Chesapeake up the peninsula between the York and James rivers. So it was that the Peninsula Campaign was launched and carried on from March 17 to July 2, 1862.

But first, the entrance to the James River had to be cleared of an important obstacle. The Confederates had ironclad a captured United States ship, the *Merrimac*, which they renamed the *Virginia*. (Even so, it has usually gone down in history as the *Merrimac*, as in the battle of the *Monitor* and the *Merrimac*.) On March 8, the *Merrimac* sank one Union warship and burned another off Hampton Roads. The next day it sallied forth again to attack another blockading Union ship, when it was met by the Union ironclad, the *Monitor*. The *Merrimac* and the *Monitor* engaged in a five-hour struggle, the first battle between ironclads in history, before the *Merrimac* limped back to port for repairs. A couple of months later it was burned to prevent Union capture when Norfolk was taken. It was only then that the James became fully accessible to Union ships, but Union forces had already long since driven up the Peninsula.

McClellan's army which embarked from Alexandria, Virginia in mid-March was probably the most impressive that had ever been assembled in America. It was well over a hundred thousand strong, well-dressed in blue uniforms, thoroughly trained, and finely equipped. Even so, it moved only slowly up the Peninsula and only removed Confederate resistance as far as Williamsburg by May 5. Its path to Richmond was blocked by a smaller Confederate army under the command of General Joseph E. Johnston. While these two large armies were jockeying for position and clashing, Stonewall Jackson with 18,000 men was tying up and often besting in skirmishes Union forces more than twice that size in the Shenandoah Valley. In late May, he routed Union forces in a battle at Winchester, and Washington was believed to be in danger.

As for McClellan, though he came within a few miles of Richmond, he never achieved his goal. Fierce battles between the opposing armies did take place in late May, early June, and late June. At the Battle of the Seven Pines, General Johnston was severely wounded and was replaced by Robert E. Lee. In him, the Confederacy had, as it turned out, its finest and most audacious field commander. In late June, in what is known as the Seven

Days' Battles, Lee made a series of assaults on Union forces in an attempt to overwhelm and drive them out. McClellan was able to maintain superior fire power by concentrating his forces where they could be supported by gunboats along the rivers. When Lee's attacks were repulsed by superior firepower, he finally withdrew to Richmond. The Union army remained nearby for more than a month longer, but it did not launch another attack. Instead, it was gradually withdrawn in August, and the field command was turned over to General John Pope.

Pope's command was short-lived. He had some success in the west commanding small forces and envisioned himself a great leader of troops commanding a victorious army. It did not work out. In late August he concentrated his forces for a march directly on Richmond by land. Pope was badly defeated at the Second Battle of Bull Run (August 29, 30). First, he was cut off from his supply base by Stonewall Jackson, and when he tried to attack Lee's army at Bull Run, General James Longstreet overwhelmed his flank and he was badly defeated.

Lee determined to follow up on this victory and take the war into the North before the disorganized Union army was likely to be in shape to defend. In mid-September, he led the Army of Northern Virginia into Maryland west of Washington with several objects in mind: (1) to sever rail connections between the Northeast and Midwest, probably at Harrisburg, Pennsylvania; (2) to obtain foreign recognition of the Confederacy by the stunning invasion of the North; (3) possibly to draw Maryland on to the side of the Confederacy and isolate Washington; and (4) to obtain badly needed supplies for his army. However, General McClellan was restored to the command of the Union army, and because of his popularity with the soldiers, he was able to rally it much more quickly than Lee had expected.

Thus, he was able to intercept Lee in Maryland, aided in the undertaking by a copy of the campaign plans of the Confederate army which had been captured. The main result was the Battle of Antietam on September 17. Before that occurred, however, Stonewall Jackson succeeded in taking the garrison at Harper's Ferry and the large arsenal of weapons stored there. Antietam was the single bloodiest day of battle in the war. Lee's army was badly outnumbered, but he fought boldly, as usual, and at the end of the day neither side had gained ground. McClellan undoubtedly held the upper hand, but he did not renew the attack the next day. Instead, he allowed the Confederate army to withdraw and cross the Potomac into Virginia.

Even so, Antietam was a blow to Southern hopes. Lee had been turned back; he had failed to demonstrate to the world the superiority of Southern arms and thus gain foreign recognition and aid. It was *not* the turning point of the war, but thereafter expectations of foreign aid dimmed.

Armies in the East did not usually undertake campaigns once winter was coming on, but Lincoln was determined to make yet another attempt on Richmond before the end of 1862. Faced with a reluctant McClellan,

Lincoln replaced him with General Ambrose Burnside as commander of the Army of the Potomac. Burnside's sartorial contribution was greater than his military one in high command. He wore hair down the sides of his face, and "sideburns" were named after him. At any rate, Burnside brought an army of 113,000 into Virginia to attack Lee with 70,000. The battle took place at Fredericksburg on December 13. Lee's army was positioned on the south side of the Rappahanock river on the high ground above it. Burnside's troops crossed the river on pontoons and attacked Lee head on across open ground. They met withering artillery and deadly rifle fire from the entrenched Confederates. Yet on they came in wave after wave, as each succeeding wave was mowed down. The carnage was frightful to behold, as the dead and wounded lay piled on one another. None could question the bravery of the Union soldiers, but the attack was suicidal, and the Union army was fortunate to be able to withdraw.

Burnside was shortly replaced with General Joseph Hooker, nicknamed "Fighting Joe" for earlier exploits. Hooker was competent enough at the task of rallying and training an army, but he was a braggart nonetheless. He was free with his criticism of other generals and boasted of what he would do to Lee when he met him in battle. He got his opportunity at the Battle of Chancellorsville, May 2–4, 1863. Lee had kept his army near Fredericksburg after the battle there. Hooker brought an army of 130,000 to attack Lee's army of 60,000 near there. Confronted by overwhelming numbers, Lee decided on one of his most daring maneuvers. He divided his army, keeping only 10,000 troops to face Hooker's force, and sent Stonewall Jackson with 30,000 men to attack the right flank. The flank attack came late in the day and, though balloonists had observed Jackson's maneuvering (Hooker thought he was retreating), took the corps under attack by complete surprise. The right flank of the Union army panicked, so that only a rally within the remainder of the army prevented a rout. Even so, Hooker had enough and retreated, though a considerable portion of his army had not been engaged in action.

Lee had now become a paragon in the eyes of his Southern admirers (nor was he any less feared in the North than he was glorified in the South). His army now appeared to be invincible; he had faced time after time the best that the Union could send and had turned them back. But Chancellorsville was a disastrous battle for Lee; he lost his strong right arm, the irreplaceable Stonewall Jackson. Jackson was returning to the lines at dusk after the battle, from a reconaissance mission, when he was mistaken by his men for the enemy, shot down, and mortally wounded. What Lee could conceive, Jackson could execute, could execute swiftly, effectively, and brilliantly. He excelled in the rapid movement of an army. A lesser man would have lost six armies performing his daring maneuvers, yet he never lost one. His secret was surely in the devotion of his troops, and that may well have been a reflex of his own religious devotion.

The Confederate army stood out for the devoutness of its leaders, and Jackson was probably the most devout. Hardly a day in his camp was without a religious service, and he was as much at home on his knees in prayer as in the saddle of his horse, Little Sorrel. Lee spent the night in prayer for him as Jackson's life hung in the balance. As death gripped him, Jackson's last words were, "Let us cross over the river and rest under the shade of the trees." A year later, General Grant said of Jackson: "He was a gallant soldier, and a Christian gentleman."[116] His death foreshadowed the fall of the Confederacy, for never again would Lee win a decisive victory.

Behind the Lines

Life goes on in the midst of war as at other times. People grow old and die; babies are born; weddings take place; people must still busy themselves with getting a living; scientific discoveries are made; newspapers are published; and politicians still contend over policies and position. That is not to suggest that the war did not alter lives or that people were not often engrossed with it.Indeed, the Civil War probably had a greater impact on the lives of Americans than any war in which the United States have been involved. This was especially so for the South. Most of the war was fought in the South; most of the destruction occurred there; and the strain on resources and wealth was much greater in the South than elsewhere. But Americans in the North were also caught up in the war, and changes occurred there as well. Southern nationalism gave rise to the Confederacy. Northern nationalism changed the character of the country.

There had long been considerable desire to use the United States government to promote national economic development, particularly national banking, transportation, and industrialization. Efforts to do this had thus far been frustrated over any extended period of time, first by the Jeffersonian Republicans and then by the Jacksonian Democrats. While both the Jeffersonians and Jacksonians both had a national following, the leadership was primarily Southern. When the Confederacy was formed, Southern Representatives and Senators withdrew from Congress, with an exception or so. They thus provided the Republicans with control of Congress and gave them a free hand to institute their national programs. The constitutional objections to some of the programs could still be voiced, but the power had shifted to others.

There had been a thrust to have a high protective tariff, usually on the grounds that it would promote manufacturing, going back to Hamilton and advanced in later years by Henry Clay and the Whigs. At last, those seeking a high tariff had their opportunity, and it was in keeping with the Republican platform to pass one. Indeed, even before the war began or the bulk of the Southerners had withdrawn from Congress, the Morrill Tarriff Act was passed in 1861. However the tariff was raised much higher in 1862, and again in 1864. The average rate on goods covered was 37 per cent by the act of 1862, and it was raised to 47 per cent in 1864. While there was some talk of these as revenue measures, it is clear that such high rates would discourage imports and tend to decrease revenues.

The Republicans rewarded their followers in the West by passing a Homestead Act in 1862. This act provided 160 acres of land free within the public domain to any head of household who would settle on the land and improve it over a period of five years. The only charge to be made, if the conditions were complied with, was a small registration fee. This fulfilled the long-time hope for free land for homesteaders on the public domain. There was not any great rush generally, however, to take up the land.

Another act made possible by the secession of the south was the Morrill Land Grant Act of 1862. Congressman Justin Morrill had earlier pushed a similar bill through Congress, but President Buchanan had vetoed it, on the grounds of its unconstitutionality, among other things. Lincoln entertained no such objections, and a new bill became a law in 1862. It provided that each state would receive 30,000 acres for each of its Representatives and Senators from the public domain. The proceeds of the sale of the land were to provide funds to enable states to found agricultural and technical colleges. At the time it was passed, of course, only loyal states would participate (though later reconstructed states also received land). This act not only expanded the role of the national government but also might be expected to attach some people more firmly to the Union.

The idea of a transcontinental railroad had been in the wind ever since the acquisition of California. It was not reckoned to be a commercially feasible project, and no private investors came forward to undertake the project. Small wonder, for it would have to cross hundreds upon hundreds of miles sparsely inhabited by Indians and somewhat more thickly by buffalo and other wild animals. In any case, the building of a railroad to the Pacific became a political issue, since it appeared that it would have to be subsidized by government. Southerners generally opposed a more northerly route, and nothing was done until they were gone from Congress. The Pacific Railway Act of 1862 authorized two corporations to undertake the building and operation of the railroad: the Union Pacific from Omaha, Nebraska westward, and the Central Pacific to build from the west coast eastward. Each was granted a hundred foot right-of-way, 5 sections of land in alternate sections along either side of the track, and a construction loan figured at the rate of $16,000 per mile in level country, $32,000 in the foothills, and $48,000 in the mountains. In 1864, Congress doubled the amount of the land grants, in the hope of spurring the building. Very little work was done until after the war. No such grants for private undertakings had ever been made before by the United States government, and several Presidents had vetoed measures in aid of road building that were much less comprehensive on the grounds that they were unconstitutional.

The power of the national government was extended into the matter of slavery in new ways in the course of the war. The war was fought, Lincoln insisted at the outset, to preserve the Union, not to free the slaves. The Constitution conferred no power on the federal government to interfere with property in slaves. Yet the war did become a crusade for freeing the slaves, and active measures were taken during the war pointing in that direction. The Confiscation Act, passed in August, 1861, provided for the emancipation of slaves used by the Confederacy in the war effort. In April, 1862, Congress abolished slavery in the District of Columbia and provided compensation to their owners. In June, Congress abolished slavery in the territories without compensation. Some military commanders had made moves to free slaves who came under their authority, but that was generally discouraged.

The most dramatic act, however, was Lincoln's Emancipation Proclamation, which went into effect January 1, 1863. He made the preliminary announcement of it September 22, 1862. The announcement came on the heels of the Union army's turning Lee back at the Battle of Antietam. There was a reason for this. Lincoln had been pondering and considering such a proclamation for months, but he had been advised not to do it so long as it might appear to be a desperate war move to recoup the declining fortunes of the Union army. Antietam made it clear that the Union was in no immediate peril, and Lincoln acted. The proclamation was made official on January 1, 1863. In its language, the Emancipation Proclamation was bold. It declared that "on the 1st day of January, A.D. 1863, all persons held as slaves within any State or designated part of a State, the people whereof shall then be in rebellion against the United States shall be then, thenceforward, and forever free. . . ."[117]

It should be noted, however, that as of the moment it was issued and to the best of Lincoln's knowledge, the proclamation did *not* free a single slave. It did not free a slave in Maryland, Delaware, Kentucky, Missouri, West Virginia, nor in any state or portions of a state within the Confederacy occupied by Union troops. These last, including West Virginia, were excluded by name, including a listing of occupied counties. In short, Lincoln freed all those slaves over which he had no control. No doubt, this was by design. The proclamation was justified "as a fit and necessary war measure for suppressing . . . rebellion," as Lincoln said, and was done by "power in me vested as Commander-in-chief of the Army and Navy of the United States. . . ."[118] It was intended to relieve the slaves within the Confederacy of their bonds and allegiances, and thus to remove the slaves from aid and help to the Confederate cause. Lincoln did not in words incite the slaves to rebel against their masters, but he certainly offered them an incentive to do so.

The immediate effects of the Emancipation Proclamation were mixed. It aroused the deepest resentment in the Confederacy, of course, and probably prolonged the war as well as contributing to the ferocity of the fighting in the last two years. Nor was it well received by a goodly number in the North. Determined abolitionists were disgruntled because Lincoln had restricted its application to territory over which he had no control. Many Democrats were unhappy that the President had acted in a way to make slavery the issue and exceeded any clear constitutional authority. The legislature of Lincoln's home state, Illinois, declared that the administration had "at once converted the war . . . into the crusade for the sudden, unconditional and violent liberation of 3,000,000 negro slaves; a result which would not only be a total subversion of the Federal Union but a revolution in the social organization of the Southern States. . . ."[119] On the other hand, it might have bound some in the North closer to the Union cause, and it probably did undermine the Confederate drive for foreign recognition by England and France. As for the slaves within the Confederacy, they generally remained loyal to their masters.

Yet the Emancipation Proclamation was a symbolic event, and it was big with importance for the future. Lincoln had, after all, said more than he had appeared to say. He had said that the slaves within the Confederacy were "thenceforward and forever free." If the proclamation meant anything, it had to mean that as the Union armies advanced, the slaves would be freed (as indeed they often were). Moreover, it presaged a coming end to slavery in the United States. Actually, however, neither Lincoln nor most politicians believed that emancipation could be constitutionally effected by presidential fiat. Thus, a movement got underway in 1864 to add the 13th Amendment to the Constitution, which would abolish slavery. The Senate approved it in April, 1864, but the House failed to muster the necessary two-thirds majority to pass it at that time. It did so in January, 1865. The ratification of the amendment, however, belongs to the Reconstruction period, where it will be told.

One other series of Federal actions needs to be discussed here—those having to do with financing the war and creating a national banking system. Although Congress levied a number of new taxes (including an income tax) to help finance the war, a large portion of the cost of the war was paid by borrowing the money. The national debt increased from $66.5 million in 1861 to $2.67 billion at the end of 1865. Much of the money was raised by floating loans from the general public. These bonds were sold mainly by private firms, notably by Jay Cooke, a Philadelphia banker. However, the government used two other devices for raising money which are of particular interest. One was by issuing treasury notes, which were known as greenbacks, and were used as money. They were fiat money, since they could not be redeemed at the time, and they were made legal tender for public and private debts, with a couple of exceptions.

The other device for raising money was involved in the creation of a national banking system. The national banking system was, however, more far reaching than that. A National Bank Act was passed in 1863 and considerably revised in 1864. These acts provided for the chartering of the banks by the federal government with the power to issue currency—i.e., national bank notes. These bank notes were backed by government bonds; thus, the government could get money by monetizing, i.e., issuing bank notes on the basis, of its debt. After the demise of the Second National Bank in the 1830s, there was no national banking system nor any national paper money system. State-chartered banks usually issued paper money, but it was not legal tender, and could be accepted or not as people chose. Congress attempted to drive state-chartered banks out of the business of issuing paper. It did so, first, by making the national bank notes legal tender for most purposes. Second, it taxed the state bank notes. When a minimal tax did not have the desired effect, Congress raised the tax on them to 10 per cent in 1865. Thus, state banks had to become national banks, or go out of the business of issuing paper money.

Three things need to be pointed out about these methods of financing. First, they were mostly of doubtful constitutionality. The income tax was not in accord with the requirement that direct taxes be apportioned among the states. Second, the issuing of treasury notes and national bank notes was not authorized by the Constitution, and when the power to issue such bills of credit had been proposed in the Constitutional Convention, it had been rejected. Moreover, the members of the Convention had understood that no power had been granted to make paper money legal tender. Second, the greenbacks and national bank notes were inflationary, i.e. increased the money supply. The effects could be noted in two ways: one, the decline in the value of the money in relation to gold; two, the rise in prices. Third, the national banking system tender laws were a major extension of the power of the federal government.

Even so, the most important development in the economy, in relation to the war, was the great growth and expansion of production within the Union. Whatever the long-term effects of debasing the currency—the impact was felt particularly in the 1870s—, the short-run effect was a glow of prosperity, increasing investment, and expansion of production. Moreover, whatever the weaknesses in the methods of financing the war in the Union were, they were dwarfed by the methods employed by the Confederacy. The Confederate government financed only a small portion of the cost of the war by taxation. Instead, it resorted to borrowing and to issuing paper money. More than $1.5 billion in Confederate treasury notes were issued in the course of the war. The more they issued, the less that the money was worth, so that by April, 1865, it took 60 Confederate dollars to buy 1 dollar in gold, if anyone could be found to make the exchange.

Basically and more broadly, as the Union economy expanded and grew the Confederate economy contracted and produced less and less. The Southern economy had always been based on trade with foreign countries and the North. The South produced mainly raw materials for manufactur and staple crops, and relied heavily on the import of finished goods. Trade between the North and South was prohibited as soon as the war broke out, and the Union blockade or control of Southern ports made foreign trade difficult and costly, when it was not virtually impossible. There were efforts to change the Southern economy during the war by producing more goods for consumption as well as war materials, and these met with some success. The production of cotton, for example, fell drastically in the course of the war, for despite blockade running and illegal trade not much could get to any market. And, considerable efforts were made to produce war materials, consumer goods, and other things needed. But such a drastic change could hardly be made in the short period of time by a people under siege with definite ideas about limited government.

The general tendency was that as the war continued, the Southern economy deteriorated and less and less was produced. By contrast, the Union grew stronger, more self-sufficient, and more powerful. Though both sides adopted conscription, the Southern manpower was being exhausted in the last two years of the war, while Union manpower was steadily increasing. For one thing, hundreds of thousands of immigrants came into the North, but few came into the South. During the long war, the Union economic superiority increased, and the Southern economy deteriorated.

The Fall of the Confederacy

The turning point of the war came on successive days in early July, 1863. On July 3, Pickett's charge at the Union center at Gettysburg failed to crack the army, and Lee's foray into the North failed. On July 4, Vicksburg fell, and with that blow the Southwest was cut off by land from the Southeast. The war would continue for nearly two years longer, but the chances of a Confederate victory declined steadily after those July days.

Following his victory at Chancellorsville, General Lee decided upon another venture into the North. The victories at Fredericksburg and Chancellorsville had revived Southern hopes, and Lincoln's Emancipation Proclamation aroused outspoken opposition in the North. There was still at least a possibility of foreign recognition. A victory in the North might sharpen differences in the North, give new impetus to the peace movement, and produce foreign recognition. At any rate, Lee moved his army northward through western Virginia and Maryland into Pennsylvania in June. General Hooker led the main body of the Union army into the same general area, but resigned at the last moment and was replaced by General George G. Meade.

On July 1–3, 1863, the Battle of Gettysburg took place, an engagement which has been described as the greatest battle ever fought in the Americas. On the first day, the Confederate army drove Union forces through the town of Gettysburg, and the armies took up positions on ridges facing each other and separated by lower ground. On the second day, Lee intended to envelop the Union army by attacks on the left and the right. General Ewell did take territory on the right, but Longstreet was too late to succeed in the other movement. On the morning of the third Ewell renewed his assault but was driven off the ridge. A silence had descended on the battlefield by noon, and Meade strengthened his center anticipating a Confederate assault. Lee did not disappoint him. First came a heavy bombardment by Confederate artillery. Then came 15,000 Confederate soldiers, led by Pickett's division, in an assault on the main body of Meade's army. Halfway across the mile separating the armies, Union artillery opened up a withering fire on the oncoming troops. Undaunted, Pickett's force moved at double time into the assault upon Union forces. For a brief moment a small number of men in the attacking force broke into Union lines, but they were shot down or captured, and the rest of the force was decimated. Two of Pickett's brigadiers were killed, and all of his regimental commanders were killed or wounded.

The remains of the attacking force returned as best they could to Confederate lines. Meade's forces did not counterattack. Nor did they do so on the next day, as Lee's army remained in position. Orders from Washington urged Meade not to allow the Confederates to escape, but these were of no avail. On July 5, Lee began his withdrawal toward Virginia, and though the Potomac was too swollen to be crossed for several days after the army reached it, Meade did nothing of consequence to prevent the return of the Confederates to their home base.

Even so, Gettysburg was an irreparable loss for the Confederacy. The main body of the Army of Northern Virginia would never again leave that state, and Lee remained mostly on the defensive thereafter.

The fall of Vicksburg was of greater strategic importance, however. In early 1863, General Grant had brought an army to the vicinity of Vicksburg with a view to taking Vicksburg and thereby gaining Union control over the whole Mississippi River. It would be no easy task. His troops were outnumbered by troops under the command of General Joseph Johnston, which opposed him. Yet he broke the surrounding forces in a series of brilliant battles before laying Vicksburg under siege (May 22–July 4). On July 4, Confederate General Pemberton surrendered the city and the 30,000 troops in it to Grant. A few days later Port Hudson in Louisiana fell, and the whole of the Mississippi was under Union control.

Union attention in the lower South then shifted to Chattanooga. Both as a rail center and for its location on the Tennessee River, it was the key transportation point in the south. On September 9, 1863, Confederate General Braxton Bragg abandoned the city to Union forces and occupied the high ground above the city. President Davis rushed reinforcements to Bragg and the Battle of Chickamauga was fought in late September. The Union army remained in control of Chattanooga, but it was surrounded and the supplies cut off by the Confederates. Grant was made commander of all Union forces west of the Appalachians, and he placed General George

Thomas in command at Chattanooga. In the Battles of Lookout Mountain and Missionary Ridge (November 23–25), Thomas routed Bragg's Confederate forces, and the whole area around Chattanooga was securely in Union hands.

In March, 1864, the character of the war changed dramatically, or, more precisely, it changed in the East to match what had been going on in the West. It did not change instantaneously, of course, but the stage was set for the change. Ulysses S. Grant was made commanding general of the Union army in March. He took personal command of the Army of the Potomac, and Sherman succeeded him as commander in the West. Grant and Sherman differed significantly from the Union commanders in the East thus far. These latter fought battles, not campaigns, battles from which, win or lose, they withdrew to fight again, perhaps, another day. That had been the case at Bull Run, at Antietam, at Fredericksburg, at Chancellorsville, and at Gettysburg. It was almost as if in this gentleman's war you did not kick your opponent when he was down. You stepped aside, waited for him to recover

William T. Sherman
(1820–1891)

Courtesy New York Historical Society

Sherman was born in Ohio and trained at West Point. After graduation, he entered the military service where, as luck would have it, he spent much of his early military career in the Southern states. His Mexican War service was in California. In the 1850s, Sherman left the service, went into banking for a while, practiced law, and then became superintendant of a military academy in Louisiana. When the Civil War broke out, he joined the Union army and eventually became one of the highest ranked generals and most successful commanders in the war. Most of his fighting was done in the western theater, and he rose to eminence under Grant's command at Vicksburg and Chattanooga. He is most famous for his sweep through Georgia from Chattanooga to Atlanta to Savannah, but he also conquered the Carolinas, and ended the war second in command to Grant. When Grant became President, he made Sherman commanding general of the army, a position he held for the remainder of his military career.

fully, and joined the battle again at some later time. Neither Grant nor Sherman fought that way. They fought campaigns; they fought to crush the enemy, and to end the war, to destroy his will to fight and resist, They turned the tenor of the war toward total war.

True, Grant had never yet fought such a brilliant adversary as Lee, nor had he fought much on the scale of the battles in Virginia. But, though victory did not come quickly in Virginia, as it had elsewhere, Grant was no less dogged and determined to fight it through to the defeat of his adversary. From early May through the middle of June, Grant fought a series of battles with Lee in the futile attempt to take Richmond. They fought the Battle of the Wilderness, at Spotsylvania, Cold Harbor, and finally at Petersburg. Grant's losses were frightening; over a one-month span, he lost—killed, wounded, and captured—60,000 men, a number equal to the whole of Lee's army. Yet Grant fought on, conscious that Lee could not replace his losses, and he could. However, when he failed to take Petersburg in mid-June, 1864, his army dug in and placed Lee's army under siege for the next 9 months, in a trench warfare prelude to World War I.

Meanwhile, Sherman had assembled an army of 100,000 men to begin his march into Georgia in May, 1864. General Joseph Johnston was now in command of the Confederate army opposing his march. Although several battles were fought along the way, Sherman moved resolutely toward Atlanta, and reached the outskirts on July 17. J. B. Hood replaced Johnston, but he could not hold out long, and Sherman's army occupied Atlanta on September 2. Rather than trying to prevent Sherman from moving on, Hood headed back toward Tennessee, hoping to cut the supply lines of the Union army and force Sherman to pursue him. It was to little avail. Sherman simply sent a portion of his army under the command of General Thomas to deal with Hood. They met at the Battle of Nashville in mid-December, and Hood's army was virtually destroyed.

Meanwhile, the main portion of Sherman's army remained at Atlanta until the middle of November. As it marched out of Atlanta on its famous march through Georgia to Savannah, the city was burned. This was the scene as described by a reporter:

> On Sunday night a kind of long streak of light . . . marked the line of march and the burning depots, stores, and bridges in the train of the army. . . . "The streets" were soon in one fierce sheet of flame, houses were falling on all sides, and fiery flakes of cinders were whirled about. Men plunged into the houses, broke windows and doors with their muskets, dragging out armfuls of clothes, dressing themselves with some, and flinging the rest into the fire. Occasionally shells exploded, excited men rushed through the choking atmosphere to escape the ruin. At a distance the burning city seemed overshadowed by a cloud of black smoke. The sun looked like a blood-red

ball of fire; and the air for miles around felt oppressive and intolerable.[120]

Sherman's army was unopposed on its 300-mile march to Savannah. It cut a 60-mile wide swath of destruction along the way, living off what could be taken along the way, burning, pillaging, and destroying as it went. Railroad tracks were systematically torn from the crossties, heated, and twisted so thoroughly that they could not be restored to use. Cotton gins, the symbol of Southern rebellion, were wrecked and burned as a rule. But any- and everything might be, and sometimes was, taken or destroyed. As a contemporary newspaper reported:

> Dead horses, cows, sheep, hogs, chickens, corn, wheat, cotton, books, paper, broken vehicles, coffee-mills, and fragments of nearly every species of property that adorned the beautiful farms of this county, strew the wayside. . . . The Yankees entered the house of my next door neighbor, an old man of over three score years, and tore up his wife's clothes and bedding, trampling her bonnet on the floor, and robbing the house and pantry of nearly everything of value.[121]

Nor was the March through Georgia the worst. In January, Sherman headed north through South Carolina, the very seat of rebellion. Town after town was put to the torch, and the capital, Columbia, was burned as well.

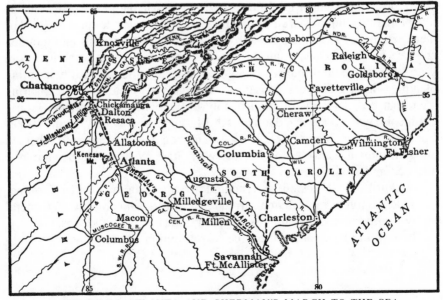

CAPTURE OF ATLANTA AND SHERMAN'S MARCH TO THE SEA

There was method in Sherman's apparent madness. He meant, as he said, to demonstrate the impotence of the Confederate government to protect its people and property. He meant, too, to destroy the will of the South to resist and to remove the means for it to do so. Nor was Sherman alone in permitting or decreeing the destruction of property. Armies had wrought destruction in many parts of the South. The Shenandoah Valley of Virginia was the scene in 1864 of vigorous contests between Union and Confederate cavalry. Grant ordered General Sheridan to destroy the resistance there by laying the countryside bare, and it was done rather thoroughly.

Lee was finally appointed commanding general of all Confederate armies in February, 1865. Unfortunately, for the South, there were no longer any large armies to command. The South was now broken, divided, cut apart, and all but conquered. Lee restored Joseph E. Johnston to command what army he could muster to oppose Sherman as best he could in North Carolina. But the days of Lee's own army were now numbered, as the long war of attrition had taken its toll in its thinning ranks. In late March, Lee made his last two attempts to break the Union lines. He was outnumbered three to one, and the efforts failed. He withdrew his forces from Petersburg on April 2, and abandoned the effort to defend Richmond. Jefferson Davis set out for the lower South with such of his cabinet as would follow him, still exhorting the armies to fight on. Lee tried to break through to get to rail transportation but he was cut off by Sheridan's cavalry. His army was reduced now to little more than 25,000 men with rations for only a few days, and unable to get away.

Lee surrendered his army on April 9, 1865 to Grant at Appomatox Courthouse. Dressed in his finest uniform, immaculate in appearance, he rode to the meeting on his striking white horse, Traveler, to meet Grant. His men were paroled, his officers allowed to keep their sidearms and mounts, and Lee made only one request: that his common soldiers be permitted to keep such horses and mules as they had to enable them to do their spring planting. Grant graciously consented. Lee bade his men farewell, assuring them that they had finally yielded only to overwhelming numbers.

Lincoln was assassinated on April 14, gunned down by John Wilkes Booth, while watching a play. The assassination plot encompassed others in the government as well, for Secretary of State William H. Seward was attacked and wounded.

On April 18, Johnston surrendered to Sherman in North Carolina. Confederate forces in Alabama surrendered May 4, and on May 26 General Kirby Smith surrendered for his force in Texas at New Orleans.

The fighting was ended; the time of retribution was at hand.

Chapter 9
Reconstruction

The future condition of the conquered power depends on the will of the conqueror. They must come in as new States or come in as conquered provinces.
—Thaddeus Stevens, 1865

The acts of Congress in question are not only objectionable for their assumption of ungranted power, but many of their provisions are in conflict with the direct prohibitions of the Constitution. . . . [T]he system of measures established by these acts of Congress does totally subvert and destroy . . . the substance of republican government in the ten States to which they apply. It binds them hand and foot in absolute slavery, and subjects them to a strange and hostile power, more unlimited and more likely to be abused than any other now known among civilized men.
—Andrew Johnson, 1867

. . . State rights were exalted and the nation was humbled. . . . Anything for slavery was constitutional. Vain are all our victories, if this terrible rule is not reversed. . . . This will be the crowning victory of the war. Beyond all question the true rule under the national Constitution . . . is that anything for human rights is constitutional.
—Charles Sumner, 1869

Chronology

July, 1865—Johnson's Reconstruction Proclamation.

December (4), 1865—Congress rejects Southern representatives.

December (18), 1865—13th Amendment Ratified.

April, 1866—Civil Rights Act.

December, 1866—*Ex parte Milligan* (Supreme Court decision).

1867—First Reconstruction Act.

March–May, 1868—Impeachment Proceedings against Johnson.

November, 1868—Grant elected President.

1869—''Black Friday.''

1870—Ku Klux Klan Acts.

1871—Exposure of the Tweed Ring.

1872—Exposure of Credit Mobilier.

1873—Panic of 1873.

1875—Resumption of Specie Payments.

1876—Impeachment of Belknap.

1877—Hayes becomes President (End of Military Reconstruction).

Reconstruction was a sorry episode in American history. Perhaps, it would be more accurate to say that Reconstruction *is*, not *was*, a sorry episode, for the animus behind Reconstruction was revived in the 1950s and 1960s, and is still very much at work at present. But let that wait, for the better part of a hundred years separates the two episodes. The word "reconstruction" was first used in the early 1860s to refer to the reuniting of the United States. That is, it referred to the means by which the Southern states could become a part of the Union once again. But in the course of Reconstruction it became a "remaking" of the South, and that by military force at the height of the effort. It was this continued and extensive use of force that made Reconstruction such a sorry episode.

Historians usually treat the period of Reconstruction as falling mainly between April, 1865—Lee's surrender and Lincoln's assassination—and April, 1877—the removal of the last occupying troops from the South, a twelve-year period. It is not that neat, of course. The beginnings of Reconstruction go back to 1862, at the latest, and it was well into the 1880s before the effort largely ground to a halt (only to be revived much later, as already noted). In one sense, much of Reconstruction was a continuation of the Civil War and could be fruitfully viewed in that way. There was no treaty of peace, as there had been no declaration of war, and the South had no definite terms by which the exertion of force could be removed. In any case, the seeds of Reconstruction lay in the justification of the war, in the shift in the course of the war to make it a crusade against slavery, and in the war's becoming a total war. Sherman's destructive march through Georgia was a prelude to a total attempt to make over the South.

Lincoln had attempted to justify the war on the grounds that secession was unconstitutional. The Union was perpetual, indissoluble, he held, and the Constitution provided no means whereby a state might withdraw or secede. He was certainly right that there was no provision in the Constitution describing how and under what conditions a state might secede. But President Buchanan had been equally right in declaring that the Constitution did not authorize the use of force upon a state. The question of using force on states had come up several times in the Constitutional Convention, and it was rejected each time, mainly because, as it was argued, to use force on a state would mean war. It was agreed that the power of the United States would be used on individuals (and combinations of them), not upon states as entities. Thus, if the states had acted unconstitutionally in seceding, an equally good case could be made that the United States government acted unconstitutionally in making war on them.

Of course, that was not the official viewpoint. Officially, Lincoln declared the people of the Confederacy to be in a state of rebellion, and he acted on the assumption that both the state governments and the Confederacy were illegal. In his last public address, April 11, 1865, President Lincoln described the situation this way: "Unlike a case of war between independent nations, *there is no authorized organ for us to treat with*—no one man has authority to give up the rebellion for any other man. We simply must begin with and mould from disorganized and discordant elements."[122] This may have been consistent with Lincoln's view all along, but it certainly opened up a large can of worms. If each person was on his own and there were no state governments or other organizations with which to deal, then the people of the South were at the mercy of the federal government to be dealt with as it would. And given the animosities aroused during the war, the reformist zeal of the abolitionists, and the lack of restraint shown by the Union armies in the last stages of the fighting, the way would appear to be open for a massive effort to remake the South, i.e., for wholesale Reconstruction.

Lincoln did try to gather up some of the worms and put them back in the can as he proceeded with his speech. He noted that he had received a letter in which he was taxed for not having made up his mind whether the seceded states were in or out of the Union. He indicated that he had intentionally avoided a public statement on the question. He thought the question raised involved a pernicious abstraction. "We all agree," he said, "that the seceded States, so called, are out of their proper practical relation with the Union, and that the sole object of the Government, civil and military, in regard to these States, is to again get them into their proper practical relation. I believe that it is not only possible, but in fact easier, to do this without deciding or even considering whether those States have ever been out of the Union, than with it."[123] Andrew Johnson, President after Lincoln's assassination, said the next year, "Now that the rebellion has been put down . . . there is an issue made that the States are still out of the Union, which is precisely what the rebels undertook to effect. . . . The States were never out of the Union."[124]

Actually, neither Lincoln nor anyone else could square what had taken place with the Constitution. Undoubtedly, he hoped to get the states firmly within the Union as soon as possible. He had been and was conciliatory toward the South. In his Second Inaugural Address, March 4, 1865, Lincoln used the famous words: "With malice toward none, with charity for all, with firmness in the right as God gives us to see the right, let us strive to finish the work we are in, to bind up the nation's wounds. . . .'' But somebody had sowed the wind—whether the Confederate states in seceding, the Union in deciding to use force to preserve the Union, the Confederacy in resisting for so long, Lincoln in issuing the Emancipation Proclamation, the Union in departing from the Constitution at various points in the course of the war—and the South reaped the whirlwind. The whirlwind was Reconstruction, and the way was prepared for it, however unwittingly, by steps taken during the war.

Devastation at the South

Indeed, the South had already reaped one whirlwind before Reconstruction had hardly begun. The destruction wrought by the Union armies, particularly in the last year and a half of the war, had left much of the South in ruins. Many cities—Atlanta, Columbia, parts of Richmond, and others— had been virtually destroyed. Long stretches of what had once been railroads were no more, their rail ripped up and bent beyond use. Numerous houses had been burned, both in cities and through the countryside. Indeed, so common was the sight of bare chimneys standing where once there had been houses that it gave rise to the poor joke that the South was the only place in the world where people built chimneys without attaching houses to them. Fences were frequently down, cotton gins burned or dismantled, cattle lost, strayed, or stolen, and plows burned or broken.

General Sherman described the ruin and desolation in the South this way:

> Look to the South, and you who went with me through that land can best say if they too have not been fearfully punished. Mourning in every household, desolation written in broad characters across the whole face of this country, cities in ashes and fields laid waste, their commerce gone, their system of labor annihilated and destroyed. Ruin, poverty and distress everywhere, and now pestilence adding the very cap-sheath to their stack of miseries; her proud men begging for pardon and appealing for permission to raise food for their children; her five million of slaves free and their value lost to their former owners forever.[125]

Many plantations, homes, and other buildings had been sacked of their treasures by Union soldiers. A reporter described one such situation in the wake of Sherman's army: ''. . . came up to a retired plantation house, just set on fire. The soldiers were rushing off on every side with their pillage. An old lady and her two grandchildren were in the yard alarmed and helpless. The flames and smoke were shooting through the windows. The old lady rushed from one to another beseeching them at least to save her furniture.

They only enjoyed the whole thing, including her distress. . . ."[126] The extent of treasures taken was so great that Southerners long claimed that "the houses of volunteer officers, and chaplains especially, in almost every New England and Northern villages" had "stolen plate, pictures, and even wearing apparel . . . proudly displayed as 'rebel trophies,' or 'confiscated' property'."[127]

Many people—indeed, virtually all who had possessed any wealth—were financially ruined at the end of the war. The South was virtually bereft of capital. Confederate currency was worthless. Bonds issued by the Confederate States of America were worthless, and destined never to be redeemed. State bonds, too, were often next to worthless. Many private stocks and bonds, such as those of railroads, would ordinarily bring only a fraction of their face value. The most extensive capital investment of all, that in slaves, vanished with the emancipation of the slaves. Land, cotton, and other goods were often confiscated or taken in lieu of taxes. A South Carolinian, Henry William Ravenel, described in his diary both the general and his personal loss of property, as of May 22, 1865:

> We begin now to realize the ruin to property which the war has entailed upon us. All classes and conditions of men will suffer who had property, except the small farmers who owned no negroes. Confederate securities, I consider a total loss. Bank stock, confederation and private bonds, are all more or less dependent for their availability upon Confederate securities, & upon the value of negro property; both of which are lost. . . . The only money now in possession of our people is coin in small quantities which had been hoarded through the war, & some bills of the local banks. There will be but little means of increasing this amount for some time to come, as provisions are scarce, & the cotton has been mostly burnt, captured or sold. The financial prospect is a gloomy one, & there will be much distress before our conditions can improve.[128]

Actually, Ravenal underestimated the extent of his poverty and distress, along with that of others. He clung as long as he could to the remnants of his former life, for he was a man of middling years, and it is difficult to change. But one by one, he had to give up virtually everything that remained from his former station. He discovered, too, that few things, not even land, would bring anything like their former value in such market as existed. The decline in wealth relative to the other states is shown in the following figures for per capita wealth in the former Confederate states. "Louisiana had been second in the nation in per capita wealth in 1860. By 1880 she would be in thirty-seventh place. South Carolina dropped in the same twenty years from third to forty-fifth in per capita wealth; Mississippi from fifth to forty-sixth, Georgia from eighth to fortieth, Texas from ninth to thirty-sixth, Alabama from sixteenth to forty-fourth, Arkansas from nineteenth to forty-third, and Virginia from twentieth to thirty-fifth.''[129] Much of the south has not recovered its earlier financial position in the United States economy from that day to this.

But beyond the material destruction and deprivation resulting from the war, there was a spiritual devastation wrought by defeat and what became known as ''the lost cause.'' In one sense, at least, the North had suffered as well as the South, if not proportionately as much. That was in the loss of young men in battle, to disease, and those who suffered wounds, such as loss of limbs, from which there is no ultimate recovery. Actually, the Union lost more men than did the Confederacy, but in terms of relative population, not nearly so many, so that Southern families suffered more generally the loss of sons, fathers, brothers, and uncles in the war. But the material destruction and deprivation caused by armies was confined almost entirely to the South, since the war was fought there almost entirely. Even more, the spiritual malaise following the war was entirely Southern. The North was victorious; the South was utterly defeated.

Visitors to the South frequently commented on the sense of hopelessness that pervaded the South. A traveler from Chattanooga to Atlanta says that he did not see a smile on a single face along his journey. Some Southerners gave voice to the disorientation, to the grief over the lost cause, to the feeling of not knowing where to go from defeat. A man in Mississippi wrote his brother, ''Our fields everywhere lie untilled. Naked chimneys and charred ruins all over the land mark the spots where happy homes, the seats of refinement and elegance, once stood. Their former inhabitants wander in

poverty and exile, wherever chance or charity affords them shelter or food. Childless old age, widows, and helpless orphans beggared and hopeless, are everywhere.''[130] A former slave described the situation of his former master as he left the old plantation: ''The massa had three boys to go to war but there wasn't one to come home. All the children he had was killed. Massa, he lost all his money, and the house soon began dropping away to nothing. Us niggers one by one left the old place, and the last time I seed the home plantation I was a standing on a hill. I looked back on it for the last time through a patch of scrub pines, and it looked so lonely. There wasn't but one person in sight, the massa. He was a-setting in a wicker chair in the yard looking out over a small field of cotton and corn. There was four crosses in the graveyard in the side lawn where he was a-setting. The fourth one was his wife. . . .''[131]

Some expressed their disconsolate feelings in poignant poetry. So it was with this writer in his farewell to the Stars and Bars of the Confederacy:

> Furl that Banner, softly, slowly!
> Treat it gently—it is holy—
>   For it droops above the dead.
> Touch it not—unfurl it never,
> Let it droop there, furled forever,
>   For its people's hopes are dead.[132]

There were those who believed that the South had suffered enough. There was no doubt that the Confederacy had been defeated, and that those who had fought and survived were more than ready to stop fighting. Desertions had decimated the ranks of the Confederate armies in the last months of the war. Once the generals had surrendered, men laid down their arms and as quickly as they could made their way to their homes. What most wanted and hoped for was peace and order in which to take up their lives and make a living as best they could. That the slaves were freed, there was no doubt, and Southerners were prepared to acquiesce in it, though there was still hope for compensation.

But in many ways the worst was yet to come. The trials of Reconstruction lay ahead. Of these days, an Alabamian wrote in 1890:

> The days during which the reconstruction governments ruled in the several Southern states were the darkest that ever shrouded any portion of our country.
>
> The slaughter and sacrifices during our great civil war were terrible indeed, but those dark days were lighted by the shining valor of the patriot soldier; the storm clouds were gilded with glory.
>
> But there was in the scenes of [Reconstruction] . . . nothing but wretchedness and humiliation, and shame, and crime begetting crime. . . .[133]

There were those in the North ready to forgive and forget, eager for reunion, but there were others who believed that the South must be not only broken but also changed, and changed radically. Thus, there was reconstruction.

Presidential Reconstruction

Congress was not in session when the war ended and would not normally meet (and did not) until December, 1865. Thus, if steps were to be taken to restore the states to their place in the Union the initiative would lie with the President. Most likely, that is the way Lincoln would have wanted it, and Johnson made no move to call Congress into special session. Indeed, Lincoln had already made tentative moves toward bringing several states back into the Union well before the fighting was over. The record is not clear as to whether or not Lincoln had an overall plan for all of the states. In his last messages, he had indicated a willingness to be flexible as to the terms under which states could resume their places. Nothing that he had done suggests that he had in mind any extensive program of reconstruction. Probably, it would be better to think of both his acts and those of Johnson after him as "resumption" rather than "reconstruction."

At any rate, Lincoln had issued a "Proclamation of Amnesty and Reconstruction" in 1863. He offered amnesty to those who had "rebelled" against the United States who would take an oath of allegiance to the United States and agree to support the government. There were some exceptions: notably, high ranking military and naval officers of the Confederacy, civil and diplomatic officers of the Confederacy, former United States members of Congress who joined the Confederate effort, and army and navy officers of the United States who resigned their commissions to take part in the Confederacy. His plan for bringing states back into the Union is known as the "Ten Per Cent Plan." When as many as 10 per cent of those who had voted in the presidential election of 1860 within a state should take the oath of loyalty, the state could form a government and begin to act.

Louisiana and Arkansas complied with President Lincoln's terms and formed "loyal" governments. However, Congress rejected the members they elected to Congress, and they were not by their acts restored to the Union. In July, 1864, Congress passed the Wade-Davis Bill setting forth much more complex and harder terms for readmission of the states. In addition, the bill proclaimed the emancipation of the slaves, which Lincoln believed to be beyond the constitutional authority of Congress. He pocket vetoed the bill, but issued a proclamation to the effect that if any state wished to comply with its terms, he would work with it. None did so. That is how matters stood when Lincoln was assassinated. He was still making a case for his program a couple of days before the end of his life.

Andrew Johnson
(1808–1875)

Johnson was the 17th President of the United States, and the third to succeed to that office after the death of the President. He was born in North Carolina but settled in Tennessee as a young man. Although Johnson never attended any school, he managed to learn to read and write as a youth and received help from his wife in extending his learning. He worked as a tailor for a while, but before long he became involved in local politics. From there, he went on to state politics, and in 1843 he began a stint in the House of Representatives. He was a Democrat and a Southerner, but he never had much sympathy with slavery or slaveholders. Johnson did not approve of secession, and when Tennessee left the Union he remained in the Senate. Lincoln named him provisional governor of his state in 1862 and his running mate on a Union ticket in 1864. His state returned him to the Senate in 1875, but he died shortly afterward.

It was widely believed that had Lincoln lived Reconstruction would have been accomplished much more easily and with less disruption of the South. Certainly, his plan, so far as it had been expressed, was the mildest proposed, and it did not undertake to punish the South. But it is only conjecture that Lincoln could have succeeded in overcoming congressional resistance or that he would have stuck to his program in the face of determined congressional resistance. One thing is certain: he was at odds with Congress over reconstruction at the time of his assassination. Anything more would be speculation.

Undoubtedly Andrew Johnson had two difficulties in dealing with a Congress dominated by Northern Republicans that Lincoln did not have. He was a Southerner from Tennessee, and he was a Democrat, elected on a Union ticket with the Republican Lincoln. Even so, there was no reason to doubt his loyalty to the Union; it had been tested by fire and proven in ways that most politicians in the North had not. When his state had seceded from the Union, he had refused to go along with it. Moreover, he had remained in his Senate seat until 1862, when Lincoln appointed him provisional governor of that portion of Tennessee under Union control.

It should be said, too, that some of those who were for dealing with the South much more firmly than Lincoln was doing believed that Johnson would do just that. The *National Anti-Slavery Standard,* commenting on Lincoln's assassination, said, "We believe that this cruel calamity will be blest by a sterner line of treatment of the slaveholding rebels than the humane and generous heart of Lincoln liked to present."[134] Johnson had given cause for people to believe that he would be harsh in his treatment of the South. He was known to despise the planter class and to believe that those who had led the rebellion were traitors. As late as 1868, he wrote that "I shall go to my grave with the firm belief that Davis, Cobb, Toombs and a few others of the arch-conspirators and traitors should have been tried, convicted and hanged for treason. . . ."[135]

As it turned out, however, Johnson was his own man as President, and while the program which he followed did have some sterner features than the one Lincoln had advanced, in the main he followed Lincoln's direction. As already noted, Johnson held that the states had never been outside the Union. Therefore, they did not have to be brought back into the Union, only to form governments that were loyal so that they could take up their place within the United States. He acted as quickly as he could to make it possible during 1865, while Congress was still recessed, to get the states organized for resuming their position in the Union. On May 29, he issued an Amnesty Proclamation, pardoning most of those who had participated in what he termed the "late rebellion." It was very similar to the earlier proclamation issued by Lincoln, excepting all of those from its terms that Lincoln had done, requiring the taking of an oath of loyalty, but creating some new classes who were not automatically pardoned. Perhaps, the most significant new class excepted was those who had participated in the Confederate undertaking who had property valued at $20,000 or more. Those who were not automatically pardoned (by taking the oath, of course) could, however, apply to the President for one, and many such pardons were issued during the year.

In those states which did not yet have provisional governors or been authorized to organize governments, Johnson appointed such governors and instructed them to have conventions held in their states, the members of which would be elected by loyal citizens. These conventions would amend their constitutions so as to conform with the United States Constitution, ratify the 13th Amendment abolishing slavery, revoke the ordinances of secession, and repudiate all debts contracted for fighting the war, etc. By December, 1865, all the former Confederate states, except Texas (which did not complete its compliance until April, 1866) had governments in operation, and had elected Senators and Representatives to Congress.

When Congress met in December, however, Johnson's efforts were brought to a halt. None of the Senators or Representatives from the former Confederate states were admitted to the respective houses of Congress. There was never any doubt the houses were empowered by the Constitution to determine the qualifications of their members, and if one or the other houses determines that those who have been chosen by the electorate are not qualified, there is no appeal. The President could not make Congress admit members which it refused, and since Johnson could not get Congress to admit those elected by the former Confederate states, he could not restore them to their place in the Union. A Committee of Fifteen Senators and Representatives was appointed to deal with questions of Reconstruction, including the admission of their representatives to Congress. Over the next year, they admitted only the delegation from Tennessee.

Congress waged a contest with the President from December, 1865 to 1866 over which should reconstruct the South. Actually, however, Congress was far from being united in the contest during that year, if it ever was. The leaders in the contest, and they were very nearly united, were the Radical Republicans. Charles Sumner was the outstanding spokesman for the Radicals in the Senate, and Thaddeus Stevens was the leader in the House. Both men held that the Congress alone had the power to lay down the rules for reconstructing the South. Sumner held that the states had committed suicide by their acts of secession and that they had reverted to territorial status. Stevens, on the other hand, maintained that they were conquered provinces. In either case, both maintained Congress must set the terms for

Thaddeus Stevens
(1792–1868)

Stevens was the leader of Radical Reconstruction (1866–1868), during the crucial period when Congress took control. He was born in Vermont, educated at Dartmouth, and practiced law at Gettysburg, Pennsylvania. He first went to Congress as a Whig in 1849, but he became a Republican and helped to organize the party in Pennsylvania. Stevens was an abolitionist, in effect, if not in name, during most of his career, and he was intent upon making over the South after the war. As Chairman of the House Ways and Means Committee during the war, he played a critical role in war finance. Much of Radical Reconstruction can be attributed to, as well as blamed on, him.

their admission to the Union. As Stevens said, "They must come in as new states or remain as conquered provinces. Congress . . . is the only power that can act in the matter."[136] The crucial point they were making was that Congress must act, not the President, to re-establish the Confederate states.

Undoubtedly, two developments within the Southern states during 1865 greatly disturbed the Radicals in Congress and their followers. One development was that most of the states enacted what were called Black Codes governing the employment and work of Negroes. When the slaves were freed, they were footloose and fancy free, so to speak, and many may have envisioned the great life that was to follow now that they were free. At the same time, however, they had no visible means of making a living, especially if they left the plantations and farms to which they were attached. At first, many of them became camp followers of Union armies. Generally speaking, most were illiterate; they might or might not have marketable skills, and they had little or no property. The United States government established a Freedmen's Bureau in early 1865 to protect the rights of Negroes in the South, and to provide medical care and food for them at first.

The Black Codes, however, were attempts by the state governments to define the position of the freed Negro. While codes varied from state to state, in general Blacks were treated differently from whites. No state provided for any of them to vote. Johnson suggested to the governor of Mississippi that it would be a good idea to "extend the elective franchise to all persons of color who can read the Constitution of the United States in English and write their names, and to all persons of color who own real estate valued at not less than $250 and pay taxes thereon. . . ,"[137] but no action was taken on it. Vagrancy laws were usually quite strict, and Mississippi, for example, provided that after a specific date those Blacks who were unemployed would be put out under contract to white employers. Racial intermarriage was forbidden, and, though Blacks were permitted to sue in the courts on their own behalf, they could not testify in criminal cases against whites.

These Black Codes aroused considerable opposition in the North. It should be noted that at the time they were adopted they were not contrary to the laws or the Constitution of the United States; some of their provisions did not differ much from rules Union army officers had adopted for Blacks, nor were vagrancy laws any harsher than those in some states in the North. The states of the former Confederacy had no reason to doubt, either, that they had full authority to legislate regarding such matters. Even so, the Black Codes were the occasion of acrimonious comment from the North. The Chicago *Tribune* declared, "We tell the white men of Mississippi that men of the North will convert the State of Mississippi into a frog pond before they will allow such laws to disgrace one foot of soil in which the bones of our soldiers sleep. . . ." Charles Sumner thundered, "Strike at the Black Codes as you have already struck at the Slave Codes. There is nothing to choose between them."[138]

Alexander H. Stephens
(1812–1883)

Stephens was Vice-President of the confederate States of America. He was born
in Georgia, graduated from what became
the University of Georgia, and taught
school until he was admitted to the bar.
Elected to the state legislature in 1836, he
was active in politics for most of the rest
of his life. Before the Civil War Stephens
was usually a Whig, and, though he opposed secession, he left the Union with
his state and served the Confederacy.
Indeed, he was the conscience of the
Confederacy, for if secession was to be
justified by a strict construction of the
Constitution, then the Confederacy must
strictly adhere to its own constitution.
This position often embarrassed President
Davis in his conduct of the war. His
study, *A Constitutional View of the Late
War,* is considered to be the best statement of the Southern position. Although
Stephens was imprisoned for a short while
after the war, he returned to Congress in
1873 and served there for most of the rest
of his life.

The second development which exasperated vocal elements in the North
was that a goodly number of ex-Confederates, some who had been in high
position, were elected to Congress in the first election. Alexander H.
Stephens, Vice-President of the Confederacy was elected to the Senate from
Georgia; Mississippi elected a man who had been a general in the Confederate army; and North Carolina chose a man who had been in the
congress of the Confederacy. Four former Confederate generals were
elected to the House and as many as eight men who had reached the rank of
colonel. There should have been no surprise that Southerners would elect to
office men whom they considered leaders, and that certainly included many
who had served in the Confederacy. But that was not the angle from which
Radicals looked at it. "The Government has thrown open the gates of
political power to unrepentant rebels," in the opinion of *The Independent.*[139]

But there was much more behind the congressional rejection of the President's efforts to restore the Southern states than these developments. There was, first of all, a desire for vengeance against Southern whites that began to grow and spread after the war. The Southern leaders especially must be punished. Senator John Sherman of Ohio said, "We should not only brand the leading rebels with infamy, but the whole rebellion should wear the badge of the penitentiary, so that for this generation at least, no man who has taken part in it would dare to justify . . . it."[140] Any signs that the South did not remain repentant were intolerable.

Second, the South must be made over, changed, reformed, in a word, reconstructed. James Russell Lowell, the poet, thought the South should be "Americanized." "Is it not time," he asked, "that these men be transplanted at least into the nineteenth century, and, if they cannot be suddenly Americanized, made to understand something of the country which was too good for them. . . ."[141] A religious paper declared that the North would have to "teach the South line upon line, precept upon precept, by military garrisons, by Bureau courts, by Congregational churches, by Northern settlers, by constitutional amendments, by Christian missionaries, by free schools, lectures, newspapers and reading rooms, what be the first principles of social order, political eminence, moral worth and industrial success."[142] Thaddeus Stevens declared, "It is intended to revolutionize their principles and feelings . . . , to work a radical reorganization in Southern institutions, habits, and manners."[143]

The guiding aim of much of this proposed effort to make the South over was the achievement of Negro equality with the whites. Indeed, they were perhaps to be made superior politically in the South. Stevens said that the "true doctrine of reconstruction is that defeated rebels have no civil or political rights . . ., and that all loyal men without regard to race or color, are entitled to equal rights as citizens."[144] Chief Justice Salmon P. Chase gave it as his opinion that "If all the people feel as I do you will not have to wait long for equal rights at the ballot box. . . ."[145]

How sincere the Radical Republicans might have been about punishing the South or remaking it is at least questionable. But there is no reason to doubt that they meant business about the third point. It is this: they were determined to maintain the continued dominance of the Republican Party in power for as long as possible. This certainly underlay the rejection of the Southern nominees for Congress. The Republican Party was a sectional party; it had no following among voters in the South. If Negroes should be fully counted, rather than according to the three-fifths rule, the South would gain in electoral votes and representation in the House. Even without that, the South had often dominated politically before the Civil War and might well do so again in alliance with northern Democrats. Even in 1865, the Radicals might have lost their control had the Southerners been admitted to Congress, though the Republicans would have had a majority.

Salmon P. Chase
(1808–1873)

Courtesy National Archives

Chase was born in New Hampshire, graduated from Dartmouth, studied law, and began the practice of it in Ohio. Although Southern sympathy was widespread in Cincinnati, where Chase settled, he was an outspoken opponent of slavery, and gained fame as a lawyer in defending fugitive slaves. Chase shifted his political alliances several times, from the Whigs to the Liberty Party to the Free Soilers, until he found a home in the Republican Party, which he helped to organize in 1854. In the Senate, Chase opposed the Compromise of 1850, the Kansas-Nebraska Act, and any effort to expand slavery. He left the Senate in 1855 to become the first Republican governor of Ohio. Lincoln called on him to be Secretary of the Treasury during most of the war, and Chase was instrumental in establishing the national banking system and the issuance of the Greenbacks. In 1864, he was appointed Chief Justice of the Supreme Court, a position he held until his death.

In any case, the radicals made no secret of the fact that they intended to use Reconstruction so as to assure Republican dominance for the future. Thaddeus Stevens held that the Southern states must not be readmitted to the Union until a constitutional amendment had been adopted "so as to secure perpetual ascendancy to the party of the Union . . . ,"[146] To that end, those who had supported the Confederacy must be denied the vote, at least for a time. This was one of the prime purposes of the first version of the 14th Amendment, which was approved by Congress in 1866 and sent to the states. It was sent to the Southern states for ratification as well, though how states which were "defunct" or were dead because they had committed suicide could be permitted to participate in amending the Constitution was never made clear. The Radical leadership was hardly in a mood to be restrained by reason, in any case. None of the states which had been in the Confederacy ratified the amendment, and it was not adopted at this time. Southern rejection of the amendment only increased the determination of the Radicals to put the South in its place.

The contest between President Johnson and the Radicals in Congress became more and more heated until the Congressional elections in the fall of 1866. Johnson was as determined to stand his ground and have the Southern states fully restored to the Union as the Radicals were to take over Reconstruction. When Congress passed a bill in February adding to the powers of the Freedmen's Bureau, Johnson vetoed it on the grounds that it gave unconstitutional powers to the military. The leaders in Congress mustered enough support by July to pass the bill over his veto. Congress passed a Civil Rights bill in April which Johnson also vetoed on the grounds of its unconstitutionality. This, too, was passed over his veto. The President took to the railroad in August and September to try to get congressional candidates of his persuasion elected. His speaking tour was preceded by a National Union Convention in Philadelphia, at which those favorable to the President's program rallied behind him. However, both this effort and the speaking tour failed to turn the tide in the congressional elections. In several cities, the President was baited, provoked, and heckled intolerably. It was a sorry campaign in which Johnson was charged with being traitorous, insolent and a drunken brute. The Republicans won handily, and, in the absence of the former Confederate states, had two-thirds majorities in both houses of Congress. Thereafter, the Radicals were in the saddle.

Congressional Reconstruction

Congress now strove to take complete control of Reconstruction, and, in effect, the whole government. Ultimately, the constitutional powers of Congress are greater than those of either (or perhaps both) of the other two branches. But ordinarily there is a counterweight to the exercise of this power other than the other two branches. Congress is divided into two houses, independent of each other, and either house may negate any action by the other. Moreover, the members of each branch are independently chosen and may vote as they will, subject finally to their own electorates. To put it another way, power is ordinarily dispersed among the members, especially in the Senate, so as to make any extended and concerted action by Congress exceedingly difficult. The Radicals overcame these difficulties, or most of them, from late 1865 into the early 1870s. A Radical cabal (combination) controlled the actions of Congress most of the time over these years. The cabal cut across the lines separating the House and the Senate with the Committee of Fifteen, composed of members from both houses. The Radical cabal was dominated by such men as Thaddeus Stevens, George W. Julian, Benjamin F. Wade, Charles Sumner, Henry Wilson, George S. Boutwell, and Benjamin F. Butler.

At its core, Radical Republicanism arose out of the abolitionist fervor which preceded the war and had its roots in the reformism and perfectionism of the 1840s. The strength of the Radicals lay in the fact that they had a purpose and a mission, a cause. Theirs was a righteous cause, in their opinion, to forge a new Union, to avenge the Union men who had died in the war, to punish the South, to not only free the slaves but also elevate them to a condition of equality with others, and to remake the South so that the rebellious spirit could never again arise there. Slavery had been a crime and a sin; the South must repent and be converted. Anyone who opposed the efforts of the Radicals was a Southern sympathizer, wanted Union soldiers to have died in vain, was not a true Republican, and supported treason. Democrats were denounced as being the party of disunion. The Radicals intimidated other Republicans, browbeat Democrats, beset the President and eventually tried to remove Johnson from office, and hamstrung the courts. Thus, they ruled.

Once they had consolidated their position, the Radicals took over Reconstruction. In early March, 1867, Congress passed the First Reconstruction Act. It declared that the existing state governments, except for Tennessee, in the former Confederacy were illegal. The ten states involved were divided into five military districts, and the President was ordered to send military forces to each under the command of a general. Responsibility for maintaining order was placed under the authority of the

Benjamin F. Wade
(1800–1878)

Wade was born in Massachusetts, migrated to Ohio, studied law, and began the practice of it. He served in the Senate from 1851 to 1869, first as a Whig and then as a Republican. He was an anti-slavery man from the beginning and emerged as a radical during the Civil War. During the war, he opposed Lincoln's go-slow policy on slavery, favored the immediate emancipation and arming of the slaves, the execution of the Southern leaders, and confiscation of Confederate property. Wade was a bitter opponent of Johnson's reconstruction program as well and was a leader in thrusting for thorough going reconstruction of the South. As president *pro tem* of the Senate, he voted for the removal of Johnson from office, although he was in line to succeed him as President.

military, who were empowered to arrest, try, and enforce sentences against those convicted. The act prescribed that the voters of these states, voting without regard to race or color, should choose delegates to a constitutional convention, which should frame a constitution to be submitted to the voters for their approval. When they had done so, and when they had approved the proposed 14th Amendment to the Constitution, they might then organize governments and take up their place in the Union.

Johnson vetoed the bill and sent to Congress a long list of particulars in which it violated the Constitution in a great variety of ways. It placed these peoples, Black and white, under military rule, Johnson pointed out, in time of peace, subjected them to military courts in violation of the Constitution, and forced people to act in certain ways in order to be permitted to govern themselves. "The negroes have not asked for the privilege of voting," he said; "the vast majority of them have no idea what it means. This bill not only thrusts it into their hands, but compels them, as well as the whites, to use it in a particular way."[147] No matter, the Radicals were hardly interested in the President's opinion, much less the provisions of the Constitution. They acted quickly to pass the measure over the veto. Late in March, Congress passed another reconstruction bill, providing in detail for registering voters by the military and completing the work of reconstruction. Johnson also vetoed it, and it was passed over his veto.

Despite other reconstruction acts which were supposed to clear up the matter of who was eligible to vote, it never was made entirely clear who was eligible. There was no doubt that many of the leaders in the secession and the war were ineligible, but how many others was uncertain. In the final analysis, who could and could not vote was left to military registrars, and their decisions were final. At any rate, Negro registered voters were in a majority in South Carolina, Florida, Alabama, Mississippi, and Louisiana. Of the total number registered, 627,000 were whites and 703,000 Blacks. In June, 1868, by an Omnibus Act, seven states—Alabama, Florida, Georgia, Louisiana, Arkansas, North Carolina, and South Carolina—were restored to the Union. However, after military forces were removed from Georgia, Negroes were expelled from the state legislature, and Georgia was removed from the Union and military occupation restored. Georgia, along with Mississippi, Texas, and Virginia, were all readmitted to the Union in the course of 1870. These four states were required to ratify the 15th Amendment as well as the 14th to attain readmission. How the Radicals could justify on constitutional grounds the counting of ratification of amendments by states which by their own logic were not in the Union remains a mystery to this day.

Meanwhile, the Radicals continued to work to discredit President Johnson and reduce his power over affairs as much as they could. On the same day—March 2, 1867—that the First Reconstruction Act was passed, Congress passed two bills curtailing the President's power. One was the Tenure of Office Act, which provided that cabinet members particularly (including the Postmaster General and Attorney General) might serve during the term of the President who had appointed them and could be removed from office during that time with the consent of the Senate. Johnson vetoed the measure on the grounds that by practice and precedent it had been established that the power of removal belonged to the President, but it was passed over his veto. On the same day, Congress attached to an appropriation bill a provision that the General of the Army could not be removed or assigned elsewhere without the consent of the Senate and requiring that all orders of the President or Secretary of War relating to military operations would have to go through that general. Although Johnson did not veto the bill, because of the appropriations, he did protest the interference with his powers as commander-in-chief, as well he might.

Johnson suspended Secretary of War Edwin M. Stanton in August, 1867. There was little doubt that Stanton was the Radicals' man in the cabinet, that he served, in effect, as a spy for the Radical leaders. Indeed, Stanton had not been above ignoring Lincoln's wishes, and he had even less reason to be loyal to Johnson. Stanton had used the army in the latter part of the war to take over churches of Southern whites and turn them over to Northern ministers of the same denomination. According to many in the Northern churches, Southerners and the ministers who supported them were sinners,

Edwin M. Stanton
(1814–1869)

Courtesy New York Historical Society

Stanton was best known as Secretary of War for Lincoln and Johnson, but he also served briefly as Attorney General under Buchanan. He was born in Ohio, graduated from Kenyon College, and became a lawyer. He was a Democrat up until the Civil War, was opposed both to Lincoln and the Republican platform, yet Lincoln appointed him to a cabinet position. As head of the war department, however, he became much more radical in his views. Stanton opposed Johnson's position on reconstruction and was closely allied with the Radicals in Congress. Although Johnson first suspended and then dismissed him from his post, he clung to his position with the support of Congress and the military. His obstinacy probably led to the impeachment proceedings against Johnson.

and until they had purged themselves of their sins they were unfit to preside over churches. Lincoln ordered the practice stopped, but it made little difference. When the Senate refused to give its approval to the suspension, Grant, who had been appointed in the interval, resigned, and Stanton took over once again as Secretary of War. In February, 1868, Johnson dismissed Stanton from office.

The Radicals, many of whom had been eager to impeach Johnson, believed that they now had their case. Johnson had violated the Tenure of Office Act. The House agreed by voting impeachment of Johnson on eleven charges, including violation of both the Tenure of Office and Command of the Army acts. The case then went to the Senate for trial before Chief Justice Salmon Chase in the spring of 1868. A Senate vote was taken first on the eleventh charge which was the most general. The vote was 35 for removal of Johnson from office on this count to 19 against. Since a two-thirds majority is required for conviction, it would have required the switch of one vote for the motion to carry. Votes were taken on two more of the charges, but when these also failed to get the required majorities, the remainder of the charges were dropped. Although Johnson had not been convicted of any wrongdoing neither had he been cleared resoundingly. He finished out the term, but he had little influence on events.

Constitutional Reconstruction

The Radicals made a shambles of the Constitution during their period of rule. Of that, there should be no doubt. The Civil War had fitted as readily into the Constitution as a round peg of the same size would fit into a square hole. There simply is no provision in the Constitution for the United States government to use force, i.e., make war, upon states. There are no provisions for the treatment of people within states when war is undertaken against them. And certainly there were no provisions in the Constitution for reconstructing states.

In any case, the Radicals ran roughshod over the Constitution for several years. Lincoln had maintained that the Union was indissoluble, that states could not secede from it. (The Supreme Court later ruled, in *Texas vs. White,* that this was the law.) Yet the Radicals denied to former Confederate states their place in the Union and, though they had no representation, proceeded to levy taxes upon the South. The slaves were freed well before a constitutional amendment was adopted; property was thus taken from the owners without compensation. (Lincoln had several times proposed that provision be made for compensation, but Congress did not concur.) Constitutional amendments were passed after, instead of before, the President or Congress had acted: to free the slaves, to disqualify leading Confederates, to induce the states to grant the vote to Blacks. In effect, martial law was imposed at various times without following the forms for doing so. Time and time again Congress overrode the most serious and weighty Constitutional objections raised by President Johnson.

What of the courts during these years? The first thing to note about that is that under the best of conditions it usually takes time to get a case before the courts, especially the Supreme Court on appeal. Sometimes, it takes years to get the best case before the Supreme Court. Meanwhile, a Congress determined to have its way can do a great deal of damage. For another thing, the courts were reluctant during these years to plunge into what were called "political" questions. For example, there were attempts to get the federal courts to enjoin Secretary Stanton from enforcing the reconstruction acts. The courts refused to accept the cases.

There was more to the failure of the courts to defend the Constitution very vigorously than either slowness or lack of jurisdiction, however. There is good reason to believe that the Supreme Court was afraid to confront the Congress head on. Congress made its first move to box in the court in April of 1866. Justice John Catron had died in 1865, leaving a vacancy in the Supreme Court. Johnson nominated his Attorney General for the position, but instead of giving its consent, Congress passed a bill reducing the size of the court by two members. Thus, Johnson not only no longer had a vacancy but also there would not be a vacancy when the next member retired or died. This was an attempt to prevent Johnson from affecting the character of the court. The Supreme Court itself came under fire, however, when it announced its decision, *Ex parte Milligan,* December, 1866. The Supreme Court held that the trial of a civilian by a military tribunal unless it was in connection with military operations in a state was unconstitutional. This and two other high court decisions "evoked in both houses of Congress a bitter Radical attack on the Court. Thad Stevens called the Milligan decision 'more dangerous' than the Dred Scott case, while Bingham suggested that Congress at once deprive the Court of all appellate jurisdiction. . . ."[148] In 1868, Congress passed a bill removing the Federal court jurisdiction over habeas corpus cases arising under the Habeas Corpus Act of 1867. The Court bowed to this restriction of its power.

But perhaps the most grotesque violation of the Constitution was in using Southern states declared to be out of the Union to help ratify amendments to the Constitution. Three constitutional amendments were adopted during Reconstruction. The 13th Amendment, which was adopted in 1865, prohibits slavery or involuntary servitude except as punishment for crime. The 14th Amendment, a complicated and far reaching one, was held to have been adopted in 1868. Down through the years, the crucial portion of this amendment has been the first section. It established United States and state citizenship for all persons born or naturalized in the United States. Most directly, it made Blacks citizens. The remainder of the section consists of restrictions on the states. They are prohibited to abridge the privileges or

Reconstruction Amendments

Article XIII

[Declared Ratified in 1865]

Section 1. Neither slavery nor involuntary servitude, except as a punishment for crime whereof the party shall have been duly convicted, shall exist within the United States, or any place subject to their jurisdiction.

Section 2. Congress shall have power to enforce this article by appropriate legislation.

Article XIV

[Declared Ratified in 1868]

Section 1. All persons born or naturalized in the United States, and subject to the jurisdiction thereof, are citizens of the United States and of the State wherein they reside. No State shall make or enforce any law which shall abridge the privileges or immunities of citizens of the United States; nor shall any State deprive any person of life, liberty, or property, without due process of law; nor deny to any person within its jurisdiction the equal protection of the laws.

Section 2. Representatives shall be apportioned among the several states according to their respective numbers, counting the whole number of persons in each State, excluding Indians not taxed. But when the right at vote of any election for the choice of electors for President and Vice-President of the United States, Representatives in Congress, the Executive and Judicial officers of a State, or the members of the Legislature thereof, is denied to any of the male inhabitants of such State, being twenty-one years of age, and citizens of the United States, or in any way abridged, except for participation in rebellion, or other crime, the basis of representation therein shall be reduced in the proportion which the number of such male citizens shall bear to the whole number of male citizens twenty-one years of age in such state.

Section 3. No person shall be a Senator or Representative in Congress, or elector of President and Vice-President, or hold any office, civil or military, under the United States, or under any State, who, having previously taken an oath, as a member of Congress, or as an officer of the United States, or as a member of any State legislature, or as an executive or judicial officer of any State, to support the Constitution of the United States, shall have engaged in insurrection or rebellion against the same, or given aid or comfort to the enemies thereof. But Congress may by a vote of two-thirds of each House, remove such disability.

Section 4. The validity of the public debt of the United States, authorized by law,including debts incurred for payment of pensions and bounties for services in suppressing insurrection or rebellion, shall not be questioned. But neither the United States nor any State shall assume or pay any debt or obligation incurred in aid of insurrection or rebellion against the United States, or any claim for the loss or emancipation of any slave; but all such debts shall be held illegal and void.

Section 5. The Congress shall have the power to enforce, by appropriate legislation, the provisions of this article.

Article XV

[Declared Ratified in 1870]

Section 1. The right of citizens of the United States to vote shall not be denied or abridged by the United States or by any State on account of race, color, or previous condition of servitude—

Section 2. The Congress shall have power to enforce this article by appropriate legislation.

immunities of citizens of the United States, to deprive any person of life, liberty, or property, without due process of law, or to deny any person within their jurisdictions the equal protection of the laws. Section 2 sets up a scheme for reducing the representation in Congress of any state which denies the vote to a significant portion of the males 21 or older. Section 3 disqualifies a portion of those who served in the Confederacy. This disability could be and later was removed. Section 4 declares the Confederate debt invalid, the federal debt valid, and prohibits any state to pay any portion of the Confederate debt or compensation for slaves. The 15th Amendment, which forbids the denial to the vote to any person because of race, color, or pervious condition of servitude, was adopted in 1870.

While former Confederate states, not yet enjoying the privileges of other members of the Union, were involved in the ratification of all three amendments under pressure, the ratification of the 14th was most controversial. When the amendment was submitted in its first version in 1866, it was rejected by all the former states of the Confederacy, except Tennessee, along with Delaware and Kentucky. With 12 states rejecting it, it failed of ratification. By the terms of the First Reconstruction Act in 1867, Congress required that no state could be restored to the Union until it had ratified the 14th Amendment, and further, that no state could be restored until the amendment had actually become a part of the Constitution. With this threat hanging over their heads, the new governments organized under the reconstruction acts ratified the amendment. Even counting these, it was far from clear that the amendment had been ratified. Secretary of State Seward issued an "iffy" proclamation of ratification in July, 1868. He pointed out that two states, Ohio and New Jersey, had voted to rescind their earlier ratification and indicated that there were doubts about the legitimacy of the governments of some of the Southern states. But if all these doubtful states were counted, he said, the amendment was adopted.

That was too uncertain a proclamation in the view of the leaders of Congress, and that body adopted a resolution declaring that three-fourths of the states had ratified the amendment and the Secretary of State should properly proclaim it to be ratified. This resolution had no precedent and has had no antecedent. Moreover, only 27 states were listed by Congress as having ratified, and counting the Southern states there were 37 states; thus, three-fourths had not ratified by the count of Congress. No matter, the amendment was in effect.

Regardless of the irregularity of their adoption, it should be pointed out that these amendments did give after the fact constitutional sanction to much that had already been done during the early years of Reconstruction. It should be noted, too, that the courts, Presidents, and the Democratic Party had reasserted their force sufficiently by the 1880s to restore much of the constitutional balance to the United States government. Meanwhile, too, the states were reasserting their role in the Union.

Reconstruction Politics

The Reconstruction of the South is often treated separately from national politics of the Grant period (1869–1877). Thus, what are often described as "scandals" during the Grant Administration are not dealt with in the context of Reconstruction, but as something distinct from it. That is unfortunate. Actually, virtually the whole of the Reconstruction was scandalous by any very high standards of judgment: the treatment of the Southern states and people, the behavior of the Radical politicians, the intimidation of President Johnson and the courts, the callous attitude toward the Constitution, and the use of Blacks to maintain Republican rule. Moreover, some things that were called scandals were hardly that at all. For example, what was called the "Crime of '73" was neither a crime nor unethical, immoral, or scandalous. It was simply a governmental decision not to mint any more silver dollars, followed by making silver no longer legal tender except for small payments. This made good sense, since silver did not much circulate because it had been overvalued in the fixed ratio between gold and silver. Nor was the "Salary Grab Act" so much scandalous as greedy. Congress increased the annual salary of its members from $5,000 to $7,500 by an act in 1873. It had a retroactive feature which helped to raise the cry of scandal. The act was shortly repealed.

What has been conceived of as a scandal or corruption has often been much too narrowly conceived and applied. Often it is restricted to instances when a politician has been given gifts or "bought" in one way or another or has taken bribes. In practice, what historians call scandals are what journalists or partisan politicians have uncovered and described in that way. Thus, much that is scandalous when viewed more broadly escapes detection or unfavorable notice. For example, it is surely of much greater moment to the public to have those in power violate the Constitution than for a politician to take a gift and grant a favor, though the latter possibly should bring disrepute as well.

In any case, misbehavior by politicians was widespread during the Reconstruction period, both nationally and toward or in the South. Moreover, they have common roots in what went on during the Civil War and Reconstruction. There was a great increase in national power during these years, in government taxes and expenditures, and government programs. This was so not only in the extension of Federal power over the South during Reconstruction but also in a national banking system, the fostering of railroad building, the protective tariff, and the creation of fiat money. The more extensive government activity becomes the greater opportunities there are for graft, corruption, and scandalous behavior. Moreover, at the same time these developments were taking place the usual restraints of checks and balances were reduced. During the Civil War and for several years after it, the South was removed as a restraint on the government by the absence of its representatives from the national councils. In addition, the Radicals managed not only to browbeat Republicans generally into line in both houses of Congress but also to offset the restraining hand of the President and intimidate the courts. The Radical stance of moral superiority because of their efforts to free the slaves, their loyalty to the Union, and the attempt to extend and protect the rights of the Freedmen provided an excellent cover for the power grabbing and corruption of Reconstruction.

In any case, the Reconstruction of the South was the most dramatic spectacle in the ongoing political scandal of the period. The years from 1867 to 1877 are often described as Black Reconstruction. This suggests that Blacks ruled over the South during these years. That considerably overstates the case. The only state where Negroes dominated the legislature was South Carolina. No Black ever served as elected governor of any of the states, though in at least two instances Blacks did act briefly as governors. They held office as lieutenant governors of South Carolina, Mississippi, and Louisiana, and in one state or another, most state offices. Two served as Senators for Mississippi, and a total of fifteen Blacks were elected to the House of Representatives. Nor did Blacks play even that important a role in the states down to 1877; in some states, their role was quite limited, and in most it had been greatly reduced before 1877. The heady days for Blacks in southern politics were the late 1860s and early 1870s.

Actually, rule during the time when Republicans controlled most state governments in the South was mainly by a combination of Blacks, Carpetbaggers, and Scalawags. A Carpetbagger was a Northerner who came into the South with nothing but a carpetbag for his belongings, according to legend, seeking his fortune. In fact, a considerable number of people from the North came to the South toward the close of the Civil War and the years immediately afterward. They came for a great variety of reasons: some to work for the Freedmen's Bureau, some as teachers in the schools promoted by the Freedmen's Bureau, some to establish Union Leagues to teach the Blacks to vote Republican, others to profit in one way or another from the defeat and crushing of the South.

In the chaos that prevailed in the wake of the conquering armies and the uncertain status of governments there was indeed wealth to be gained in dealing with confiscated property of Confederates and in other ways. Many Carpetbaggers, whatever their motives for coming into the South, did gain political office. Of the Southern states admitted to the Union in 1868 four of their governors and ten of their Senators were Carpetbaggers. During the period of Reconstruction, nineteen Carpetbaggers represented Southern states in the Senate.

"Scalawag" was a derogatory term applied by other Southerners to native Southern whites who participated in the Reconstruction governments. In the minds of many Southern whites they were turncoats and traitors to their people. Perhaps they were, but they were, at any rate, an important

element in the governments of some states. Since these governments ruled
by the support of military force (whether present or on call), it would be
correct also to refer to it as Military Reconstruction.

But whatever they should be called, these Reconstruction governments
were notorious for their taxing and spending and the aid and comfort they
gave to corrupt operators. Historian E. Merton Coulter described it this way:
"Saddled with an irresponsible officialdom, the South was now plunged
into debauchery, corruption, and private plundering unbelievable—
suggesting that government had been transformed into an engine of destruction. . . . Corruption permeated government from the statehouse to the
courthouse and city hall. . . . The variety of means used to debauch
government and plunder the public treasury bespeaks the vivid imaginations
and practical ability of the perpetrators. Every seceded state came under the
withering hand of Radical rule, but it was reserved to South Carolina,
Louisiana, and Arkansas to suffer most. Legislatures piled up expenses
against their impoverished states to fantastic heights."[149] The Blacks
involved were often more to be pitied than censured. After all, they had no
political experience, were often illiterate, and were more or less pawns of
the Radicals and the Union Leagues which instructed them in voting. They
certainly had no experience in managing fiscal matters, though they were
not notably more irresponsible than their Carpetbagger allies in many
instances.

Ulysses S. Grant was probably elected President in 1868 by and certainly
depended for the majority of the popular vote upon the Negro vote he
received. Grant had virtually no political experience when he came to the
highest office in the land. His only known qualification for the office was
his military leadership in the Civil War. In times past, when he had voted,
he had sometimes voted Democratic. The Republicans nominated him as
their candidate in 1868 and again in 1872 and elected him President both
times. However, he may well have won over the Democrat, Horatio
Seymour, in 1868 because so many whites in the South were disfranchised.
Although the Republican party split in 1872, and the Liberal Republicans
nominated Horace Greeley, as did the Democrats, Grant won rather easily.
But by 1876 Grant had been widely discredited.

Grant was used: used by the Radicals, used by radical regimes in the
South who depended upon him to send troops when needed, and used by
friends whom he had appointed to office. He showed no insight in choosing
his cabinet members generally, rarely rose to the defense of a battered
Constitution, and some of those around him contributed considerably to the
reputation of the period for being corrupt.

While not everything someone called a scandal was indeed scandalous, as
noted earlier, there were more than enough scandals during Grant's administrations. Grant had not been in office long when the first one broke in 1869.
It is generally known as "Black Friday" (September 24, 1869), a day when

the price of gold plunged, ruining many speculators. Jay Gould and Jim Fisk attempted to corner the available gold and profit by controlling its price. To succeed in this scheme, they needed government cooperation. They persuaded Grant's brother-in-law to use his influence with the President to prevent the government from selling gold. Grant never agreed to this, and when the crunch came, the Secretary of the Treasury, George Boutwell, released $4 million in gold for sale, with Grant's approval. This was both an effort to manipulate government one way for private profit and its use in the opposite way to produce harm to some investors.

The Credit Mobilier exposé occurred in 1872 when the New York *Sun* revealed some of the maneuvers of this company. (The revelations concerned events that had taken place prior to the time that Grant took office, however, and could not be charged to him.) Credit Mobilier was a construction company organized to build the Union Pacific Railroad. It made large profits, and those who held stock in it received high dividends. Several politicians, including a Vice-President and some Congressmen, were able to acquire stock at attractive prices. Since the Union Pacific had received government aid, there was a strong suspicion that Credit Mobilier was, in effect, buying political support. Congressman Oakes Ames of Massachusetts was censured for his involvement in the affair.

A Whiskey Ring was exposed in 1875. It involved collaboration between revenue officials and distillers to defraud the government of tax on whiskey. One of the revenue officials was a Grant appointee, and Grant's private secretary was also involved. All told, 238 persons were indicted, though not all were convicted. In 1876, Grant's Secretary of War, William W. Belknap, was impeached by the House of Representatives for accepting bribes in the sale of trading posts in Indian territory. He resigned before he could be tried by the Senate.

The End of Reconstruction

The ending of Reconstruction was as sordid and entangled with politics as the beginning. Actually, the more militant aspects of Reconstruction ended at different times in different states. Most histories treat the final removal of all troops from the South in 1877 as the end. The legal residue of Reconstruction was around for years after 1877, whereas military occupation and Black and Carpetbag control of most states ended earlier. Native Southern whites regained control of Tennessee in 1869, Virginia and North Carolina in 1870, Georgia in 1871, Arkansas, Alabama, and Texas in 1874, and Mississippi in 1875. Only Louisiana, South Carolina, and Florida had Radical governments after 1876.

As might have been expected, the disfranchisement of many whites and the organization of state and local governments by Blacks and Carpetbaggers stirred a hornet's nest of resentment among native whites and a determination to regain control of the governments. The prolonged use of force by the Union and the dispatching of troops among them prompted whites to retaliate in kind. Blacks could not legally be disfranchised after the adoption of the 15th Amendment, but they often could be and were scared away from the polls or participating in government. The most infamous of the organizations by which this was accomplished was the Ku Klux Klan, but there were a number of other similar secret organizations. Former Confederate general Nathan Bedford Forrest of Tennessee was head of the Klan, or one of them, for a time, but he disbanded it in 1869. Organizations of that stripe, and some less secret, continued to operate in the following years, however. Another means used to obtain political control by Southern whites was for them to have but one political party. Some called themselves Conservatives in the first few years, but eventually they coalesced behind the Democratic Party. It was as Democrats that the South became the Solid South, and the Democratic Party in the South served as an instrument for Southern white rule. An Amnesty Act of 1872 removed the disabilities on ex-Confederates contained in the 14th Amendment, except for a few hundred. Thereafter, officers of the Confederacy frequently were elected to political office as Southern whites regained control of the governments.

In considerable measure the Reconstruction effort ended by just petering out. For one thing, the men with the greatest zeal for reconstructing the South were no longer on the scene. Thaddeus Stevens died in 1868, and Charles Sumner was not much of a factor after 1872. Congress passed a variety of civil rights acts in the early 1870s designed to protect Negroes in the South, but those charged with enforcement eventually wearied of sending in troops and marshals. When President Grant received a request to send troops into Mississippi in 1875, he replied: "The whole public are tired out with these annual autumnal outbreaks in the South and the great majority are ready now to condemn any interference on the part of the Government."[150] The Democrats gained control of the House of Representatives in 1874, and thereafter the Radicals could no longer control what Congress would do.

Even so, Radical governments were still contending for control in Florida, South Carolina, and Louisiana in late 1876, and they were still backed by Federal troops in South Carolina and Louisiana. The ending of military occupation came to hinge on the presidential election of 1876. Rutherford B. Hayes was the Republican candidate, and Samuel Tilden was the Democratic choice. Tilden got a majority of the popular vote, but neither gained an undisputed majority of the electoral vote. To put it another way, Tilden had 184 undisputed electoral votes, one short of a majority, and Hayes had 166. Three states—Florida, Louisiana, and South Carolina—had each sent in two sets of electoral returns, one for the Republican and one for the Democratic candidate. Congress appointed an electoral commission of fifteen members: five from the House, five from the Senate, and five from

Rutherford B. Hayes
(1822–1893)

Courtesy Library of Congress, Brady-Handy Collection

Hayes was the 19th President of the United States, and he served for only one term. He was born in Ohio, graduated from Kenyon College, attended Harvard law school, and practiced law. He served in the Union army during the Civil War and rose to the rank of major general. As a Republican, he was elected to Congress after the war service and supported the party program during Reconstruction. Hayes was twice elected governor of Ohio and nominated by the Republicans for President in 1876. Probably, his Democratic opponent, Samuel J. Tilden, would have won the election, but Hayes got all the contested electoral votes and was declared the winner. He removed the troops from the South, left that section to its own devices, and administered the affairs of government well, but was not renominated by his party.

the Supreme Court. Republicans had a majority on the commission, and they awarded all the contested votes to Hayes, thus giving him a bare majority.

If that decision was accepted, it looked as if the Democrats were done out of an election they had almost certainly won. However, a behind-the-scenes agreement was worked out with Southern Democrats to make concessions to the South in return for their acceptance of the decision of the commission. One of those concessions was the promise that Hayes would remove the troops. This was done in April, 1877, and it marks the end of militant Reconstruction.

What was accomplished by Reconstruction? On the positive side, the slaves were freed, but not much that endured beyond that. But, it should be emphasized, the freeing of the slaves was achieved under Presidential Reconstruction. Radical Reconstruction did bring constitutional amendments which attempted to make Negroes equal with whites before the law and prohibited excluding them from voting as a class. A goodly number of Blacks were taught to read and write during Reconstruction, and that did not vanish at the end of the period. But most of what the Radicals attempted to do was shortly undone by Southern whites or could not be maintained once the troops were withdrawn. Thus, it is a reasonable conclusion that not much aside from the freeing of the slaves on the positive side was accomplished by Reconstruction, and that a great deal of damage was done by Radical Reconstruction. It exacerbated feelings between the North and the South.

It took a hundred years before the Methodists and Presbyterians would achieve reunion, and the Baptists still have not reunited. It aroused animosity between Blacks and whites and fortified the determination of Southern whites to keep the Blacks from power or anything that signified equality. Reconstruction finished the work of the economic destruction of the South begun by the war. Politically, the South languished so far as its role in the United States government was concerned. It was a hundred years before a President could be elected who came from a Southern state.

On the whole, then, Radical Reconstruction was a debacle.

Notes

1. Charles A. and Mary R. Beard, *The Rise of American Civilization* (New York: Macmillan, 1934, 2 volumes in one, rev. and enl.), vol. II, pp. 52–54.

2. Wilbur J. Cash, *The Mind of the South* (Garden City, N. Y.: Doubleday, 1954), p. 113.

3. Henry S. Commager, *Documents of American History,* vol. I (New York: Appleton-Century-Crofts, 1962, rev. ed.), p. 237.

4. Marvin Meyers, Alexander Kern, and John G. Cawelti, *Sources of the American Republic,* vol. I (Chicago: Scott, Foresman and Co., 1960), pp. 263–64.

5. Commager, *op. cit.,* vol. I, p. 251.

6. Quoted in "Introduction" of James L. Bugg, ed., *Jacksonian Democracy: Myth or Reality?* (New York: Holt, Rinehart and Winston, 1962), p. 1.

7. Robert V. Remini, *The Age of Jackson* (Columbia: University of South Carolina Press, 1972), p. 18.

8. Quoted in Samuel F. Morison and Henry S. Commager, *The Growth of the American Republic,* vol. I (New York: Oxford University Press, 1942), p. 471.

9. Remini, *op. cit.,* pp. 16–17.

10. James Parton, "A Evaluation of Andrew Jackson," Bugg, *op. cit.,* p. 15.

11. Edward Dumbauld, ed., *The Political Writings of Thomas Jefferson* (New York: Liberal Arts Press, 1955), pp. 48–49.

12. Quoted in Glyndon G. van Deusen, *The Jacksonian Era* (New York York: Harper & Row, 1959), p. 22.

13. Joseph L. Blau, ed., *Social Theories of Jacksonian Democracy* (Indianapolis: Bobbs-Merrill, 1954), pp. 11, 16.

14. *Ibid.,* p. 27.

15. *Ibid.,* p. 28.

16. *Ibid.,* p. 75.

17. *Ibid.,* p. 76.

18. *Ibid.,* p. 87.

19. *Ibid.,* p. 131.

20. *Ibid.,* p. 132.

21. Remini *op. cit.,* p. 44.

22. *Ibid.,* p. 133.

23. *Ibid.,* p. 139.

24. *Ibid.,* pp. 147–48.

25. Commager, *Documents of American History,* vol. I, p. 259.

26. Remini, *op. cit.,* p. 64.

27. Commager, *Documents of American History,* vol. I, p. 260.

28. Remini, *op. cit.,* pp. 165, 171.

29. Commager, *Documents of American History*, vol. I, p. 272.

30. Quoted in Claude G. Bowers, *The Party Battles of the Jackson Period* (New York: Octagon-Books, 1963), p. 313.

31. Quoted in Nelson M. Blake, *A History of American Life and Thought* (New York: McGraw-Hill, 1963), p. 273.

32. George A. Peek, Jr., ed., *The Political Writings of John Adams* (New York: Liberal Arts Press, 1954), pp. 98–99.

33. Alexis de Tocqueville, *Democracy in America*, Erik von Kuehnelt-Leddihn, intro., vol. II (New Rochelle, N.Y.: Arlington House, n.d.), pp. 114–15.

34. *Ibid.*, p. 112.

35. Quoted in Ralph E. Pumphrey and Muriel W. Pumphrey, eds., *The Heritage of American Social Work* (New York: Columbia University Press, 1961), p. 133.

36. Quoted in Frederick Rudolph, *The American College and University* (New York: Alfred A. Knopf, 1962), pp. 4–5.

37. Frederick Marryat, *A Diary in America*, Sidney Jackman, ed. (New York: Alfred A. Knopf, 1962), p. 309.

38. Merle Curti, *et. al., American Issues* (New York: Lippincott, 1960, 4th edition), p. 151.

39. Quoted in Daniel Boorstin, *The Americans, The National Experience* (New York: Vintage Books, 1965), p. 58.

40. Rudolph, *op. cit.*, p. 220.

41. Robert H. Bremmer, *American Philanthrophy* (Chicago: University of Chicago Press, 1960), p. 56.

42. Thomas C. Cochran, "Business Organization and the Development of an Industrial Discipline," *Views of American Economic Growth: The Agricultural Era*, Thomas C. Cochran and Thomas B. Bremer, eds. (New York: McGraw-Hill, 1966), p. 216.

43. Constance M. Green, "Light Manufactures and the Beginnings of Precision Manufacture," *The Growth of the American Economy*. Harold F. Williamson, ed. (Englewood Cliffs, N.J.: Prentice-Hall, 1951), p. 195.

44. Quoted in Gilbert C. Fite and Jim E. Reese, *An Economic History of the United States* (Boston: Houghton Mifflin, 1965, 2nd edition), p. 225.

45. Meyers, Kern and Cawelti, *op. cit.*, p. 454.

46. Raymond S. Inman and Thomas W. Koch, eds., *Labor in American Society* (Glenview, Ill.: Scott, Foresman and Co., 1966), pp. 23–24.

47. Commager, *Documents of American History*, vol. I, p. 296.

48. Quoted in John Herman Randall, Jr., *The Making of the Modern Mind* (Boston: Houghton Mifflin, 1954, rev. ed.), p. 402.

49. *Ibid.*, p. 400.

50. Quoted in Blake, *op. cit.*, p. 243.

51. Gerald N. Grob and Robert M. Beck, eds., *American Ideas*, vol. I (New York: The Free Press of Glencoe, 1963), p. 236.

52. Blake, *op. cit.*, p. 244.

53. Grob and Beck, *op. cit.*, p. 258.

54. Quoted in Blake, *op. cit.*, p. 245.

55. Robert E. Spiller, *et. al.*, eds., *Literary History of the United States* (New York: Macmillan, 1953), pp. 527–28.

56. Ralph Waldo Emerson, "Self-Reliance," *Collected Works of Ralph Waldo Emerson* (New York: Greystone Press, n.d.), pp. 16–18.

57. Ernst Cassirer, *Rousseau, Kant and Goethe* (New York: Harper Torchbooks, 1963), pp. 2–3.

58. Perry Miller, ed., *The American Transcendentalists: Their Prose and Poetry,* p. 371.

59. Quoted in Blake, *op. cit.,* p. 250.

60. Henry D. Thoreau, *Walden* and *On the Duty of Civil Disobedience,* Norman H. Pearson, intro. (New York: Rinehart, 1948), p. 281.

61. Vernon L. Parrington, *The Romantic Revolution in America* (New York: A Harvest Book, 1954), p. 100.

62. *Ibid.,* p. 101.

63. Quoted in Alice Felt Tyler, *Freedom's Ferment* (New York: Harper & Row, 1962), p. 37.

64. *Ibid.,* p. 68.

65. *Ibid.,* p. 71.

66. *Ibid.,* p. 73.

67. *Collected Works of Ralph Waldo Emerson,* pp. 211–12.

68. Grob and Beck, *op. cit.,* vol. I, p. 334.

69. *Ibid.*

70. Quoted in Samuel L. Blumenfeld, *Is Public Education Necessary?* (Old Greenwich, Conn.: Devin-Adair, 1981), p. 211.

71. Charles Crowe, ed., *A Documentary History of American Thought* (Boston: Allyn and Bacon, 1965), pp. 112–13.

72. Tyler, *op. cit.,* p. 486.

73. *Ibid.,* p. 494.

74. Quoted in Leonard D. White, *The Jacksonians: A Study in Administrative History* (New York: Macmillan, 1954), p. 14.

75. Norman A. Graebner, *Empire on the Pacific* (New York: Ronald Press, 1955), p. 9.

76. Edward C. Kirkland, *A History of American Life* (New York: Appleton-Century-Crofts, 1958), p. 38.

77. Robert S. Hunt, *Law and Locomotives* (Madison: State Historical Society of Wisconsin, 1958), p. 38.

78. Russell E. Westmeyer, *Economics of Transportation* (Englewood Cliffs, N.J.: Prentice-Hall, 1952), pp. 47–48.

79. Commager, *Documents of American History,* vol. I, p. 308.

80. Quoted in Graebner, *op. cit.,* pp. 27–28.

81. Commager, *Documents of American History,* vol. I, p. 311.

82. Curti, *op. cit.,* p. 520.

83. Quoted in Allan Nevins, *The Ordeal of the Union,* vol. I (New York: Charles Scribner's Sons, 1947), p. 276.

84. Richard B. Morris, ed., *Encyclopedia of American History* (New York: Harper & Bros., 1953), p. 210.

85. Nevins, *op. cit.,* vol. I, p. 270.

86. *Ibid.,* p. 290.

87. *Ibid.,* pp. 300–01.

88. *Ibid.*, pp. 276–77.

89. J. G. Randall and David Donald, *The Civil War and Reconstruction* (Boston: D. C. Heath, 1961), p. 95.

90. Beard and Beard, *op. cit.*, vol. I, p. 635.

91. Quoted in Fite and Reese, *op. cit.*, p. 277.

92. Commager, *Documents of American History,* vol. I, p. 334.

93. James Buchanan, "Republican Fanaticism as a Cause of the Civil War," *The Causes of the American Civil War,* Edwin C. Rozwenc, ed. (Boston: D. C. Heath, 1961), pp. 66–67.

94. Nevins, *op. cit.*, vol. II, pp. 440–41.

95. *Ibid.*, pp. 446–47.

96. Quoted in James F. Rhodes, *History of the United States from the Compromise of 1850,* vol. II (New York: Harper & Bros., 1893), p. 437.

97. Roy F. Nichols, *The Disruption of American Democracy* (New York: The Free Press, 1967), p. 206.

98. Rhodes, *op. cit.*, vol. II, p. 73.

99. William H. Seward, "The Irrepressible Conflict," Rozwenc, *op. cit.*, p. 13.

100. Quoted in Rozwenc, *op. cit.*, p. 64.

101. Commager, *Documents of American History,* vol. I, p. 345.

102. Abraham Lincoln, "The House Divided," Rozwenc, *op. cit.*, p. 25.

103. Quoted in Rhodes, *op. cit.*, vol. II, p. 432.

104. Commager, *Documents of American History,* vol. I, p. 385.

105. *Ibid.*, p. 388.

106. *Ibid.*, p. 414.

107. *Ibid.*, pp. 395–96.

108. Alexander H. Stephens, *A Constitutional View of the Late War Between the States,* vol. I (Philadelphia: National Publishing Co., 1868), pp. 9–10.

109. Quoted in James M. McPherson, "The Abolitionists Fight on in Civil War and Reconstruction," *The Age of Civil War and Reconstruction.* Charles Crowe, ed. (Homewood, Ill.: Dorsey Press, 1966), p. 227.

110. Quoted in Randall and Donald, *op. cit.*, p. 438.

111. *Ibid.*, p. 233.

112. *Ibid.*, p. 232.

113. Commager, *Documents of American History,* vol. I, p. 428.

114. Samuel E. Morison, *The Oxford History of the American People* (New York: Oxford University Press, 1965), p. 621.

115. Quoted in *ibid.*, p. 636.

116. *Ibid.*, p. 677.

117. Commager, *Documents of American History,* vol. I, p. 420.

118. *Ibid.*, p. 421.

119. *Ibid.*, p. 422.

120. Quoted in Avery Craven, *Reconstruction: The Ending of the Civil War* (New York: Holt, Rinehart and Winston, 1969), p. 54.

121. Quoted in Randall and Donald, *op. cit.*, p. 428.

122. Commager, *Documents of American History,* vol. I, p. 448.

123. *Ibid.*, p. 449.

124. Quoted in Claude G. Bowers, *The Tragic Era* (Cambridge: The Riverside Press, 1929), p. 132.

125. Craven, *op. cit.*, p. 55.

126. *Ibid.*

127. Quoted in E. Merton Coulter, *The South During Reconstruction* (Baton Rouge: Louisiana State University Press, 1947), p. 4.

128. Quoted in Hodding Carter, *The Angry Scar: The Story of Reconstruction* (Garden City, N.Y.: Doubleday, 1959), pp. 35–36.

129. *Ibid.*, p. 33.

130. Coulter, *op. cit.*, p. 16.

131. Carter, *op. cit.*, p. 35.

132. Quoted in Paul H. Buck, *The Road to Reunion* (Boston: Little, Brown and Co., 1937), p. 33.

133. Hilary A. Herbert, "A Justification of the Solid South," *Reconstruction*, Richard N. Current, ed. (Englewood Cliffs, N.J.: Prentice-Hall, 1965), pp. 377–78.

134. Quoted in Buck, *op. cit.*, p. 13.

135. Carter, *op. cit.*, p. 74.

136. Thaddeus Stevens, "The Fruit of Foul Rebellion," Current, *op. cit.*, p. 16.

137. Quoted in Craven, *op. cit.*, p. 92.

138. *Ibid.*, p. 121.

139. *Ibid.*, p. 116.

140. Quoted in Buck, *op. cit.*, p. 14.

141. *Ibid.*, p. 23.

142. Quoted in Coulter, *op. cit.*, p. 80.

143. Craven, *op. cit.*, p. 126.

144. *Ibid.*, p. 127.

145. Quoted in Bowers, *The Tragic Era*, p. 57.

146. Stevens in Current, *op. cit.*, p. 16.

147. Commager, *Documents of American History*, vol. I, p. 484.

148. Alfred H. Kelly and Winfred A. Harbison, *The American Constitution: Its Origins and Development* (New York: W. W. Norton, 1955), p. 479.

149. Coulter, *op. cit.*, p. 148.

150. Francis B. Simkins, *A History of the South* (New York: Alfred A. Knopf, 1956), p. 289.

Glossary

Annexation—to attach something to another body, usually a larger one. Thus, those who sought to bring Texas into the Union favored the "annexation" of that state. The term was particularly appropriate because Texas was an independent nation at the time.

Cabal—a group of persons engaged in more or less secret intrigues. The Radicals who controlled Congress during Reconstruction did so sometimes by preparing their positions in advance in exclusive meetings with one another—resembling the action of a cabal. Indeed, the Committee of Fifteen took on some of the aspects of a cabal.

Carpetbagger—A Northerner who came into the South after the Civil War seeking his fortune. Carpetbaggers were usually despised by native whites because they took advantage of Reconstruction programs to gain wealth and political power.

Caucus—a meeting of members of a political party to nominate a candidate. During the first third of the 19th century, presidential candidates were usually nominated by a congressional caucus of those belonging to a particular party. The practice of nominating candidates by caucus at the local level continued in some states into the 20th century.

Chartered Monopoly—a term used to describe companies which possessed a monopoly by government charter. The term was often used to describe national banks. The Jacksonians opposed chartered monopolies and generally favored free enterprise.

Communism—a political and economic system based on common ownership of property. In the 19th century, many communists did not envision government ownership of property, but in 20th-century Communist countries that is the rule. In the 19th century, communist organizations were usually small groups of people living in separate communities.

Communitarian—a term devised to distinguish arrangements in which small groups of people live together, usually owning their property in common, from 20th century communism, where the power of government is used to impose communal arrangements on whole peoples.

Confederacy—used to describe the Confederate States of America, an organization composed of the 11 Southern states which seceded from the Union. While the Confederate Constitution was modeled after the United States Constitution, its makers insisted theirs was a confederation restrained by the basic independence of the states, not a consolidated system, such as they believed the United States was becoming.

Conservatism—an outlook which emphasizes the importance of preserving continuity with the values of the past. This attitude was formulated during the French Revolution, and is opposed to radical or revolutionary change.

Continental Divide—an imaginary line at the crest of the Rocky Mountains. East of this line water flows to the Gulf of Mexico, and west of it to the Pacific.

Conscription—the drafting of men into the armed forces—compulsory military service. Both the Union and the Confederacy conscripted men to be soldiers during the latter part of the Civil War, but it was possible to hire a substitute rather than go in person.

"Dark Horse"—in politics, the nomination of a candidate who was not expected to be chosen. Democrats were most likely to nominate a "dark horse" or compromise presidential candidate because they required more than a simple majority of the delegate votes to achieve nomination, and where there was heated contest among contenders none could get the necessary votes. Thus, they turned to a "dark horse" when none of the contenders could be chosen.

Democracy—means rule by the people. However, the Democratic Party was often referred to as "the Democracy" from its beginning to the middle of the 19th century.

Democratic Party—a political party formed and led by Andrew Jackson and his followers. It claimed to be a continuation of the Jeffersonian Republican Party. The party usually stood for states' rights, private enterprise, strict construction of the constitution, free trade, and opposed Federal aid for internal improvements and national banks.

Emancipation—the act of setting free, especially slaves. When an owner sets his slaves free, he emancipates them; when government sets them free, that is the abolition of slavery.

Faction—what is now usually described as an interest group. Political parties not in power were sometimes referred to and even denounced as factions in the early years of the Republic.

Fractional Reserve Banking—is the practice by banks of holding only a portion of the money on deposit in reserve. In the early 19th century, most banks were banks of issue—i.e., issued their own currency—and they often kept only a fraction of the amount needed to redeem their currency on hand. After the Civil War, only national banks issued currency, and other banks handled mainly saving and checking accounts.

Geopolitics—the practice of taking geography into major consideration when deciding the political course of a nation. Geopolitical considerations are often used to justify territorial expansion. For example, the purchase of Louisiana was motivated by the desire of the United States to control the Mississippi and its outlets.

Graft—using political position to obtain dishonest gain, as when a politician takes a kickback for awarding a contract.

Greenbacks—were fiat money issued by the United States Treasury during the Civil War. They were put into circulation by making them legal tender, and they were fiat money because they were not redeemable in gold or silver at the time.

Individualism—a social theory which gives first place to the rights, liberty, and responsibility of the individual. The opposite theory is collectivism, in which the emphasis is on the group or whole body of the people.

Intellectual—one who primarily uses ideas in his work, for example, a poet, a journalist, a teacher, a social thinker. The term is sometimes used in the special sense of one who is bent on reforming or transforming society to conform with his ideas. For example, William Lloyd Garrison could be described as an intellectual because he used the power of ideas in the reforming abolitionist movement.

Internal Improvements—used to refer to the building of roads, digging of canals, dredging of harbors or rivers, and the like. Whether the United States government could constitutionally or should provide aid for such projects was often an issue in the first half of the 19th century.

Interposition—a doctrine connected with the nullification theory. It was the belief that a state which nullified a Federal law could use its power—"interpose" it—to protect its citizens from the operation of the law. This doctrine was never really put into effect.

"Ironclad"—a wooden warship covered with iron plate to protect it from cannon fire. A few such vessels were used during the Civil War.

Irrepressible Conflict—the idea that the existing political conflict between the slave and free staes was unavoidable, and that it would continue until the United States were all either slave or free. The idea has survived since the Civil War mainly as a way of raising the question of whether or not the war was inevitable.

"King Cotton"—a phrase that gained currency before the Civil War of the leading role of cotton in domestic, but especially in foreign, trade. Cotton was king, some Southerners held, and through her control of it the South would be invincible because of the foreign support she would receive in a war against the North.

Liberalism—in the 19th century, it referred to the beliefs of those who favored extending individual liberty by limiting government. Liberals also tended to favor universal suffrage. In the 20th century, American liberals have shifted toward expanding government power which often curtails individual liberty.

Manifesto—a strong public statement of the intentions or purposes, usually of some group or organization. Examples, the Ostend Manifesto and the *Communist Manifesto*.

Mason-Dixon Line—the boundary between Pennsylvania and Maryland. It has been thought of, however, as the boundary between slave and free states and thus as separating the North and the South.

Mount Olympus—a mountain in Greece which, in ancient times, was said to be the dwelling place of the gods. Nowadays, those whose attitudes indicate that they believe they are above the attachments and prejudices of mere mortals are described sometimes as being Olympian, i.e., godlike, in their postures.

Nationalism—devotion to the interest and well being as well as attachment to a nation. In the 19th century, a growing nationalism led more and more peoples to want to have their own independent nation. Viewed from that perspective, the Southern nationalism that gave rise to the Confederacy was the reflex of a widespread spirit of the period.

Old Northwest—the territory north of the Ohio, east of the Mississippi, and west of the Appalachians in the early 19th century. Before states were organized, it was also known as the Northwest Territory. When the United States acquired territory to the Pacific, the Oregon country became *the* Northwest.

Old Southwest—the area out of which the states of Alabama, Tennessee, Mississippi, and part of Louisiana were carved. Once Texas and the Mexican Cession were acquired, the southern portion of this became *the* Southwest.

Omnibus—in legislation it means a catch-all bill, or one that covers a variety of matters.

Perfectionism—the belief that perfection is attainable here on earth. It undergirds utopianism—the vision of a perfect society—and gives thrust to reforms and revolutions for making over society. Reforms are pushed by comparing current conditions with some perfect model, not with what has ever been.

Popular Sovereignty—the belief in allowing the people within a politically organized area to make the decisions. Stephen A. Douglas applied this doctrine to the slavery issue in the territories, and advocated letting the people decide the question in each territory.

Pre-emption—the privilege of moving on to unclaimed land and establishing a claim to being given the first opportunity to purchase it. The United States began to recognize this privilege for the first settlers on unclaimed government lands in the 1830s and 1840s.

Radical—literally, means going to the root or origin of the problem. Radical change, then, is change that basically alters customs, traditions, laws, and constitutions. The Radicals during Reconstruction advocated such changes in the South.

Romanticism—an attitude which exalts feeling above reason, spirit over matter, and substance over form. It was at its center a literary and aristic movement in the 19th century, but the attitudes associated with it spread through the society.

"Scalawag"—a native white Southerner who cooperated with Carpetbag and Black-dominated governments during Reconstruction.

Secession—the withdrawal of Southern states from the Union. Southern leaders argued that the United States was a union of states which had voluntarily come into the Union and that they could leave it by the reverse procedure from the one by which they had entered it.

Sectionalism—an attachment to a region or section of a country, New England was the first region in which sectionalism became pronounced. In the pre-Civil War era, it became common to speak of three sections: the North, the South, and the West.

Socialism—a social and political system based on common or government ownership of the means of production of goods. The main point, in practice, is governmental control over the distribution of goods.

"Spoils System"—a derogatory term used by those who oppose it to describe the practice of victorious politicians appointing their favorites to office. Those who oppose this practice prefer a merit system, such as the Civil Service, for the appointment of government workers. Andrew Jackson was accused of initiating the spoils system, but earlier Presidents had also found occasion to appoint their favorites.

Suffrage—the privilege of voting. The term is usually used in connection with the class of persons which has the privilege of voting, for example, property holders, white males 21 years of age or older, women, and so forth.

Technology—the techniques and tools used in the production and distribution of goods.

Total War—a war in which all the resources of the involved countries involved are called upon in order to obtain unconditional surrender from the enemy. It entails, too, the destruction of the enemy's potential to make war. The Civil War was becoming a total war during the last two years.

Transcendentalism—a belief in transcending, going beyond, or rising above. It was especially the belief that man can transcend his bodily limitations by attending to his feelings, insights, and intuitions.

Transcontinental—literally means extending across a continent. However, what have been called transcontinental railroads in the United States did not cross the country from the Atlantic to the Pacific, but rather usually extended from the Mississippi to the Pacific.

Utopia—an imaginary place described in literature, usually one where perfect social conditions have been achieved. The idea took hold among some people in the 19th century that it would be possible to have such perfect societies here on earth.

Voluntarism—the belief in accomplishing as many things voluntarily as possible, rather than forcing them through compulsion. For example, the voluntarist usually favors supporting churches, schools, and charities by voluntary efforts instead of government support.

Whig Party—a party which emerged in the 1830s, led by Henry Clay, Daniel Webster, and others. Whigs tended to favor a more active role by the federal government in developing industry and transportation than did the Democrats; thus, they stood for protective tariffs, Federal aid for internal improvements, and a national bank. They ceased to play a role in national affairs after around 1855.

Suggestions for Additional Reading

The Civil War and Reconstruction are such dramatic and engrossing events that they tend to dominate this period long before they come to the center of the stage. Events as much as 30 or 40 years before the outbreak of the war are often seen in retrospect as portending the war. Nearly half of the text in this book is devoted in one way or another to the background to and the Civil War and Reconstruction. Yet they should not be allowed to overshadow or crowd out many other important events and developments: westward expansion, the explorations of the West, the treks westward in Conestoga wagons or through the wilds to Utah, the removal of the Indian tribes, the coming of the railroad, the development of an American literature, and many others. This was truly an era of American expansion and growth and the development of the kind of diversity we might expect with extensive freedom. There is a large literature on hundreds of aspects of this period, both original and secondary, ranging from journals, diaries, collections of speeches, poetry, and novels to biographies, histories, and specialized studies.

The politics of the "Age of Jackson" has called forth a considerable literature. The prelude to that in the election of 1824 can be studied in George Dangerfield, *The Era of Good Feelings;* Samuel F. Bemis, *John Quincy Adams and the Union;* and Clement Eaton, *Henry Clay and the Art of Politics. The Election of Andrew Jackson* has been closely examined by Robert V. Remini. There is much material on Jackson himself and his period. See, for example, Marvin Meyers, *The Jacksonian Persuasion;* Glyndon G. Van Deusen, *The Jacksonian Era*; John W. Ward, *Andrew Jackson: Symbol for an Age;* and Joseph L. Blau, ed., *Social Theories of Jacksonian Democracy.* For the men who were with or against Jackson (people tended to side one way or another), see Thomas P. Govan, *Nicholas Biddle: Nationalist and Public Banker;* volume II of Charles M. Wiltse, *John C. Calhoun;* James C. Curtis, *The Fox at Bay: Martin van Buren and the Presidency;* Sydney Nathans, *Daniel Webster and Jacksonian Democracy;* and George R. Peage, *Henry Clay and the Whig Party.*

Vernon L. Parrington's *The Romantic Revolution in America* covers both literary developments and political thought, 1800–1860. He has given more attention to Southern literature than is usual. Perry Miller, *The Transcendentalists,* deals primarily with New England, as does Van Wyck Brooks, *The Flowering of New England.* For particular romantics, see Octavius B. Frothingham, *Theodore Parker*; Joseph W. Krutch, *Henry David Thoreau,* Mason Wade, *Margaret Fuller: Whetstone of Genius;* Ralph L. Rusk, *The Life of Ralph Waldo Emerson;* and Randall Stewart, *Nathaniel Hawthorne.* On the reform movements spurred by the romantic movement, see Alice Felt Tyler's *Freedom's Ferment* for detailed coverage of many of them. The revival movement is treated in T. L. Smith, *Revivalism and Social Reform*. Arthur E. Bestor's *Backwoods Utopias* tells the story of various utopian communities. Mormon history can be studied in Nels Anderson, *Desert Saints: The Mormon Frontier in Utah* and Leroy R. Hafen and Ann W. Hafen, *Hand Carts to Zion: The Story of a Unique Western Migration*. Abolition is the subject of G. H. Barnes, *The Anti-Slavery Impulse* and Louis Filler, *The Crusade Against Slavery*. Public education is discussed in Sidney Jackson, *America's Struggle for Free Schools* and Samuel L. Blumenfeld, *Is Public Education Necessary?*

The westward movement and the frontier have occupied much of the attention of historians. General works on the subject include Ray A. Billington, *Westward Expansion;* Frederick J. Turner, *Rise of the New West;* and Thomas D. Clark, *The Rampaging Frontier*. On the development of transportation, see Balthaser H. Mayer, *History of Transportation in the United States Before 1860;* Carter Goodrich, *Government Promotion of Canals and Railroads;* Stewart H. Holbrook, *The Story of American Railroads;* and Sidney L. Miller, *Inland Transportation*. The story of early Texas emerges in William C. Binkley, *The Texas Revolution;* Marquis James, *The Raven: A Biography of Stephen F. Austin;* and Walter Lord, *A Time to Stand*. The acquisition of Oregon is told in Norman A. Graebner, *Empire on the Pacific: A Study in American Continental Expansion;* Bernard DeVoto, *The Year of Decision;* and Frederick Merk, *The Oregon Question*. The war with Mexico and the related diplomacy are described in Otis A. Singletary, *The Mexican War;* volume II of Charles G. Sellers, *James K. Polk;* and Justin H. Smith, *The War with Mexico,* in two volumes.

There is indeed a bountiful literature of every sort on the background to and history of Civil War and Reconstruction. There is no single subject in American history on which scholars and writers have lavished more attention or spilled more ink. The material on Lincoln alone would fill a good-sized library, and the end is not in sight of books and articles on him. So popular are books on Lincoln, doctors, and dogs that someone once suggested that a book entitled *Lincoln's Doctor's Dog* ought to be a runaway best seller. The following can only suggest the variety and extent of works on this era.

Among the general histories, there are J. G. Randall and David Donald, *The Civil War and Reconstruction* and the multi-volumned work by Allan Nevins, *Ordeal of the Union, The Emergence of Lincoln,* and *The War for the Union*. The general background to the war is discussed in the following: Avery Craven, *The Coming of the Civil War* and *Civil War in the Making;* Henry H. Simms, *A Decade of Sectional Controversy;* Arthur C. Cole, *The Irrepressible Conflict;* and Arthur Y. Lloyd, *The Slavery Controversy*. The immigration of the mid-19th century is covered in Maldwyn A. Jones, *American Immigration;* William F. Adams, *Ireland and Irish Immigration to the New World from 1815 to the Famine;* and Marcus L. Hansen, *Refugees of Revolution*. For many years, Ulrich B. Phillips—*Life and Labor in the Old South* and *American Negro Slavery,* among others—dominated on the subject of plantation life and Negro slavery. These have been modified somewhat by Kenneth M. Stampp, *The Peculiar Institution* and Frank L. Owsley, *Plain Folk of the Old South*. Avery

O. Craven, *The Growth of Southern Nationalism,* tells of an important development in the history of the South. The Compromise of 1850 is the subject of
Holman Hamilton's *Prologue to Conflict: The Crisis and the Compromise of
1850.* On Kansas-Nebraska, there is James C. Malin, *The Nebraska Question.*

The Civil War itself is described in such works as Bruce Catton, *This
Hallowed Ground;* Carl R. Fish, *The American Civil War;* and Bruce Catton, *A
Stillness at Appomattox.* For the Confederacy, see E. Merton Coulter, *The
Confederate States of America;* Clement Eaton, *A History of the Southern
Confederacy;* and Robert S. Henry, *The Story of the Confederacy.* On the
economic measures of the Union government, see Wesley C. Mitchell, *A
History of the Greenbacks;* Andrew M. Davis, *The Origin of the National
Banking System;* Earle D. Ross, *Democracy's College;* and Robert W. Fogel,
The Union Pacific Railroad.

Histories dealing with Reconstruction include E. Merton Coulter, *The South
During Reconstruction;* Claude G. Bowers, *The Tragic Era;* Robert S. Henry,
The Story of Reconstruction; Eben G. Scott, *Reconstruction During the Civil
War;* William R. Brock; *An American Crisis: Congress and Reconstruction;*
John H. Franklin, *Reconstruction After the Civil War;* Avery O. Craven,
Reconstruction: The Ending of the Civil War; and Eric L. McKitrick, *Andrew
Johnson and Reconstruction.* Special studies on the subject are: Fawn M.
Brodie, *Thaddeus Stevens; Scourge of the South;* Howard K. Beale, *The
Critical Year;* and Joseph B. James, *The Framing of the Fourteenth Amend-
ment.* On the scandals of the Grant period, see William B. Hesseltine, *Ulysses
S. Grant: Politician;* Seymour J. Mandelbaum, *Boss Tweed's New York;* and
Allan Nevins, *Hamilton Fish: The Inner History of the Grant Administration;*
The drawing together once again of the people North and South is told in Paul
H. Buck, *The Road to Reunion.*

INDEX